The Time-Life Book of
Elegant Everyday Cooking

Time-Life Books Inc.
is a wholly owned subsidiary of
THE TIME INC. BOOK COMPANY

TIME-LIFE BOOKS INC.

EDITOR: George Constable
European Editor: Ellen Phillips
Design Director: Louis Klein
European Design Director: Ed Skyner
Fresh Ways Series Director: Dale M. Brown
Series Designer: Herbert H. Quarmby
Book Manager: Blaine Marshall
Production Manager: Prudence Harris

PUBLISHER: Joseph J. Ward

THE COOKS

Adam DeVito
Henry Grossi
John T. Shaffer
Lisa Cherkasky
Pat Alburey
Joanna Farrow
Carole Handslip
Rosemary Wadey
Jane Suthering
Anthony Kwok
Nigel Slater
Janice Murfitt

THE CONSULTANTS

Carol Cutler
Janet Tenney
Patricia Judd
Pat Alburey
Mary Jo Feeney
Norma Macmillan

Library of Congress Cataloging in Publication Data
Main entry under title:
The Time-Life Book of elegant everyday cooking
  Includes index
ISBN 0-8094-9150-8
ISBN 0-8094-9151-6 (lib. bdg.)

The Time-Life Book of Elegant Everyday Cooking

BY

THE EDITORS OF TIME-LIFE BOOKS

TIME-LIFE BOOKS / ALEXANDRIA, VIRGINIA

Contents

Just Plain Good

This cookbook is dedicated to the proposition that healthful food can be easy and delicious. It keeps that happy thought in mind as it lays out an array of mouth-watering, light, uncomplicated dishes. Here you will find 274 recipes for soups and starters, poultry, fish and shellfish, beef, veal, lamb and pork, pasta, vegetables, salads, and low-calorie, scrumptious desserts, as well as suggestions for picnics, brunches, and barbecues. All the dishes are low in saturated fats, cholesterol, and salt. Yet not one stints on flavor. They take advantage of fresh ingredients, and many can be prepared ahead of time and served cold—a boon for the busy cook.

Drawn from the pages of Time-Life Books' successful series, *Fresh Ways,* the recipes make eating wisely but well a pleasure instead of a chore. In their sensibleness, they are never grim. They recognize, for example, that the strictures of modern nutritionists are not directed against fat itself but rather against the quantity of fat in our diet. Even if it were possible to eliminate fat altogether, this would not be a desirable goal. Fat is an essential nutrient—especially for children—because it provides certain fat-soluble vitamins and helps the body to absorb these; it contains essential fatty acids that the body cannot produce itself but that are converted by the body into the basic material of cell membranes; and it is the most concentrated source of energy available. In addition, fat contributes to flavor and palatability, and because it takes longer to digest than either protein or carbohydrates, it is chiefly responsible for the comfortable feeling of satisfaction that comes after eating well.

Fat becomes culpable only when we eat too much of it—which most adults in the Western world tend to do. About 40 percent of our caloric intake is accounted for by fat, compared with about 10 percent in developing countries, and studies have shown that this high proportion is not only more than we need but is also associated with the high incidence of obesity and coronary disease in the more affluent societies.

Closely linked with the issue of fat in the diet is that of the notorious compound cholesterol. Excess cholesterol deposited within the walls of blood vessels can lead to circulatory problems and hence to arterial and heart disease, but the problem is not as simple as this connection implies. Present in all animal tissue, cholesterol is a fatty substance that is needed for the fluidity of our cell membranes and for the synthesis of certain hormones and vitamin D. The amount of cholesterol we take in with our food is normally far less than is produced by the body and does not by itself raise the cholesterol in our blood to unacceptable levels. The villain is really saturated fat, which stimulates the body's own synthesis of cholesterol. (In contrast, polyunsaturated fats, present in certain plant and vegetable oils, can actually reduce cholesterol by aiding the body's mechanisms for getting rid of it.) For this reason, although it is sensible to be aware of the cholesterol levels in our diets and to eat cholesterol-rich foods such as liver and kidneys only occasionally, the main precaution we should take against raising the amount of cholesterol in our blood is to reduce our intake of fat, and especially of saturated fat.

Foods that are good for you

What this means for health-conscious cooks is patently simple—we should choose and prepare our foods carefully. Keeping the amounts of fat and cholesterol in each dish within reasonable limits is something that, happily enough, these recipes all manage to do. Moreover, they often include foods rich in fiber. Dietary fiber is itself indigestible, yet it assists the digestion of food and bulks up waste material, thus speeding the passage of waste through the intestines. Extravagant health claims have been made for this improbable nutritional hero; nevertheless, it is likely that fiber helps prevent diseases of the intestine—possibly including colon cancer—and reduces the body's absorption of cholesterol.

You will find plenty else in this book to be pleased about. The dishes are all original, the inventions of health-minded, creative cooks working under the guidance of nutritionists in the Time-

Life test kitchens in the United States and in Great Britain. Each recipe comes with a photograph of the finished dish so that you can see what it looks like.

As welcome light fare, poultry, fish, shellfish, and salads crop up frequently in these pages. Even the ancient Greeks knew that salads were healthful; they held salad to be a food of the gods. In Shakespeare's England, so-called fountains of youth, assembled from the first tender herbs and lettuces of spring, were eagerly consumed as antidotes to the grim winter diet. The great French gastronome Brillat-Savarin summed it up nicely: "Salad refreshes without weakening and comforts without irritating," he wrote in 1825, "and it makes us younger."

Whether truly rejuvenating or not, salad is, with its endless choice of ingredients, a bountiful source of minerals, vitamins, and other nutrients. And when it is dressed with care, salad will be low in fat as well, and thus in calories. The fact that most lettuces are between 90 and 95 percent water is bound to give some weight-conscious people reason to cheer.

Salads made with grains, dried beans, or pasta—as many are, in this book—will be loaded with protein and complex carbohydrates, the main source of energy for the body. Dried beans offer a particularly generous supply of fiber and protein; but for their protein to be utilized by the body, they must be coupled with other foods that offer complementary proteins.

When chicken and turkey are skinned, both become remarkably low in fat and in calories. Indeed, with its skin removed and any excess visible fat scraped away, chicken loses at least 40 calories per three-ounce serving. Better yet, a three-ounce serving of skinned turkey breast contains even less saturated fat than skinned chicken, and it has fewer calories to boot.

About cooking methods

For the other meat dishes presented in this book the cuts come from the least fatty parts of the animals. Yet it is fat, of course, that gives meat, especially red meat, much of its flavor and juiciness. Because the recipes avoid the fattier cuts, cooking methods and ingredients have been employed that ensure flavor and moistness. And care has been taken to see to it that the meat is not overcooked—which is easy to do with lean cuts, particularly when pieces are small. Prolonged high heat is the surest way to toughen meat, and to dry it out and shrink it as well. To further keep fat and cholesterol levels within healthful limits, the recipes make little use of cream, butter, and cheeses in sauces. The sauces themselves are often created by reducing the liquids in which the meat and other ingredients have simmered, and thus many of their nutrients are retained. Be sure, however, to skim off any fat before proceeding with your reduction.

When it comes to the vegetable recipes, the favored cooking methods are boiling and steaming. Most vegetables benefit from being cooked in only enough water to cover them. The water should be boiling before the vegetables are plunged into it, then allowed to come back to a boil before the saucepan is covered and the heat reduced. For maximal nutritional benefit, steaming is actually sounder than boiling. This is because the vegetables cook in the water vapor rather than in the water itself, which leaches out nutrients. The color is also better; the volatile acids in the vegetables rise with the steam to the lid and then run down the sides of the pan into the water below, and thus do not have any sustained contact with the vegetables. To ensure that the vegetables will cook evenly, distribute them loosely in the steamer; this allows the vapor to circulate around them. And since those at the bottom can overcook, it pays to use a steamer large enough to spread the vegetables out evenly. A metal vegetable steamer or steaming basket is a good investment—but a steamer can easily be improvised from a colander or a strainer positioned over a saucepan. Add the vegetables to the steamer only after the water is boiling; the high temperature helps to inactivate enzymes that would otherwise destroy the vitamin C.

The proof in the pudding

Healthful procedures and ingredients might seem beside the point when it comes to desserts, which by nature are supposed to be sinful. But you will be pleasantly surprised by those in this book; they quite literally allow you to have your cake and eat it too. The recipes strive to limit sugar, honey, and other sweeteners to no more than two tablespoons per serving. (In some instances, such as the frozen desserts that dominate the selection, more sugar is needed to guarantee the end result—a matter of chemistry, not taste.) Of course, sugar is not the sole caloric ingredient in a dessert. Surprisingly, a teaspoonful of it contains only 16 calories. Fat, with about 33 calories per teaspoonful, weighs in at double that amount.

The fats in desserts—usually in the form of butter, cream, or egg yolks—have traditionally made piecrusts flaky, mousses smooth, custards rich. All are of animal origin, however, and all therefore contain saturated fats. But as the recipes demonstrate, fats can be curbed without marring a dessert's appeal. You will find butter, cream, and egg yolks included in many of the desserts, but in moderate amounts—enough, certainly, to lend flavor or texture or both. Butter is generally limited to half a tablespoon per serving; sometimes it is paired with margarine to achieve flakiness in pastry without increasing saturated fat. Cream is by and large restricted to a tablespoon per portion, and a single egg yolk is divided among four servings. Such well-thought-out, yet delicious desserts can bring a well-planned, well-balanced meal to a happy and most satisfying conclusion.

The Key to Better Eating

Calories **180**
Protein **21g.**
Cholesterol **65mg.**
Total fat **8g.**
Saturated fat **4g.**
Sodium **230mg.**

Better eating is an achievable goal for everyone. This book makes it possible by addressing the concerns of today's weight-conscious, health-minded cooks with recipes that take into account guidelines set by nutritionists. The secret to eating well, of course, has to do with maintaining a balance of foods in the diet. The recipes thus should be used thoughtfully, in the context of a day's meals. To make the choice easier, the book presents an analysis of nutrients in a single serving, as at right. The counts for calories, protein, cholesterol, total fat, saturated fat, and sodium are approximate.

Interpreting the chart
The chart below shows the National Research Council's Recommended Dietary Allowances of calories and protein for healthy men, women, and children, along with the council's recommendations for the "safe and adequate" maximum intake of sodium. Although the council has not established recommendations for either cholesterol or fat, the chart does include what the National Institutes of Health and the American Heart Association consider the daily maximum amounts of these substances for healthy members of the general population.

The book does not purport to be a diet book, nor does it focus on health foods. Rather, it expresses a common-sense approach to cooking that uses salt, sugar, cream, butter, and oil in moderation while including other ingredients that also provide flavor and satisfaction. Herbs, spices, and aromatic vegetables, as well as fruits, peels, juices, wines, and vinegars are all employed toward this end.

The recipes make few unusual demands. Naturally they call for fresh ingredients, offering substitutes when these are unavailable. (Only the original ingredient is calculated in the nutrient analysis, however.) Most of the ingredients can be found in any well-stocked supermarket. The presence now in many communities of farmers' markets, health-food stores, and gourmet shops enlarges the range of choice and adds new dimensions of excitement to cooking.

In order to simplify meal planning, most of the recipes offer accompaniments. These accompaniments are intended only as suggestions, however; cooks should let their imaginations be their guide and come up with ideas of their own to achieve a sensible and appealing balance of foods.

In the test kitchens where the recipes were developed, heavy-bottomed pots and pans were used to guard against burning the food whenever a small amount of oil was called for and where there was danger of the food adhering to the hot surface, but nonstick pans can be utilized as well. Both safflower oil and virgin olive oil were favored for sautéing. Safflower oil was chosen because it is the most highly polyunsaturated vegetable fat widely available in supermarkets, and polyunsaturated fats reduce blood cholesterol. Virgin olive oil was used because it has a fine fruity flavor lacking in the lesser grade known as "pure." When virgin olive oil is unavailable, or when its flavor is not essential to the dish, "pure" may be substituted.

About cooking times
To help the cook plan ahead, the book takes time into account in its recipes. While recognizing that everyone cooks at a different speed and that stoves and ovens differ, it provides approximate "working" and "total" times for every dish. Working time stands for the minutes actively spent on preparation; total time includes unattended cooking time, as well as time devoted to marinating, steeping, or soaking ingredients. Since the recipes emphasize fresh foods, they may take a bit longer to prepare than "quick and easy" dishes that call for canned or packaged products, but the payoff in flavor, and often in nutrition, should compensate for the little extra time involved.

Recommended Dietary Guidelines

		Average Daily Intake		Maximum Daily Intake			
		CALORIES	PROTEIN grams	CHOLESTEROL milligrams	TOTAL FAT grams	SATURATED FAT grams	SODIUM milligrams
Children	7-10	2000	22	240	67	22	2000
Females	11-14	2200	37	220	73	24	2200
	15-18	2200	44	210	73	24	2200
	19-24	2200	44	300	73	24	3000
	25-50	2200	44	300	73	24	3000
	50+	1900	44	300	63	21	3000
Males	11-14	2500	36	270	83	28	2500
	15-18	3000	56	280	100	33	3000
	19-24	2900	56	300	97	32	3000
	25-50	2900	56	300	97	32	3000
	50+	2300	56	300	77	28	3000

1 *Mussels on the half shell coated with a fragrant tomato and fennel relish make an appealing and quickly prepared party dish (recipe, page 39).*

Soups and Openers

Chilled Snow-Pea Soup

Serves 6
Working time: about 40 minutes
Total time: about 3 hours and 30 minutes
(includes chilling)

Calories **70**
Protein **3g.**
Cholesterol **0mg.**
Total fat **4g.**
Saturated fat **1g.**
Sodium **70mg.**

2 tbsp. polyunsaturated margarine
¾ lb. snow peas, stems and strings removed
8 scallions, trimmed and chopped
one 3-oz. potato, peeled and grated
4 tsp. unbleached all-purpose flour
2½ cups unsalted chicken stock
⅛ tsp. salt
freshly ground black pepper
1¼ cups skim milk
10 fresh basil leaves

Melt the margarine in a heavy-bottomed saucepan over medium heat. Set aside four of the snow peas; add the remaining snow peas to the pan, with the scallions and potato. Stir the vegetables for one minute, then add the flour and stir for one minute more. Gradually mix in the stock, and bring it to a boil, stirring continuously. Add the salt and some freshly ground black pepper. Cover the pan, lower the heat, and simmer the mixture for 15 minutes, stirring it occasionally. Remove the pan from the heat.

Purée the mixture in a food processor or blender with the skim milk. Press the purée through a sieve. Finely chop four of the basil leaves and stir them into the soup; reserve the remaining basil leaves for garnish. Allow the soup to cool, then chill it in the refrigerator for at least two hours.

Blanch the reserved snow peas in a saucepan of boiling water. Drain them, refresh them under cold running water, and drain them again thoroughly. Cut the snow peas into thin, diagonal strips.

Garnish each serving with a few slivers of snow pea and a basil leaf.

Carrot and Cardamom Soup

Serves 8
Working time: about 35 minutes
Total time: about 3 hours (includes chilling)

Calories **75**
Protein **3g.**
Cholesterol **trace**
Total fat **2g.**
Saturated fat **1g.**
Sodium **275mg.**

8 cardamom pods
2 tsp. virgin olive oil
1 onion, coarsely chopped
2 celery stalks, coarsely sliced
1½ lb. carrots (6 to 8 medium), cut into chunks
3 cups unsalted chicken or vegetable stock
¼ lb. cucumber (about ½), peeled and cut into chunks
¾ cup plain low-fat yogurt
½ tsp. salt
freshly ground black pepper
1 tsp. sugar
2 slices whole-wheat bread, crusts removed
celery leaves for garnish
ice cubes for garnish (optional)

Wrap the cardamom pods in a double layer of paper towels and crush them lightly with a rolling pin, to split them. Heat the oil in a large, heavy-bottomed saucepan over medium heat. Add the onion, celery, carrots, and split cardamom pods, and cook the mixture, stirring it occasionally, until the vegetables begin to soften—about three minutes. Stir in 2 cups of the stock, and bring the liquid to a boil. Lower the heat, cover the pan, and simmer the vegetables until the carrots are soft—8 to 10 minutes. Remove the pan from the heat, and let the mixture cool for about 10 minutes.

Purée the cucumber chunks with the cooked vegetable mixture in a food processor or blender. Pour the purée into a bowl and add the remaining stock, then stir in ½ cup of the yogurt, the salt, some pepper, and the sugar. Pass the soup through a coarse sieve to remove the cardamom pods. Refrigerate the soup in a tightly covered container until it is thoroughly chilled—at least two hours, or overnight.

Toast the bread on both sides, then cut it into ¼-inch dice.

To serve, pour the soup into individual bowls and add a few cubes of ice to each bowl, if you wish. Swirl a spoonful of yogurt on the surface of each portion. Garnish the soup with the celery leaves, and serve with the diced whole-wheat toast.

Chilled Tomato-and-Shrimp Soup

Serves 4
Working time: about 20 minutes
Total time: about 1 hour and 20 minutes (includes chilling)

Calories **120**
Protein **14g.**
Cholesterol **97mg.**
Total fat **1g.**
Saturated fat **0g.**
Sodium **150mg.**

2 cups unsalted veal or chicken stock
4 ripe tomatoes, peeled, seeded and coarsely chopped
½ cucumber, peeled, seeded and coarsely chopped
1 scallion, trimmed and sliced into thin rounds
2 tbsp. red wine vinegar
¼ tsp. white pepper
1 tsp. Dijon mustard
4 to 8 drops hot red-pepper sauce
¾ lb. baby shrimp
½ cup croutons

Pour the stock into a serving bowl. Stir in the tomatoes, cucumber, scallion, vinegar, pepper, mustard and red-pepper sauce. Add the shrimp and stir again. Cover the bowl and refrigerate it for at least one hour.

Serve the soup in chilled soup bowls; if you wish, garnish each portion with a few croutons.

Cold Curried Vegetable Soup

Serves 4 as a first course
Working time: about 20 minutes
Total time: about 2 hours and 20 minutes
(includes chilling)

Calories **130**
Protein **5g.**
Cholesterol **1mg.**
Total fat **4g.**
Saturated fat **1g.**
Sodium **220mg.**

2 tsp. safflower oil
1 small onion, thinly sliced
2 tbsp. mild curry powder
2 garlic cloves, finely chopped
14 oz. canned unsalted tomatoes, coarsely chopped, with their juice
3 cups unsalted chicken stock
1 tsp. chopped fresh thyme, or ¼ tsp. dried thyme leaves
1 green pepper, seeded, deribbed and cut into ½-inch pieces
1 cup cauliflower florets, thinly sliced lengthwise
1 small carrot, thinly sliced
1 small zucchini, thinly sliced
1 small yellow squash, halved lengthwise and thinly sliced across
1 tbsp. balsamic vinegar or red wine vinegar
¼ tsp. salt
freshly ground black pepper

Heat the safflower oil in a large, heavy-bottomed saucepan over medium heat. Add the onion slices and sauté them, stirring, until they are translucent — about four minutes. Sprinkle in the curry powder and cook the mixture, stirring constantly, for one minute. Add the garlic and cook it for 30 seconds. Stir in the tomatoes with their juice and cook them, stirring frequently, until the liquid is reduced by about one third — 10 to 15 minutes.

While the tomatoes are cooking, pour the stock into a pot over medium-high heat. Add the thyme and place a steamer in the pot. Arrange the green pepper, cauliflower, carrot, zucchini and squash in the steamer. Cover the pot and steam the vegetables until they are tender — five to seven minutes. Transfer the vegetables to the tomato mixture and pour in the steaming liquid. Add the vinegar, salt and some black pepper, then gently stir the soup to incorporate the vegetables. Refrigerate the soup, partially covered, for at least two hours before serving.

EDITOR'S NOTE: *This soup may be prepared as much as two days in advance.*

Vegetable-Broth Minestrone

Serves 6
Working time: about 30 minutes
Total time: about 2 hours

Calories **305**
Protein **16g.**
Cholesterol **0mg.**
Total fat **2g.**
Saturated fat **0g.**
Sodium **205mg.**

1 cup dried pinto beans, picked over

2 onions, unpeeled, halved crosswise

½ cup dry white wine

8 oz. mushrooms, wiped clean, stems removed and reserved, the caps sliced

1 lb. ripe tomatoes, peeled, seeded and chopped, the peels, seeds and juice reserved, or 14 oz. canned unsalted tomatoes, seeded and chopped, the seeds and juice reserved

2 carrots, sliced

2 celery stalks, sliced, leaves chopped and reserved

1 cauliflower, broken into florets, the leaves and core coarsely chopped and reserved

2 broccoli stalks, the florets broken off (about 2 cups), the leaves and stalks coarsely chopped and reserved

1 whole garlic bulb, the unpeeled cloves separated and crushed with the side of a heavy knife, plus 4 garlic cloves, chopped

24 black peppercorns

1 tsp. fresh rosemary, or ¼ tsp. dried rosemary

2 bay leaves

2 lemon-zest strips, each about 2 inches long

4 oz. ziti or other tubular pasta

juice of ½ lemon

¼ tsp. salt

1 cup sliced fresh basil leaves, or ¼ cup chopped fresh parsley

freshly ground black pepper

½ cup freshly grated Parmesan cheese

Rinse the beans under cold running water. Put the beans into a large pot and pour in enough cold water to cover them by about 3 inches. Discard any beans that float to the surface. Boil the beans for two minutes, then turn off the heat, cover the pot, and soak the beans for at least an hour. (Alternatively, soak the beans overnight in cold water.)

At the end of the soaking time, pour in enough additional water to cover the beans by about 3 inches. Bring the liquid to a boil, reduce the heat to maintain a strong simmer, and cook the beans until they are tender — about 30 minutes. Then drain the beans and set them aside.

While the beans are simmering, start the vegetable broth. Heat a large, heavy-bottomed pot over medium-high heat and place the onions flat sides down in the pot. Cook the onions until their cut surfaces turn dark brown — about 10 minutes. (The onions will help to color the stock.) Pour in the wine, stirring with a wooden spoon to dislodge the onions and dissolve their caramelized juices. Add the mushroom stems, the tomato peels, seeds and juice, half of the carrots, the sliced celery, the chopped cauliflower leaves and cores, the chopped broccoli leaves and stalks, the crushed garlic cloves, peppercorns, rosemary, bay leaves, lemon zest and 12 cups of water. Bring the liquid to a boil, then reduce the heat to maintain a simmer and cook the broth for one hour.

While the broth is simmering, add the ziti to 6 cups of boiling water with 1 teaspoon of salt. Start testing the pasta after eight minutes and cook it until it is *al dente*. Drain the pasta, rinse it under cold running water to keep it from sticking together, and set it aside.

In a small bowl, mix the chopped tomato and the chopped garlic with the lemon juice and salt, and set the mixture aside.

When the vegetable broth has simmered for one hour, strain it into a bowl and discard the solids. Rinse the pot and return the strained broth to it. Bring the broth to a boil. Reduce the heat to medium, then add the sliced mushroom caps and the remaining carrots, and simmer them for four minutes. Add the cauliflower florets and simmer them for four minutes more. Add the broccoli florets, celery leaves and beans, and simmer them for an additional three minutes.

Transfer the drained ziti to the pot and cook for two minutes to warm the pasta through. Stir in the tomato-garlic mixture and the basil or parsley. Season the minestrone with a generous grinding of pepper, and serve it with the grated cheese alongside.

Gazpacho Blanco

Serves 4 as a first course
Working time: about 10 minutes
Total time: about 40 minutes

Calories **165**
Protein **7g.**
Cholesterol **7mg.**
Total fat **2g.**
Saturated fat **1g.**
Sodium **220mg.**

1 lb. seedless white grapes
3 cucumbers
1 shallot, sliced
1 small garlic clove, finely chopped
¼ tsp. salt
¼ tsp. white pepper
2 cups plain low-fat yogurt
5 to 8 drops hot red-pepper sauce

Wash and stem the grapes. Cut several grapes in half lengthwise and set them aside. Purée the remaining grapes in a food processor or blender. Strain the purée through a sieve and return it to the food processor or blender.

Cut several very thin slices from the center of a cucumber and set them aside. Peel the cucumbers, halve them lengthwise, and seed them. Cut the cucumbers into thick slices and add them to the grape purée in the processor or blender. Add the shallot, garlic, salt and pepper, and briefly process the mixture until the cucumbers are reduced to fine pieces.

Pour the mixture into a chilled serving bowl and whisk in the yogurt and red-pepper sauce. Cover the soup and refrigerate it until it is well chilled — about 30 minutes. Serve the soup in chilled bowls, garnished with the reserved cucumber slices and grape halves.

Gazpacho with Roasted Peppers

Serves 4 as a first course
Working time: about 50 minutes
Total time: about 1 hour and 50 minutes

Calories **70**
Protein **2g.**
Cholesterol **0mg.**
Total fat **4g.**
Saturated fat **1g.**
Sodium **170mg.**

1 large sweet red pepper
1 large green pepper
2 ripe tomatoes, peeled, seeded and coarsely chopped
2 celery stalks, thinly sliced
1 cucumber, peeled, halved lengthwise, seeded and cut into large chunks
2 garlic cloves, chopped
1 cup coarsely chopped fresh watercress, plus 4 whole sprigs for garnish
½ cup unsalted veal or vegetable stock
¼ cup fresh orange juice
1 tbsp. fresh lemon juice
1 tbsp. virgin olive oil
¼ tsp. salt
freshly ground black pepper

Preheat the broiler. Broil the peppers 2 to 3 inches below the heat source, turning them often, until they are uniformly blistered and blackened — 12 to 15 minutes. Transfer the peppers to a bowl and tightly cover the bowl with plastic wrap. Let the peppers stand for five minutes — the trapped steam will loosen their skin.

Make a slit in one of the peppers and pour the juices that have collected inside it into the bowl. Peel the pepper from top to bottom. Halve the pepper lengthwise, then remove and discard the stem, seeds and ribs. Repeat the procedure with the other pepper.

Put the peppers and their juices into a food processor or blender along with the tomatoes, celery, cucumber, garlic, chopped watercress, stock, orange juice, lemon juice, oil, salt and some pepper. Process the mixture in short bursts until a coarse purée results. Transfer the gazpacho to a bowl; refrigerate it for at least one hour, then garnish it with the watercress sprigs and serve.

EDITOR'S NOTE: *This soup may be prepared as much as 24 hours in advance.*

Dilly Avocado Soup

Serves 6
Working time: about 15 minutes
Total time: about 1 hour and 15 minutes (includes chilling)

Calories **110**
Protein **5g.**
Cholesterol **5mg.**
Total fat **7g.**
Saturated fat **2g.**
Sodium **165mg.**

1 avocado, halved, peeled and cut into chunks (about 1 cup firmly packed), the pit reserved
2 cups plain low-fat yogurt
1½ cups unsalted chicken stock
2 scallions, trimmed and cut into ¼-inch lengths (about ¼ cup)
1 tbsp. finely cut fresh dill, or ½ tbsp. dried dillweed
¼ tsp. dry mustard
¼ tsp. salt
dill sprigs for garnish (optional)

Put the avocado chunks, yogurt, stock, scallions, cut dill or dillweed, mustard and salt in a blender or food processor and purée the mixture until it is completely smooth. Transfer the soup to a nonreactive container (include the avocado pit, if you like) and tightly cover the container. Chill the soup in the refrigerator for at least one hour. If you wish, garnish each serving with a small sprig of dill.

EDITOR'S NOTE: *Because avocado darkens when exposed to air, cut it just before you purée the soup. The yogurt will help keep the soup from discoloring as it chills, but you may also want to try the Mexican trick of leaving the avocado pit in the soup until serving time.*

carrots are soft — eight to 10 minutes.

While the soup is boiling, bring the remaining 1½ cups of stock to a simmer in a small saucepan over medium heat. Add the diced carrots and the raisins and simmer them, covered, until the carrots are tender — about five minutes. Set the saucepan aside.

Purée the soup in batches in a blender, food processor or food mill. Return the soup to the pot over medium heat and add the diced carrots and raisins with their cooking liquid. Stir in the cream, salt, some pepper and the parsley. Simmer the soup until it is heated through — about two minutes — and serve at once.

Cream of Carrot Soup with Fresh Ginger

Serves 8 as a first course
Working time: about 30 minutes
Total time: about 1 hour

Calories **155**	2 lb. carrots
Protein **4g.**	2 tsp. safflower oil
Cholesterol **15mg.**	2 tsp. unsalted butter
Total fat **8g.**	2 onions, chopped (about 1½ cups)
Saturated fat **3g.**	¼ cup grated fresh ginger
Sodium **350mg.**	8 cups unsalted chicken stock
	¼ cup golden raisins, chopped
	½ cup light cream
	¾ tsp. salt
	freshly ground black pepper
	2 tbsp. chopped fresh parsley

Cut two of the carrots into small dice and set them aside. Slice the remaining carrots into thin rounds.

Heat the oil and butter together in a large, heavy-bottomed pot over medium heat. Add the onions and cook them, stirring occasionally, until they are golden — about 10 minutes. Add the carrot rounds and the ginger, and stir in 1½ cups of the stock. Reduce the heat, cover the pot, and cook the mixture until the carrots are tender — about 20 minutes.

Pour 5 cups of the remaining stock into the pot and bring the liquid to a boil. Reduce the heat, cover the pot, and simmer the stock for 10 minutes. Remove the lid and increase the heat to high. Boil the soup, skimming the impurities from the surface several times, until the liquid is reduced by about one third and the

Chilled Curried Cucumber Soup

Serves 6 as a first course
Working time: about 20 minutes
Total time: about 1 hour and 20 minutes (includes chilling)

Calories **95**	1 cup loosely packed cilantro, a few leaves reserved for garnish
Protein **5g.**	1 onion, quartered
Cholesterol **10mg.**	2 large cucumbers, peeled, quartered lengthwise, seeded and cut into chunks
Total fat **5g.**	½ cup sour cream
Saturated fat **3g.**	1½ cups plain low-fat yogurt
Sodium **165mg.**	1 tsp. curry powder
	¼ tsp. salt
	¼ tsp. white pepper
	3 to 5 drops hot red-pepper sauce
	1¼ cups unsalted brown or chicken stock

Chop the cilantro in a food processor. Add the onion and cucumber chunks, and process them until they are finely chopped but not puréed. (Alternatively, chop the cilantro by hand and grate or finely chop the onion and cucumbers.)

In a bowl, whisk the sour cream with 1 cup of the yogurt, the curry powder, salt, white pepper and red-pepper sauce. Whisk in the cucumber mixture and the stock. Refrigerate the soup for at least one hour. Serve the soup in chilled bowls; garnish each portion with a dollop of the remaining yogurt and the reserved cilantro leaves.

EDITOR'S NOTE: *This soup is even better when it is made a day in advance.*

Cold Parsley Soup with Icy Tomato Granita

GRANITA IS THE ITALIAN NAME FOR A WATER ICE.
THE CRYSTALLINE TEXTURE OF THE TOMATO-MINT GRANITA
USED HERE PROVIDES A SUBTLE COUNTERPOINT TO THE
SOUP'S SMOOTHNESS.

Serves 6 as a first course
Working time: about 45 minutes
Total time: about 3 hours and 45 minutes
(includes chilling)

Calories **100**
Protein **4g.**
Cholesterol **1mg.**
Total fat **4g.**
Saturated fat **1g.**
Sodium **255mg.**

1 tbsp. virgin olive oil
4 scallions, trimmed and thinly sliced
1 onion, thinly sliced
2 garlic cloves, finely chopped
¼ tsp. salt
freshly ground black pepper
4 cups unsalted chicken or vegetable stock
1 potato, peeled and thinly sliced
4 cups parsley leaves, preferably Italian
6 mint sprigs for garnish
Tomato granita
1 lb. ripe tomatoes, peeled, cored and quartered
¼ tsp. salt
1 tbsp. fresh lemon juice
2 tbsp. finely chopped fresh mint

To prepare the granita, purée the tomatoes in a blender or food processor, then strain the purée through a sieve into a bowl. Stir in the salt, lemon juice and mint. Pour the mixture into ice-cube trays and freeze it for two to three hours.

Meanwhile, heat the oil in a large, heavy-bottomed pot over medium heat. Add the scallions, onion, garlic, salt and some pepper. Cook the mixture, stirring often, until the onion is translucent — about five minutes. Pour in the stock, then add the potato slices. Reduce the heat, cover the pot, and simmer the liquid until a potato slice can be easily crushed with the back of a fork — 25 to 30 minutes.

While the stock is simmering, bring a large pot of water to a boil. Add the parsley leaves; as soon as the water returns to a boil, drain the leaves and refresh them under cold running water.

Purée the parsley and the stock-vegetable mixture together in a blender or food processor. Strain the purée through a sieve into a bowl and let it cool to room temperature. Cover the bowl with plastic wrap and refrigerate it until the soup is thoroughly chilled — at least two hours.

Purée the cubes of granita in a food processor just until the mixture is grainy. Transfer the cold parsley soup to six chilled soup bowls. Spoon some of the granita into each bowl; garnish with the mint sprigs and serve immediately.

Corn and Cilantro Soup

Serves 4 as a first course
Working (and total) time: about 20 minutes

Calories **160**
Protein **5g.**
Cholesterol **6mg.**
Total fat **5g.**
Saturated fat **2g.**
Sodium **330mg.**

2 tsp. unsalted butter
1 tsp. safflower oil
1 onion, finely chopped
3 garlic cloves, finely chopped
1 tsp. cumin seeds, ground with a mortar and pestle, or 1 tsp. ground cumin (optional)
1 green pepper, seeded, deribbed and chopped
1 sweet red pepper, seeded, deribbed and chopped
1 jalapeño pepper (optional), seeded and finely chopped
1 ripe tomato, peeled, seeded and chopped
2 cups fresh or frozen corn kernels
2 cups unsalted chicken stock
½ tsp. salt
2 tbsp. chopped cilantro

Heat the butter and the oil together in a large, heavy-bottomed saucepan or skillet over medium heat. Add the onion, garlic and, if you are using it, the cumin. Cook, stirring often, until the onion is translucent — about five minutes. Stir in all the peppers and cook them until they soften slightly — about two minutes

more. Add the tomato, corn, stock and salt. Reduce the heat and simmer the soup for five minutes. Stir in the cilantro just before serving.

Toasted Onion Dip

Serves 12
Working time: about 30 minutes
Total time: about 2 hours and 30 minutes
(includes chilling)

Calories **45**	3 large Spanish onions, 2 coarsely chopped
Protein **5g.**	⅔ cup low-fat ricotta cheese
Cholesterol **trace**	6 oz. low-fat cream cheese
Total fat **2g.**	6 tbsp. finely cut chives
Saturated fat **trace**	freshly ground black pepper
Sodium **30mg.**	

Preheat the oven to 375° F., and line a baking sheet with aluminum foil.

Put the coarsely chopped onions into a heavy-bottomed saucepan and cover them with cold water. Bring the water to a boil, cover the pan, and simmer the onions gently until they are very soft and tender—30 to 40 minutes.

Meanwhile, cut the remaining onion into slices ¼ inch thick and spread them out on the prepared baking sheet. Toast the onion slices in the oven for about 20 minutes, turning them so that they brown evenly and removing them as they brown; do not let the onions burn. Alternatively, toast the onion slices under a pre-heated, medium-hot broiler, again watching carefully to be sure that they do not burn. Set the toasted onion slices aside.

When the chopped onions are cooked, drain them well and allow them to cool. Transfer them to a food processor and blend them to a smooth purée. Add the cheeses and process the mixture briefly to combine the ingredients. Turn the dip into a bowl.

Crumble the toasted onion slices. Reserve 1 table-spoon for garnish, and add the remainder to the bowl with the chives and some black pepper. Gently fold these ingredients into the dip. Cover the bowl and chill the dip for at least one hour. Just before serving, sprinkle the surface with the reserved toasted onion.

SUGGESTED ACCOMPANIMENT: *a selection of crunchy fresh vegetables for dipping.*

Cucumber Dip

Serves 6
Working time: about 15 minutes
Total time: about 1 hour and 45 minutes (includes chilling)

Calories **60**	½ cucumber, peeled, seeded, and grated
Protein **1g.**	½ tsp. salt
Cholesterol **15mg.**	⅔ cup sour cream
Total fat **5g.**	1 cup loosely packed watercress, leaves only,
Saturated fat **3g.**	washed, dried, and finely chopped
Sodium **25mg.**	2 scallions, trimmed and finely chopped
	freshly ground black pepper

Place the cucumber in a shallow bowl, sprinkle it with the salt, and let it stand for 30 minutes. Rinse the salt off under cold running water, and drain the cucumber well; lightly squeeze out any excess water.

Put the cucumber into a bowl with the sour cream, watercress, scallions, chopped chili pepper, and black pepper, and mix everything together well. Let the dip rest in the refrigerator for at least one hour before transferring it to a container with a tightfitting lid. Keep the dip in its container in the refrigerator until you are ready to go to the picnic. Pack the container upright in a cooler.

SUGGESTED ACCOMPANIMENT: *a selection of crunchy fresh vegetables.*

Red-Pepper Dip

Serves 6
Working time: about 15 minutes
Total time: about 1 hour and 15 minutes (includes chilling)

Calories **40**	2 sweet red peppers (about 7 oz. each)
Protein **3g.**	½ cup plain low-fat yogurt
Cholesterol **trace**	½ tsp. salt
Total fat **3g.**	¼ tsp. cayenne pepper
Saturated fat **1g.**	
Sodium **130mg.**	

Place the peppers 2 inches below a preheated broiler and roast them, turning them frequently, until their skin is blistered on all sides. Transfer the peppers to a bowl and cover the bowl with plastic wrap; the trapped steam will loosen the skin. Using a small, sharp knife, peel off the pepper skin in sections. Seed and derib the peeled peppers, and chop the flesh coarsely.

Place the chopped red peppers in a food processor and blend them until they are smooth. Put the pepper purée into a bowl and stir in the yogurt. Add the salt and cayenne pepper, mixing well. Let the dip rest in the refrigerator for at least one hour before transferring it to a container with a tightfitting lid. Keep the dip in its container in the refrigerator until you are ready to go to the picnic. Pack it upright in a cooler.

SUGGESTED ACCOMPANIMENT: *a selection of crunchy fresh vegetables.*

Asparagus Strudel

Serves 4
Working time: about 40 minutes
Total time: about 1 hour and 10 minutes

Calories **225**
Protein **10g.**
Cholesterol **60mg.**
Total fat **13g.**
Saturated fat **5g.**
Sodium **380mg.**

¾ lb. asparagus, trimmed, peeled, and sliced diagonally into ¼-inch thick pieces
½ cup part-skim ricotta cheese
2 tbsp. finely cut fresh chives
2 tbsp. chopped fresh marjoram
1 tbsp. chopped parsley
1 egg, separated
¼ tsp. salt
freshly ground black pepper
5 sheets phyllo pastry, each about 18 by 12 inches
2 tbsp. polyunsaturated margarine, melted
¼ cup fresh whole-wheat breadcrumbs

Preheat the oven to 400° F. Lightly grease a baking sheet. Place the asparagus pieces in a steamer set over a saucepan of boiling water and steam them until they are tender—four to five minutes. Refresh them under cold running water and drain them well. Pat the asparagus pieces dry on paper towels.

Put the ricotta into a mixing bowl with the chives, marjoram, parsley, egg yolk, salt, and some black pepper. Beat the ingredients together well and stir in the drained asparagus. In a clean bowl, whisk the egg white until it is stiff, then fold it carefully into the asparagus mixture.

Lay one of the sheets of phyllo pastry out flat on the work surface, with a long side toward you. Keep the other sheets covered with a clean, damp cloth to prevent them from drying out. Brush a little of the melted margarine over the sheet on the work surface and sprinkle it with one-fifth of the breadcrumbs. Lay another sheet of phyllo on top of the first; brush it with margarine and sprinkle it with crumbs in the same way. Repeat this process with the remaining three sheets of phyllo pastry.

Spoon the asparagus mixture onto the top sheet of phyllo, mounding it in a neat line about 1 inch in from the edge nearest to you, and leaving about 1 inch clear at each side.

Fold the sides of the pastry in, over the asparagus mixture, then loosely roll the pastry to enclose the filling. Place the strudel, with the seam underneath, on the greased baking sheet. Brush the remaining margarine over the top of the pastry.

Bake the strudel until it is golden brown and puffed up—25 to 30 minutes. Serve it sliced, warm or cold.

SUGGESTED ACCOMPANIMENT: *salad of curly endive and red onion rings.*

Spinach and Nappa Cabbage Pie

Serves 6
Working time: about 30 minutes
Total time: about 1 hour and 20 minutes

Calories **170**
Protein **12g.**
Cholesterol **90mg.**
Total fat **10g.**
Saturated fat **5g.**
Sodium **430mg.**

1 lb. Nappa cabbage, leaves separated and washed
1 lb. spinach, washed, stems removed
2 eggs
1 egg white
⅔ cup low-fat cottage cheese
3 tbsp. cut fresh chives
2 tbsp. chopped fresh marjoram or oregano
¼ tsp. salt
freshly ground black pepper
6 sheets phyllo pastry, each about 18 by 12 inches
3 tbsp. unsalted butter, melted

Bring a large saucepan of water to a boil, add the Nappa cabbage leaves, and cook them until they wilt—about one minute. Using a slotted spoon, lift the leaves out of the water into a colander and drain them well. Blanch the spinach leaves in the same water for 20 seconds, then pour them into a colander and refresh them under cold running water. Squeeze the spinach dry in a piece of cheesecloth. Coarsely chop the cabbage and the spinach.

Put the eggs and egg white into a large mixing bowl, and whisk them lightly together. Add the chopped cabbage and spinach, the cottage cheese, chives, marjoram or oregano, salt, and some black pepper. Mix the ingredients together well.

Preheat the oven to 375° F. Grease a 9-by-13-inch ovenproof dish.

Cut the sheets of phyllo pastry in half crosswise. Place one piece of phyllo in the bottom of the prepared dish and brush it with a little melted butter. Add another three pieces of phyllo, brushing each one lightly with melted butter. Pour the cabbage and spinach mixture into the dish, and level the surface. Cover the filling with the remaining eight pieces of phyllo pastry, brushing each piece with melted butter as before. Using a small, sharp knife, mark the top layer of phyllo with a diamond pattern.

Bake the spinach and cabbage pie until the top is golden brown—50 to 55 minutes.

SUGGESTED ACCOMPANIMENT: *mushroom salad with a yogurt and dill dressing.*

Zucchini Soufflés

Makes 40 soufflés
Working time: about 20 minutes
Total time: about 30 minutes

Per soufflé:
Calories **10**
Protein **trace**
Cholesterol **10mg.**
Total fat **trace**
Saturated fat **trace**
Sodium **20mg.**

5 zucchini, each about 7 inches long, ends trimmed
1 tsp. polyunsaturated margarine
2 tbsp. unbleached all-purpose flour
4 tbsp. skim milk
1 egg yolk
1 oz. sharp Cheddar cheese, grated (about 2 tbsp.)
¼ tsp. Dijon mustard
¼ tsp. salt
freshly ground black pepper
2 egg whites

Using a canelle knife or a vegetable peeler, cut away thin, evenly spaced strips of skin from the length of each zucchini to create a crimped effect. Cut each zucchini into eight slices, each about ¾ inch thick. Using a small spoon, scoop out the center of each slice, taking care not to pierce the base.

Preheat the oven to 425° F. Cook the zucchini slices in boiling water until they are bright green and almost tender—about one minute. Drain them well in a sieve, and arrange them on a baking sheet lined with parchment paper.

To prepare the soufflé filling, place the margarine and flour in a small saucepan over low heat, and whisk until the ingredients are well blended. Gradually whisk in the milk, increase the heat to medium, and bring to a boil. Lower the heat and cook for five minutes, still whisking continuously. Remove the saucepan from the heat, and whisk in the egg yolk, cheese, mustard, salt, and some pepper until evenly mixed.

In a clean bowl, whisk the egg whites until they are stiff but not dry. Add the egg white to the cheese sauce, one-third at a time, carefully folding it into the mixture until all the egg white has been incorporated. Place teaspoons of the soufflé mixture into the zucchini containers, filling each to the top.

Bake the soufflés on the top rack of the oven until the soufflé mixture is well risen and golden brown— five to eight minutes. Arrange the zucchini soufflés on a serving plate, and serve hot or warm.

EDITOR'S NOTE: *Variants of this recipe can be made with artichoke bottoms or hearts, mushrooms, or tomato halves in place of the zucchini slices.*

Feta and Phyllo Parcels

Makes 12 parcels
Working time: about 30 minutes
Total time: about 45 minutes

Per parcel:
Calories **75**
Protein **2g.**
Cholesterol **5mg.**
Total fat **6g.**
Saturated fat **1g.**
Sodium **130mg.**

4 sheets phyllo pastry, each about 18 by 12 inches
3 tbsp. virgin olive oil
4 oz. feta cheese, rinsed, patted dry, and cut into 12 pieces
1 tbsp. finely chopped fresh mint

Preheat the oven to 350° F.

Place one sheet of phyllo pastry on a work surface and brush it with a little of the oil. Place a second sheet on top of the first and brush with oil. Turn over the two sheets together and brush the upper surface. (Keep the other two sheets of phyllo pastry covered with a damp cloth to prevent them from becoming brittle.)

Using a saucer about 6 inches in diameter as a template, cut out six disks from the double sheet of oiled phyllo. Place a piece of feta cheese and a little fresh mint in the center of each disk. Gather up the phyllo edges carefully and twist them slightly to make a frill. Transfer the parcels to a baking sheet. Repeat with the remaining phyllo sheets.

Bake the parcels on the lower rack of the oven for five minutes, then lower the temperature to 325° F., and bake until the bottoms and sides are evenly colored—10 to 15 minutes more. Transfer the parcels to a warm serving platter and serve at once.

Stuffed Mushrooms with Goat Cheese and Spinach

Serves 6
Working time: about 30 minutes
Total time: about 1 hour and 15 minutes

Calories **84**
Protein **3g.**
Cholesterol **12mg.**
Total fat **6g.**
Saturated fat **3g.**
Sodium **112mg.**

18 large, unblemished mushrooms, wiped clean
¼ cup dry white wine
¼ cup chopped shallots
1 tsp. fresh thyme, or ¼ tsp. dried thyme leaves
1 tbsp. fresh lime or lemon juice
1 tbsp. unsalted butter
¼ tsp. salt
1 tbsp. virgin olive oil
2 garlic cloves, finely chopped
½ lb. spinach, stems removed, the leaves washed, drained, squeezed dry and coarsely chopped
freshly ground black pepper
3 oz. mild goat cheese

Carefully pull out the mushroom stems and chop them finely, either by hand or in a blender or food processor. Set the mushroom caps aside.

Preheat the oven to 350° F. In a large skillet, heat the wine, ¼ cup of water, 2 tablespoons of the shallots and the thyme over medium heat. Bring the liquid to a boil and cook the mixture for about three minutes. Add the mushroom caps, bottoms facing up, and sprinkle them with the lime or lemon juice. Cover and cook until the mushrooms have shrunk by a third — six to eight minutes. Remove the pan from the heat. Take the caps out of the pan one at a time, tilting them to let any juices run back into the skillet. Put them on a baking sheet, bottoms down, to drain them further.

Return the skillet to the burner, and reheat the contents over medium heat. Add the chopped mushroom stems, butter and ⅛ teaspoon of the salt; cook, stirring frequently, until all the liquid is absorbed — six to eight minutes. Transfer the chopped stems to a bowl.

Wash the skillet and return it to the burner. Add the oil and heat it over high heat. When the oil is hot, stir in the remaining 2 tablespoons of shallots and the garlic. Immediately place the spinach on top and sprinkle with the remaining ⅛ teaspoon of salt. Cook, stirring constantly, until all of the liquid has evaporated — about four minutes. Transfer the spinach mixture to the bowl containing the chopped mushroom stems, and sprinkle with pepper. Stir to combine. Break the goat cheese into small pieces directly into the bowl, then carefully fold it in.

With a teaspoon, mound the spinach-and-cheese mixture into the mushroom caps. Place them in a baking dish, and bake until they are browned on top and heated through — about 20 minutes. Serve warm.

Flounder-Stuffed Tomatoes

Serves 6 as an appetizer
Working time: about 35 minutes
Total time: about 45 minutes

Calories **155**	
Protein **15g.**	1 lb. flounder fillets (or halibut or sole)
Cholesterol **43mg.**	6 ripe tomatoes
Total fat **7g.**	3 carrots, peeled and thinly sliced
Saturated fat **2g.**	2 tbsp. fresh lemon juice
Sodium **200mg.**	1½ tbsp. virgin olive oil
	5 garlic cloves, crushed
	1 large shallot, chopped
	1 tsp. fresh thyme, or ¼ tsp. dried thyme leaves
	¼ tsp. salt
	freshly ground black pepper
	¼ cup light cream

Rinse the fillets under cold running water and pat them dry with paper towels. Slice the fillets crosswise into pieces about ½ inch wide.

Slice the tops off the tomatoes and reserve them. With a spoon, scoop out and discard the seeds and pulp. Set the tomatoes upside down on paper towels to drain. Preheat the oven to 400° F.

Cook the carrots in boiling water with the lemon juice until they are quite soft — about 15 minutes.

While the carrots are cooking, heat the oil in a large, heavy-bottomed skillet over medium heat. Add the garlic cloves and cook them for two minutes. Stir in the shallot and cook it for 30 seconds. Add the fish pieces, the thyme, ⅛ teaspoon of the salt and a generous grinding of pepper. Cook the mixture for 10 minutes, stirring gently with a fork to break up the fish. Stir in the cream and remove the skillet from the heat. Discard the cloves of garlic.

When the carrots are done, drain them, reserving ⅓ cup of the cooking liquid. In a food processor, blender or food mill, purée the carrots, reserved cooking liquid, the remaining ⅛ teaspoon of salt and some pepper until smooth. Add the carrot purée to the skillet and mix gently; spoon the mixture into the tomato shells.

Put the filled tomato shells on a cookie sheet or in a baking dish and cover them with the reserved tops. Bake the shells until their skin starts to crack — about 10 minutes. Remove the shells from the oven and discard the tops. Serve at once.

Thai-Style Parcels

THE INGREDIENTS FOR THIS DISH ARE PREPARED BY THE COOK AND PRESENTED AT THE TABLE FOR EACH GUEST TO ASSEMBLE INDIVIDUALLY.

Makes 48 parcels
Working time: about 1 hour
Total time: about 4 hours (includes chilling and marinating)

Per parcel:
Calories **30**
Protein **3g.**
Cholesterol **10mg.**
Total fat **2g.**
Saturated fat **1g.**
Sodium **25mg.**

12 oz. lean beef tenderloin, trimmed of fat and chilled in the freezer until firm (about 1 hour)
12 oz. boneless chicken breast, skinned
1 Nappa cabbage, washed, dried, and finely shredded
1 large head of lettuce, leaves washed and dried
½ cucumber, peeled in alternate strips with a cannelle knife or peeler, halved lengthwise, and thinly sliced
1 bunch cilantro, leaves only
1 bunch fresh mint, large stalks removed
1 bunch fresh basil, leaves only
48 rice-paper wrappers (about 6 inches in diameter)
1 tbsp. peanut oil
freshly ground black pepper
Spicy marinade
1 oz. tamarind paste, dissolved in ½ cup water for 15 minutes
1 tsp. sambal oelek
1 tbsp. low-sodium soy sauce
1 tsp. anchovy purée
3 garlic cloves, crushed
1½-inch piece fresh ginger, peeled and finely shredded
Lemon glaze
4 tbsp. fresh lemon juice
2 tbsp. low-sodium soy sauce
1 tsp. brown sugar
Dipping sauce
¼ cup fresh lemon juice
4 tbsp. low-sodium soy sauce
2 tsp. sambal oelek
½-inch piece fresh ginger, peeled and finely shredded
1 small stick fresh lemon grass, finely chopped (optional)

To make the marinade, strain the tamarind liquid and discard the solids. Add the sambal oelek, soy sauce, anchovy purée, garlic, and ginger to the liquid, and stir well to blend the ingredients. Divide the marinade between two shallow dishes. Cut the beef into very thin slices across the grain, then cut the slices into strips about ½ inch wide. Cut the chicken breast into thin strips of the same width. Place the beef in one of the marinade dishes and the chicken in the other; stir to coat the strips evenly, and let them marinate in a cool place for three hours.

Shortly before serving, make the glaze by combining the lemon juice, soy sauce, and brown sugar with 2 tablespoons of water in a small saucepan; reduce the glaze to about 3 tablespoons—three to five minutes.

Meanwhile, make the dipping sauce by combining the lemon juice, soy sauce, sambal oelek, ginger, and lemon grass, if you are using it, with 4 tablespoons of water. Pour the sauce into dipping bowls. Arrange the Nappa cabbage, lettuce leaves, and cucumber slices on a serving platter, and the cilantro, mint, and basil on a second platter. Set out the rice-paper wrappers and bowls of tepid water for dipping the wrappers.

In a wok or a wide, heavy-bottomed frying pan, heat the oil until it is sizzling. Remove the strips of beef from the marinade, and sear them for about 20 seconds, stirring and tossing the meat with a spatula. Remove the beef from the wok and keep it warm. Cook the chicken pieces in the wok until the flesh is no longer translucent—about 45 seconds.

Arrange the beef and chicken on separate serving dishes, and brush with the glaze. Serve immediately, with the raw ingredients, pepper, and sauce, for each guest to make into parcels (box, below).

Rice-Paper Packages

MAKING A PARCEL. Dip a rice-paper wrapper in a bowl of tepid water, gently shake off any excess water, and place the softened wrapper in the palm of your hand or on a small plate. Place small quantities of ingredients in the center of the wrapper, and fold the edges over the filling to enclose it. Then dip the parcel in the sauce.

Oysters with Julienned Vegetables in Basil-Butter Sauce

Serves 4 as a first course
Working (and total) time: about 30 minutes

Calories **220**
Protein **13g.**
Cholesterol **95mg.**
Total fat **9g.**
Saturated fat **4g.**
Sodium **325mg.**

20 large oysters, shucked the liquid reserved
3 tbsp. fresh lemon juice
1 large carrot, peeled and julienned
1 celery stalk, trimmed and julienned
1 leek, trimmed, split, washed thoroughly to remove all grit, and julienned
½ cup dry white wine
1 shallot, finely chopped
¼ tsp. salt
freshly ground black pepper
2 tbsp. fresh basil, Italian parsley or cilantro cut into thin strips
1½ tbsp. cold unsalted butter
1 lemon (optional), cut into wedges

Add 2 tablespoons of the lemon juice to 1 quart of water and bring the water to a boil. Drop the carrot julienne into the boiling water; after 30 seconds, add the celery julienne; after 15 seconds more, add the leek julienne. Cook the vegetables for an additional 15 seconds, then drain them and set them aside.

Pour the wine into a large, nonreactive skillet. Add the remaining lemon juice and the shallot, and bring the liquid to a simmer. Cook the liquid until it is reduced by half — about three minutes — and turn the heat to low. Lay the oysters in the skillet in a single layer; pour in the reserved juices and cook the oysters for 30 seconds. Turn the oysters over and cook them until they are heated through — about 30 seconds more. With a slotted spoon, transfer the oysters to warmed plates. Top each oyster with some of the julienned vegetables.

With the skillet still set over low heat, add the salt, some pepper and the basil. Whisk in the butter, then ladle some of the sauce over each oyster. Garnish the plates with lemon wedges, if you like, and serve the oysters immediately.

Soft-Shell Clams
with Prosciutto and Sage

Serves 4 as a first course
Working time: about 30 minutes
Total time: about 1 hour

Calories **115**
Protein **7g.**
Cholesterol **27mg.**
Total fat **4g.**
Saturated fat **2g.**
Sodium **130mg.**

2 lb. soft-shell clams
¾ cup dry vermouth
1 oz. finely chopped prosciutto or other dry-cured ham
2 tbsp. finely chopped shallot
1 garlic clove, finely chopped
1 tbsp. chopped fresh sage, or 1 tsp. dried sage
freshly ground black pepper
2 tbsp. heavy cream
1 tbsp. finely chopped fresh parsley

Pour the vermouth into a large skillet or casserole. Bring the vermouth to a boil, then add the clams and cover the skillet. Cook the clams over high heat until they open — six to eight minutes. Discard any clams that remain closed. Do not pour out the cooking liquid.

Twist off and discard the top half of a clam shell. Slip a small, sharp knife under the clam and cut it free of the shell. Cut off the neck and set it aside. Return the clam to its half shell and set the shell in an ovenproof dish. Repeat these steps with the remaining clams. Cover the dish with aluminum foil and keep the clams warm in the oven.

Peel off and discard the blackish membrane covering the clam necks. Finely chop the clam necks.

Strain the clam-cooking liquid through a fine sieve into a smaller skillet over medium heat. Add the chopped clam necks along with the prosciutto, shallot, garlic, sage and some pepper. Cook the mixture until only about 2 tablespoons of liquid remain — approximately five minutes. Stir in the cream and bring the sauce to a simmer. Remove the clams from the oven. Stir the parsley into the sauce and spoon a little sauce over each clam. Serve immediately.

Chili and Lime Avocado Dip

Serves 12
Working time: about 15 minutes
Total time: about 3 hours and 15 minutes
(includes setting aside)

Calories **105**
Protein **2g.**
Cholesterol **0mg.**
Total fat **11g.**
Saturated fat **1g.**
Sodium **35mg.**

4 ripe avocados
1 tbsp. fresh lime juice
1 tbsp. virgin olive oil
1 pickled hot green chili pepper, finely diced (cautionary note, right)
1 garlic clove, crushed
1 scallion, finely chopped
1 tbsp. finely chopped cilantro
¼ tsp. salt
freshly ground black pepper

Cut the avocados in half and remove the pits. Spoon the flesh into a bowl and mash lightly with a fork—the texture should not be too smooth. Stir in the lime juice and oil, then the chili, garlic, scallion, cilantro, salt, and some freshly ground pepper.

Cover the mixture and set it aside for at least three hours to allow the chili to permeate the dip. Serve at room temperature.

SUGGESTED ACCOMPANIMENT: *breadsticks.*

Chili Peppers—a Cautionary Note

Both dried and fresh hot chili peppers should be handled with care. Their flesh and seeds contain volatile oils that can make skin tingle and cause eyes to burn. Rubber gloves offer protection—but the cook should still be careful not to touch the face, lips, or eyes when working with chilies.

Soaking fresh chilies in cold, salted water for an hour will remove some of their fire. If canned chilies are substituted for fresh ones, they should be rinsed in cold water in order to eliminate as much of the brine used to preserve them as possible.

Crudités on Skewers with Spiced Peanut Dip

Serves 10
Working time: about 2 hours
Total time: about 5 hours (includes chilling)

Calories **105**
Protein **5g.**
Cholesterol **2mg.**
Total fat **6g.**
Saturated fat **1g.**
Sodium **165mg.**

½ cup unsalted chicken stock
1 tsp. saffron threads
¼ lb. (about 1 cup) peanuts
1 tbsp. virgin olive oil
1 large onion, very finely chopped
4 garlic cloves, crushed
1-inch piece fresh ginger, peeled and sliced
2 tsp. ground coriander
1 tsp. ground cumin
1 tsp. ground cardamom
1 cup plain low-fat yogurt
½ tsp. salt
freshly ground black pepper
2 tsp. finely cut fresh chives
1 tsp. finely chopped parsley

Crudités
1 medium daikon radish, peeled
12-16 radishes, trimmed
2 medium carrots, peeled
2 medium celery stalks, washed and trimmed
1 small sweet red pepper, seeded and deribbed
1 small green pepper, seeded and deribbed
1 small yellow pepper, seeded and deribbed
1 small orange pepper, seeded and deribbed (optional)

Preheat the oven to 425° F. In a saucepan, bring the chicken stock to a boil; remove the pan from the heat and add the saffron threads. Stir the stock well and let it stand for about 30 minutes.

Spread the peanuts out on a small baking sheet, then roast them in the oven for six to eight minutes.

Heat the oil in a saucepan; add the chopped onion, and cook over low heat until it is very soft but not browned—8 to 10 minutes. Stir in the garlic.

Put the ginger, coriander, cumin, cardamom, yogurt, peanuts, and saffron mixture into a blender or a food processor, and blend until smooth. Pour the mixture over the onions and stir well. Cook over low heat until the mixture thickens—about 20 minutes. Season with the salt and some pepper. Pour the mixture into a bowl and cover with plastic wrap, placing the wrap directly on the surface of the dip to prevent a skin from forming; allow to cool. Chill the dip in the refrigerator for three to four hours or overnight.

Just before serving time, prepare the vegetables. Cut them into decoratively shaped slices, as shown here, or small neat cubes, and thread them onto wooden cocktail sticks.

Stir the peanut dip and spoon it into a serving bowl, then sprinkle the top with the chives and parsley. Place the bowl on a large serving platter and surround with the crudités.

EDITOR'S NOTE: *If preferred, the vegetables may be cut into sticks, about 4 inches long, and arranged attractively around the peanut dip.*

Tuna Tapenade Pizzas

IN THIS RECIPE, TUNA FISH REPLACES A LARGE PERCENTAGE
OF THE OILY INGREDIENTS OF THE TRADITIONAL PROVENCAL
TAPENADE—AN OIL, OLIVE, AND ANCHOVY PURÉE.

Serves 6
Working time: about 40 minutes
Total time: about 2 hours (includes proofing)

Calories **340**
Protein **14g.**
Cholesterol **25mg.**
Total fat **15g.**
Saturated fat **2g.**
Sodium **305mg.**

1 envelope (¼ oz.) active dry yeast
2½ cups unbleached all-purpose flour
1 tsp. salt
1 tbsp. virgin olive oil
6 cherry tomatoes, sliced, for garnish
chopped parsley for garnish (optional)
Tuna tapenade
3 anchovy fillets, rinsed, dried, and finely chopped
1 garlic clove, finely chopped
1½ tbsp. capers, finely chopped
12 black olives, pitted and finely chopped
7 oz. tuna fish packed in water, drained
1 tbsp. virgin olive oil
freshly ground black pepper

Mix the yeast with ⅓ cup of tepid water and let it stand until it is frothy—10 to 15 minutes. Sift the flour and salt into a large bowl, and make a well in the flour. Pour the yeast mixture into the well along with the oil, and mix in enough tepid water to make a soft but not sticky dough. On a floured work surface, knead the dough until it is smooth and elastic—about 10 minutes—then gather the dough into a ball and leave it in a clean bowl, covered with plastic wrap, until it has doubled in volume—about one hour.

Preheat the oven to 425° F.

Lightly oil a baking sheet. Punch the dough down to deflate it, then divide it into six balls. On a floured work surface, roll out each ball into a 5-inch-diameter circle. Press the edges of the circles to create a raised rim, then put them on the baking tray and let them rise a little—at least 10 minutes.

To make the *tapenade,* pound the anchovies and garlic together in a mortar. Add the capers, olives, tuna, oil, and some pepper in gradual stages, continuing to pound to form a paste. You may also blend the *tapenade* in a food processor. Divide the paste equally among the pizza crusts and spread it to within ¼ inch of the edges. Bake the pizzas in the oven for 15 minutes, then garnish them with the tomato slices and return to the oven for a final five minutes.

Serve warm, garnished with a little chopped parsley, if you wish.

SUGGESTED ACCOMPANIMENT: *leafy salad.*

Mussels on the Half Shell

Makes 20 mussels
Working (and total) time: 30 minutes

Per mussel: Calories **25** Protein **4g.** Cholesterol **10mg.** Total fat **1g.** Saturated fat **trace** Sodium **70mg.**	20 mussels (about 1 lb.), scrubbed and debearded
	1 lemon, cut into wedges
	Tomato and fennel relish
	2 tsp. virgin olive oil
	2 oz. (about ⅓ cup) finely chopped fennel
	2 medium tomatoes, peeled, seeded (technique, right), and chopped
	½ tsp. sherry vinegar
	1 tsp. tomato paste
	1 garlic clove, crushed
	¼ tsp. salt
	freshly ground black pepper
	2 tbsp. finely chopped parsley

Pour 4 tablespoons of water into a large pan. Add the mussels, cover the pan, and bring the water to a boil. Steam the mussels until their shells open—four to five minutes. Discard any mussels that remain closed.

Remove the top shell from each mussel and discard it. Using your fingers or a spoon, sever the connective tissue that attaches the mussel to the bottom shell. Return the mussels to their half shells and place them in an ovenproof serving dish.

Preheat the oven to 375° F.

To make the tomato and fennel relish, first pour the oil into a heavy-bottomed saucepan and sauté the fennel over medium heat until it is fairly soft—about five minutes. Add the tomatoes, vinegar, tomato paste, garlic, salt, and some freshly ground black pepper, and simmer until the mixture is well reduced—about 10 minutes. Stir in the parsley.

Spoon a little of the relish onto each half shell. Cover the dish with aluminum foil, and put it in the oven for about five minutes to allow the mussels and relish to warm through. Serve immediately, garnished with the lemon wedges.

Peeling and Seeding a Tomato

1 *PEELING THE TOMATO. Core the tomato by cutting a conical plug from its stem end. Cut a shallow cross in the base. Immerse the tomato in boiling water for 10 to 30 seconds, then plunge it into cold water. When the tomato has cooled, peel the skin away from the cross in sections.*

2 *SEEDING THE TOMATO. Halve the peeled tomato. Gently squeeze one of the halves, forcing out its seeds and juice. Rotate the tomato 90 degrees and squeeze once more. Dislodge any seeds from the inner chambers. Repeat the process with the other half.*

Stuffed Cherry Tomatoes

Makes 20 stuffed tomatoes
Working (and total) time: about 30 minutes

Per stuffed tomato:	
Calories **20**	20 cherry tomatoes
Protein **1g.**	⅓ cup low-fat ricotta cheese
Cholesterol **trace**	2 tsp. chopped fresh basil
Total fat **2g.**	⅛ tsp. salt
Saturated fat **0g.**	freshly ground black pepper
Sodium **25mg.**	parsley leaves for garnish

Slice the bottoms off the cherry tomatoes, and using a small melon baller or a teaspoon, scoop out the seeds and juice into a sieve placed over a small bowl. Press the juice from the seeds and discard the seeds. Mix the cheese with the basil, salt, some freshly ground pepper, and about 3 teaspoons of the tomato juice to make a soft paste.

Using a pastry bag fitted with a ½-inch star tip, pipe a rosette of the cheese mixture into each tomato. Garnish each filled tomato with a tiny piece of parsley and arrange the tomatoes on a serving plate.

Snow Peas with Two Purées

Makes about 36 snow peas
Working time: about 30 minutes
Total time: about 45 minutes

Per 3 carrot snow peas:	4 oz. snow peas
Calories **25**	**Cumin-scented carrot purée**
Protein **2g.**	2 small carrots, peeled and sliced into ¼-inch rounds
Cholesterol **0mg.**	¼ tsp. ground cumin
Total fat **trace**	1 tbsp. sour cream
Saturated fat **trace**	2 tsp. fresh breadcrumbs
Sodium **20mg.**	⅛ tsp. salt
	ground white pepper
Per 3 pea snow peas:	**Minted pea purée**
Calories **40**	3 shallots, finely chopped
Protein **3g.**	1 tsp. unsalted butter
Cholesterol **2mg.**	12 oz. fresh peas, shelled, or 4 oz. frozen peas, thawed
Total fat **1g.**	½ tsp. finely chopped fresh mint
Saturated fat **trace**	1 tbsp. sour cream
Sodium **15mg.**	2 tsp. fresh breadcrumbs
	⅛ tsp. salt

Place the snow peas in a deep, ovenproof bowl and pour boiling water over them. Drain immediately in a colander and refresh them under cold running water.

Leave the snow peas in the colander to drain.

To make the carrot purée, put the carrots into a saucepan with enough cold water to barely cover them; add the cumin, bring to a boil, and cook until the carrots are soft—7 to 10 minutes. Drain over a bowl. Return the cooking liquid to the pan and reduce over high heat until only about a teaspoonful remains. Purée the carrots with the reduced cooking liquid in a blender, food processor, or food mill. Pass the purée through a fine sieve if a smoother texture is preferred. If the purée is watery, cook it briefly in a saucepan over very low heat to dry it out a little. Stir in the sour cream and breadcrumbs, season with the salt and some white pepper, then set the mixture aside.

For the pea purée, sweat the shallots in the butter until they are translucent. Add the peas and 2 table-spoons of water. Heat over low heat until the water has completely evaporated, then remove from the heat, add the mint, and stir well. Purée the peas in a food processor or a blender, and stir in the sour cream, breadcrumbs, and salt. Set the mixture aside.

Arrange the snow peas on serving dishes. Using a pastry bag fitted with a fine tip, pipe the carrot purée in a line down the center of half of the snow peas. Then pipe the pea purée onto the remaining snow peas. Serve the snow peas cold.

Sauces for Artichokes

Yogurt and Pimiento

Serves 4
Working time: about 10 minutes
Total time: about 1 hour and 15 minutes

Calories **88**
Protein **5g.**
Cholesterol **3mg.**
Total fat **2g.**
Saturated fat **1g.**
Sodium **140mg.**

4 artichokes, trimmed, cooked and chilled
⅔ cup plain low-fat yogurt
1 tsp. Dijon mustard
3 oz. jar pimientos, drained and finely chopped
2 tsp. milk
1 tsp. virgin olive oil
1 garlic clove, finely chopped
1 tsp. fresh lemon juice
⅛ tsp. salt

In a bowl, blend together the yogurt and mustard with a whisk. Then whisk in the pimientos, milk, oil, garlic, lemon juice and salt, and refrigerate the mixture for at least an hour.

Serve the sauce with the artichokes, using the leaves to scoop it up.

Mustard

Serves 4
Working (and total) time: about 15 minutes

Calories **155**
Protein **4g.**
Cholesterol **2mg.**
Total fat **11g.**
Saturated fat **1g.**
Sodium **143mg.**

4 artichokes, trimmed, cooked and chilled
1 egg white
1½ tbsp. fresh lemon juice
1 tbsp. Dijon mustard
1 tbsp. grainy mustard
1 garlic clove, finely chopped
2 tbsp. safflower oil
1 tbsp. virgin olive oil
3 tbsp. milk

In a warm bowl, whisk the egg white and lemon juice to a froth. Add the mustards and garlic. Whisking vigorously, pour in the oils in a slow, thin stream. Add the milk, and whisk until the mixture thickens.

Serve the sauce with the artichokes, using the leaves to scoop it up.

Buttermilk and Tarragon

Serves 4
Working time: about 10 minutes
Total time: about 2 hours and 15 minutes

Calories **158**
Protein **4g.**
Cholesterol **2mg.**
Total fat **11g.**
Saturated fat **1g.**
Sodium **97mg.**

4 artichokes, trimmed, cooked and chilled
1 tbsp. white wine vinegar
½ tbsp. Dijon mustard
⅔ cup buttermilk
3 tbsp. safflower oil
1 scallion, trimmed and chopped
1 garlic clove, finely chopped
½ tsp. sugar
1 tbsp. chopped fresh tarragon, or 1 tsp. dried tarragon

In a bowl, whisk together the vinegar and mustard; then whisk in the buttermilk. Whisking vigorously, pour in the oil in a slow, thin stream. Add the scallion, garlic, sugar and tarragon, and combine.

Serve the sauce with the artichokes, using the leaves to scoop it up.

EDITOR'S NOTE: *Preparing this sauce a day in advance will intensify its flavor.*

Watercress

Serves 4
Working time: about 15 minutes
Total time: about 20 minutes

Calories **189**
Protein **3g.**
Cholesterol **0mg.**
Total fat **16g.**
Saturated fat **2g.**
Sodium **51mg.**

4 artichokes, trimmed, cooked and chilled
1 tbsp. chopped shallot
2 tbsp. red wine vinegar
juice of 1 lime
1 tsp. Dijon mustard
freshly ground black pepper
1 bunch watercress, washed, with stems removed
3 tbsp. safflower oil
1½ tbsp. virgin olive oil
1 garlic clove, finely chopped

Bring 1 quart of water to a boil in a saucepan. Meanwhile, combine the shallot, vinegar, lime juice, mustard and pepper in a small bowl. Let the mixture stand for 10 minutes so the flavors can meld.

Blanch the watercress in the boiling water for three minutes. Drain and then refresh under cold running water to arrest the cooking. Squeeze the watercress to remove any excess water and coarsely chop it.

Purée the shallot mixture in a food processor or blender. With the motor still running, pour in the oils in a slow, thin stream. Add the watercress and garlic, and process for about 30 seconds. Since the vivid green of the watercress quickly fades, serve the sauce as soon as possible with the artichokes; use the leaves as scoops for the sauce.

Crudités

Raw vegetables, known by the French term crudités, make the simplest and most healthful of appetizers. They are free of fat and cholesterol, amply endowed with vitamins and minerals, and high in fiber.

Let the season be your guide when choosing the vegetables. Small vegetables such as cherry tomatoes, button mushrooms, scallions, and young green beans can be left whole; others such as broccoli, cauliflower, carrots, cucumbers, sweet peppers, Belgian endive, celery, fennel, kohlrabi, and Nappa cabbage should be cut into pieces. To serve, arrange the vegetables on a platter or in a basket, and accompany with oil and vinegar or a puree, such as the ones shown here.

For an equally quick and nutritious first course, raw or blanched vegetables may be sliced or grated and tossed in a light dressing.

Bean Purée

GARLICKY PURÉES, LIBERALLY SEASONED WITH LEMON JUICE AND OLIVE OIL, ARE FOUND IN THE COOKING OF VIRTUALLY ALL THE LANDS OF THE EASTERN MEDITERRANEAN. IN THIS RECIPE, THE ADDITION OF YOGURT LIGHTENS THE PURÉE.

Serves 16
Working time: about 45 minutes
Total time: about 15 hours (includes soaking and chilling)

1½ cups dried Great Northern beans, picked over, soaked overnight in enough water to cover them
1 onion, quartered
4 large garlic cloves, peeled
2 tbsp. virgin olive oil
2 tbsp. white wine vinegar
½ tsp. salt
freshly ground black pepper
¼ cup plain low-fat yogurt
½ tsp. Dijon mustard
2 tbsp. fresh lemon juice
1 sweet red pepper, broiled, seeded, and skinned
2 tbsp. finely chopped parsley
1 tsp. chopped fresh rosemary, or ½ tsp. dried rosemary

Calories **65**
Protein **4g.**
Cholesterol **0mg.**
Total fat **2g.**
Saturated fat **0g.**
Sodium **55mg.**

Drain the beans in a colander and transfer them to a saucepan. Add the onion and garlic, cover the beans with cold water, and bring them to a boil. Boil the beans vigorously for 15 minutes, then reduce the heat to low and simmer them until they are very tender—about one and a half hours. Drain the beans in a colander and let them cool for a few minutes.

Place the bean mixture, the oil, and the vinegar in a food processor, and purée the mixture. To give the purée a smoother texture, rub it through a fine sieve. Season with the salt and some pepper.

When the bean purée has cooled, mix in the yogurt, mustard, and lemon juice. Dice the red pepper, and fold it into the bean mixture with the parsley and rosemary. Transfer the purée to a serving bowl and cover it with plastic wrap. Refrigerate it for at least four hours to allow the flavors to blend. Remove the purée from the refrigerator about an hour before serving to bring it to room temperature.

SUGGESTED ACCOMPANIMENTS: *crudités (opposite); toast fingers or strips of warm pita bread.*

Skordalia

SKORDALIA IS A RICH GREEK SAUCE CONTAINING GARLIC, OLIVE OIL, AND BREAD, WITH A CONSISTENCY RESEMBLING THAT OF MAYONNAISE. IT IS TRADITIONALLY SERVED WITH RAW VEGETABLES, SEAFOOD, OR HARD-COOKED EGGS. IN THIS LIGHTER VERSION, THE CREAMY TEXTURE IS RETAINED, BUT THE FAT CONTENT IS REDUCED BY REPLACING SOME OF THE OLIVE OIL WITH YOGURT. NEVERTHELESS, A LITTLE GOES A LONG WAY.

Serves 18
Working (and total) time: about 15 minutes

5 garlic cloves, crushed
4 slices white bread, crusts removed (about 4 oz.)
2 parsley sprigs
2 tbsp. white wine vinegar
½ tsp. salt
½ cup virgin olive oil
¾ cup plain low-fat yogurt

Calories **90**
Protein **1g.**
Cholesterol **0mg.**
Total fat **8g.**
Saturated fat **2g.**
Sodium **80mg.**

Place the garlic, bread, and parsley sprigs in a food processor, and blend until the mixture forms crumbs. Add the vinegar, salt, and 3 tablespoons of water, and process until the mixture is thoroughly blended.

With the motor still running, begin adding the oil a teaspoon at a time, so that the sauce will not separate. When the sauce begins to thicken, pour in the rest of the oil in a thin stream, then add the yogurt. Transfer the skordalia to a shallow dish to serve.

SUGGESTED ACCOMPANIMENTS: *crudités (opposite); toast fingers or strips of warm pita bread.*

Eggplant and Sesame Purée

Serves 14
Working time: about 20 minutes
Total time: about 5 hours (includes chilling)

2 eggplants (about 1¼ lb.)
1 large garlic clove, crushed
2 tbsp. virgin olive oil
4 tbsp. fresh lemon juice
2 tbsp. light tahini (sesame paste)
½ tsp. salt
freshly ground black pepper
3 tbsp. chopped fresh mint

Calories **40**
Protein **1g.**
Cholesterol **0mg.**
Total fat **3g.**
Saturated fat **1g.**
Sodium **60mg.**

Preheat the oven to 350° F. Pierce the eggplants all over with a fork, place them on a baking sheet, and bake them until they are soft and their skins are shriveled—45 minutes to one hour. Set them aside to cool.

When the eggplants are cool enough to handle, cut them in half lengthwise, scoop out the pulp, and transfer it to a food processor. Add the garlic and process the mixture to a fairly smooth purée.

Continue processing the purée while you pour in the oil, a little at a time. When all the oil has been incorporated, add the lemon juice, tahini, salt, and some black pepper, and process the purée again until it is smooth and thoroughly blended. Transfer the mixture to a bowl and stir in the chopped mint. Cover the bowl with plastic wrap, and refrigerate the purée for at least four hours to allow its flavors to develop.

Before serving, stir the mixture again and transfer the chilled purée to a serving dish.

SUGGESTED ACCOMPANIMENTS: *crudités (opposite); toast fingers or strips of warm pita bread.*

EDITOR'S NOTE: *If fresh mint is not available, flat-leaf parsley may be used instead.*

2 *Cornish hens, halved and then marinated in rum, honey, and lime juice and coated in crushed coriander seeds and pepper, cook over hot coals (recipe, page 68).*

Poultry

Chicken Cutlets with Summer Herbs and Tomato Sauce

Serves 4
Working time: about 30 minutes
Total time: about 30 minutes

Calories **278**
Protein **30g.**
Cholesterol **71mg.**
Total fat **10g.**
Saturated fat **2g.**
Sodium **327mg.**

4 chicken breast halves, boned and skinned (about 1 lb.), pounded to about ½-inch thickness
1 garlic clove, finely chopped
2 large tomatoes, peeled, seeded and coarsely chopped
1 tbsp. virgin olive oil
½ cup unsalted chicken stock
¾ tsp. tarragon vinegar
1 tbsp. each of finely chopped fresh tarragon, basil and parsley, mixed, plus sprigs for garnishing
¼ tsp. salt
¼ tsp. freshly ground white pepper
½ cup dry bread crumbs
2 egg whites
1 tbsp. safflower oil

To prepare the sauce, cook the garlic and tomatoes in the olive oil over medium-high heat in a small saucepan, stirring occasionally, until soft — about five minutes. Add the chicken stock, the vinegar and 2 tablespoons of the herb mixture, and bring to a boil. Reduce the heat, cover and simmer for five minutes. Purée the sauce in a food processor or blender and return it to the pan to keep warm.

Meanwhile, sprinkle the salt and pepper over the breasts. Mix the remaining tablespoon of herbs with the bread crumbs on a large plate. In a small bowl, whisk the egg whites vigorously and dip the breasts in the whites, then in the bread-crumb mixture.

Heat the safflower oil in a large, heavy-bottomed skillet over medium-high heat and sauté the chicken on one side until lightly brown — about three minutes. Turn the breasts, cover the skillet loosely, and sauté until they feel firm but springy to the touch — about four minutes more. Transfer the breasts to a heated platter and spoon the sauce over them. Garnish with sprigs of herbs.

SUGGESTED ACCOMPANIMENT: *corn on the cob.*

Chicken Breasts Sautéed with Cilantro

Serves 4
Working time: about 30 minutes
Total time: about 30 minutes

Calories **203**
Protein **29g.**
Cholesterol **77mg.**
Total fat **7g.**
Saturated fat **2g.**
Sodium **233mg.**

4 chicken breast halves, skinned and boned (about 1 lb.)
1 tbsp. safflower oil
freshly ground black pepper
¼ tsp. salt
⅓ cup plain low-fat yogurt
2 tbsp. light cream
1 tsp. cornstarch, mixed with 1 tbsp. water
¾ cup unsalted chicken stock
2 tbsp. fresh lemon juice
2 garlic cloves, finely chopped
2 tbsp. finely chopped shallot
1 small tomato, peeled, seeded and chopped
⅓ cup stemmed cilantro, coarsely chopped, 4 leaves reserved for a garnish

In a heavy-bottomed skillet, heat the oil over medium-high heat. Sauté the chicken breasts on one side for five minutes, then turn them and sprinkle with the pepper and ⅛ teaspoon of the salt. Sauté on the second side until firm but springy to the touch — about four minutes. Transfer the chicken to a heated platter and keep it warm.

In a small bowl, stir the yogurt and cream into the cornstarch mixture. Put the stock and lemon juice in the skillet; add the garlic and shallot, reduce the heat to low, and simmer for 30 seconds. Stir in the tomato, the yogurt mixture and the remaining ⅛ teaspoon of salt. Cook over low heat for one minute, then add the cilantro. Pour the sauce over the chicken. Garnish each breast with a fresh cilantro leaf if desired.

SUGGESTED ACCOMPANIMENT: *sautéed zucchini.*

Sautéed Chicken Breasts with Raspberry Sauce

Serves 4
Working time: about 30 minutes
Total time: about 40 minutes

Calories **226**
Protein **27g.**
Cholesterol **80mg.**
Total fat **7g.**
Saturated fat **3g.**
Sodium **153mg.**

4 chicken breast halves, skinned and boned (about 1 lb.)
⅛ tsp. salt
freshly ground black pepper
1 tsp. honey
1 tbsp. raspberry vinegar
1 tbsp. unsalted butter
½ cup dry white wine
1 shallot, finely chopped
¾ cup fresh raspberries
1 cup unsalted chicken stock
mint sprigs, for garnish (optional)

Sprinkle the chicken breasts with the salt and pepper and put them on a plate. Stir the honey into the raspberry vinegar and mix well. Dribble this mixture over the breasts and allow them to marinate for 15 minutes.

Preheat the oven to 200° F. In a heavy-bottomed skillet, melt the butter over medium-high heat, and sauté the breasts until golden — about four minutes on each side. Transfer the chicken to a serving platter and put the platter in the oven to keep warm. Add the wine and shallot to the skillet. Reduce the liquid until it barely coats the pan — there should be about 2 tablespoons. Reserve 12 of the raspberries for a garnish. Add the stock and the remaining raspberries and reduce by half, to about ¾ cup. Purée the mixture in a food processor or blender, then strain it through a fine sieve. Return the sauce to the skillet and bring it to a boil. Spoon it over the chicken and garnish with the reserved raspberries and the mint sprigs, if desired.

SUGGESTED ACCOMPANIMENTS: *green peas; steamed rice.*

Chicken Poached in Milk and Curry

Serves 4
Working time: about 15 minutes
Total time: about 1 hour and 15 minutes

Calories **499**
Protein **52g.**
Cholesterol **158mg.**
Total fat **20g.**
Saturated fat **10g.**
Sodium **492mg.**

one 3 lb. chicken, wings removed and reserved for another use, the rest skinned and cut into serving pieces
3 cups milk
2 large onions, thinly sliced (about 3 cups)
4 or 5 bay leaves
2 tsp. fresh thyme, or ½ tsp. dried thyme leaves
3 garlic cloves, crushed
1 tsp. curry powder
½ tsp. salt
freshly ground black pepper
1 cup green peas
1 tbsp. unsalted butter

In a large, heavy-bottomed saucepan over medium heat, combine the milk, onions, bay leaves, thyme, garlic, curry powder, salt and two or three generous grindings of pepper. Bring the liquid just to a simmer, then immediately remove the pan from the heat. Allow the mixture to stand for 30 minutes so that the milk can pick up the flavors; after 15 minutes, preheat the oven to 325° F.

Arrange the chicken pieces in a baking dish just large enough to hold them snugly — no larger than 9 by 13 inches. Bring the milk-and-onion mixture to a simmer again and pour it over the chicken pieces. Set the saucepan aside; do not wash it. Drape the onion slices over any chicken pieces that protrude from the liquid so that the chicken will not dry out during cooking. Put the dish in the oven and poach the chicken until the juices run clear when a thigh is pierced with the tip of a sharp knife — 35 to 40 minutes.

Take the dish from the oven and turn the oven off. Remove the chicken pieces from their poaching liquid

and distribute them among four shallow serving bowls or soup plates. Strain the poaching liquid into the saucepan, and use some of the drained onion slices to garnish each piece of chicken. Discard the remaining onions. Place the bowls in the oven to keep the chicken warm while you finish preparing the sauce.

Cook the liquid in the saucepan over medium heat until it is reduced by about one quarter; there should be approximately 2¼ cups of liquid left. Add the peas and cook them until they are tender — about five minutes. Remove the pan from the heat and whisk in the butter. Pour some of the sauce and peas over the chicken in each bowl and serve immediately.

SUGGESTED ACCOMPANIMENT: *crusty French bread to dunk in the sauce.*

Chicken Fan with Basil-Tomato Sauce

Serves 4
Working time: about 30 minutes
Total time: about 30 minutes

Calories **211**
Protein **29g.**
Cholesterol **73mg.**
Total fat **6g.**
Saturated fat **1g.**
Sodium **90mg.**

4 chicken breast halves, skinned and boned (about 1 lb.)
2 cups unsalted chicken stock
2 cups loosely packed fresh basil leaves (about 4 oz.)
1 garlic clove
2 tsp. mayonnaise
1 tomato, peeled, seeded and chopped

In a pot large enough to hold the chicken breasts snugly, simmer the stock with ½ cup of the basil leaves over medium-low heat for five minutes. Add the breasts to the stock, cover, and poach gently for eight minutes.

Turn the breasts over and poach until they feel firm but springy to the touch — about four minutes more.

Meanwhile, chop the garlic in a food processor or blender. Add the remaining 1½ cups of basil along with ½ cup of water, and purée the mixture. Pour the purée into a sieve and lightly press it with a spoon to remove excess water. To prepare the sauce, scrape the purée into a small bowl and stir in the mayonnaise and half of the chopped tomato.

Lift the chicken breasts from their poaching liquid and pat them dry. Cut each piece diagonally into slices and spread them in a fan pattern on individual serving plates. Spoon about 1½ tablespoons of the sauce at the base of each fan. Scatter the remaining chopped tomato over the top of the sauce.

SUGGESTED ACCOMPANIMENT: *spaghetti squash with Parmesan cheese.*

the heat to medium high. When the oil is hot, put the stuffed breasts in the pan and sauté them on one side until they are browned — about five minutes. Turn the breasts gently and sprinkle them with the remaining ⅛ teaspoon of salt and the pepper. Cook the breasts on the second side until they feel firm but springy to the touch — five to seven minutes more. Carefully remove the breasts from the skillet and place them on a warmed serving platter.

Prepare the sauce by stirring the stock, wine and shallot into the skillet to deglaze it. Stir frequently until the sauce is reduced by half, to about ⅓ cup. Pour some sauce over each breast and serve immediately.

SUGGESTED ACCOMPANIMENT: *snow peas with lemon butter.*

Chicken Breasts Stuffed with Garlic and Carrots

Serves 4
Working time: about 45 minutes
Total time: about 1 hour

Calories **244**	4 chicken breast halves, skinned and boned (about 1 lb.)
Protein **28g.**	1 tbsp. virgin olive oil
Cholesterol **73mg.**	24 to 32 garlic cloves, peeled
Total fat **9g.**	½ tsp. salt
Saturated fat **2g.**	1 large carrot, cut into 12 strips ¼ inch thick and 4 inches long
Sodium **362mg.**	2 tbsp. fresh rosemary leaves
	1 tsp. safflower oil
	freshly ground black pepper
	½ cup unsalted chicken stock
	¼ cup dry white wine
	1 shallot, finely chopped

Heat the olive oil in a heavy-bottomed skillet over low heat. Slowly cook the garlic cloves in the olive oil, stirring occasionally, for 20 minutes.

Sprinkle the garlic cloves with ⅛ teaspoon of the salt and continue cooking until they turn golden brown all over — about 10 minutes more. Remove the cloves with a slotted spoon and set them aside. Do not discard the oil in the skillet.

While the garlic is browning, prepare the carrots and the chicken. Blanch the carrot strips in boiling water until tender — about four minutes — then drain them and set them aside. Lay the chicken breasts on a cutting board, their smooth sides facing down. Along the thinner long edge of each breast, make a horizontal slit and cut nearly through to the opposite side. Open each breast so that it forms two flaps hinged at the center. Sprinkle the rosemary and ¼ teaspoon of the salt over the flaps. Arrange three carrot strips on the larger flap of each breast, and distribute the garlic cloves between the carrot strips. Fold the top flaps over the bottoms, align their edges, and press the breasts closed as nearly as possible.

Add the safflower oil to the oil in the skillet and turn

Chicken Riesling

Serves 4
Working time: about 30 minutes
Total time: about 1 hour

Calories **310**	4 chicken breast halves, skinned and boned (about 1 lb.)
Protein **27g.**	freshly ground black pepper
Cholesterol **79mg.**	½ tsp. salt
Total fat **11g.**	1 tbsp. safflower oil
Saturated fat **3g.**	1 tbsp. unsalted butter
Sodium **366mg.**	2 tbsp. finely chopped shallots
	1 cup thinly sliced mushrooms
	1½ cups Riesling wine
	1 tbsp. chopped fresh tarragon, or 1 tsp. dried tarragon
	1¼ cups unsalted chicken stock
	2 tsp. cornstarch
	¾ cup seedless red grapes, halved

Preheat the oven to 200° F.

Sprinkle the chicken with the pepper and ¼ teaspoon of the salt. Heat the oil over medium-high heat in a large, heavy-bottomed skillet. Sauté the pieces in the oil until brown — about five minutes on each side. Transfer the chicken to a platter and cover it with foil.

Add the butter, shallots and mushrooms to the skillet, sprinkle with ⅛ teaspoon of the remaining salt, and sauté until the shallots soften — two to three minutes. With a slotted spoon, transfer the mushrooms to the platter with the chicken, and keep it warm in the oven. Add all but ¼ cup of the Riesling to the skillet along with the tarragon, and reduce the liquid to about ¼ cup. Pour in the stock and reduce by half, to about ¾ cup. Mix the cornstarch with the remaining ¼ cup of wine. Reduce the heat so that the sauce simmers, and stir in the cornstarch mixture and the remaining ⅛ teaspoon of salt. Add the grapes and cook for two minutes. Arrange some of the mushroom mixture on each breast half, and pour the sauce over all.

SUGGESTED ACCOMPANIMENTS: *garlic bread; red leaf lettuce salad.*

Chicken with Peanuts and Ginger Sauce

Serves 6
Working time: about 20 minutes
Total time: about 2 hours and 20 minutes

Calories **261**
Protein **30g.**
Cholesterol **71mg.**
Total fat **12g.**
Saturated fat **3g.**
Sodium **200mg.**

1½ lb. chicken breast meat, cut into ½-inch cubes
½ cup dry white wine
¼ cup fresh ginger, finely chopped
1 garlic clove, crushed
¼ tsp. salt
freshly ground black pepper
1 cup unsalted chicken stock
2 tbsp. peanut butter
1 tsp. tomato paste (optional)
2 scallions, julienned
⅓ cup peanuts, crushed with a rolling pin
1 tbsp. safflower oil

Make a marinade of the wine, ginger, garlic, salt and pepper, and let the chicken stand in it for two hours.

Near the end of the marinating time, prepare the sauce. Pour the stock into a small saucepan and whisk in the peanut butter and the tomato paste, if desired. Add the scallions and simmer over low heat, uncovered, for two minutes. Remove the saucepan from the heat and set it aside.

Remove the cubes from the marinade and set them aside. Strain the marinade and add it to the sauce. Return the mixture to a simmer and cook over low heat, stirring occasionally, until the sauce is thick enough to coat the back of a spoon — about four minutes. Remove the pan from the heat.

Roll the chicken cubes in the crushed peanuts, sparsely coating the cubes. Heat the oil in a heavy-bottomed skillet over high heat. When the oil is hot but not smoking, add the chicken cubes and lightly brown them, stirring gently to keep intact as much of the peanut coating as possible — about three minutes. Re-move the skillet from the heat and allow the chicken to finish cooking as it rests in the hot pan — about two minutes more. Transfer the chicken to a warmed plat-ter and pour the sauce over it just before serving.

SUGGESTED ACCOMPANIMENTS: *steamed rice; fried bananas; cucumber salad.*

Sautéed Chicken with Mustard, Caraway Seeds and Chervil

Serves 4
Working time: about 1 hour
Total time: about 1 hour

Calories **442**
Protein **30g.**
Cholesterol **105mg.**
Total fat **18g.**
Saturated fat **8g.**
Sodium **374mg.**

4 chicken breast halves, boned and skinned (about 1 lb.), pounded to ½-inch thickness
⅛ tsp. salt
freshly ground black pepper
3 tbsp. Dijon mustard
⅓ cup plain low-fat yogurt
2 tsp. caraway seeds
5 tbsp. chopped fresh chervil or parsley
1 cup dry bread crumbs
2 tbsp. unsalted butter
1 tbsp. safflower oil
3 tart green apples, cored and cut into ¼-inch slices
2 tbsp. aquavit or kümmel (optional)
½ cup unfiltered apple cider
1 tbsp. fresh lemon juice
¼ cup heavy cream

Sprinkle the pounded breasts with the salt and pepper.

In a small bowl, whisk together the mustard, yo-gurt, caraway seeds and 4 tablespoons of the chervil or parsley. Generously coat the breasts with the mix-ture, then place them in the bread crumbs and pat on the crumbs evenly. Chill for at least 10 minutes, or for up to an hour.

Once the breasts have been chilled, heat 1 table-spoon of the butter and the oil in a large heavy-bottomed skillet over medium heat. Place the breasts in the pan and sauté, turning once, until the crumbs are golden — six to eight minutes.

Heat the remaining tablespoon of butter in a heavy-bottomed skillet over medium heat. Toss in the apple slices and cook them for four to five minutes, turning the slices occasionally. Add the aquavit or kümmel, if using, and simmer to evaporate — one to two minutes. Add the cider, the lemon juice and more pepper, and simmer for three to four minutes. Push the apples to one side of the skillet and whisk in the cream. Cook for two minutes more.

To serve, place the chicken on a heated platter and, using a slotted spoon to lift the apple slices from the pan, arrange the slices around the breasts. Continue simmering the sauce until it thickens slightly — two to three minutes. Pour the sauce over the chicken and apples and garnish with the remaining tablespoon of chervil or parsley. Serve immediately.

SUGGESTED ACCOMPANIMENT: *mashed turnips or rutabaga.*

Honey-Basil Chicken

Serves 4
Working time: 20 minutes
Total time: about 1 hour

Calories **258**
Protein **27g.**
Cholesterol **92mg.**
Total fat **12g.**
Saturated fat **3g.**
Sodium **215mg.**

4 whole chicken legs, skinned
¼ tsp. salt
freshly ground black pepper
1 tbsp. safflower oil
½ tbsp. unsalted butter
2 tbsp. honey
2 tbsp. unsalted chicken stock
2 garlic cloves, thinly sliced
30 to 40 fresh basil leaves

Preheat the oven to 400° F. Cut a piece of aluminum foil one foot square for each leg. Sprinkle the legs with the salt and pepper. Heat the oil and butter in a skillet over medium heat, then brown the legs for about two minutes on each side. Put a leg in the middle of each foil square, and drizzle 1½ teaspoons of the honey and 1½ teaspoons of the stock over each one. Lay one quarter of the garlic slices on each piece, cover with a loose layer of the basil leaves, and wrap the foil snugly over the top. Put the foil packages on a baking sheet and set it in the oven.

After 30 minutes, remove a foil package from the oven and unwrap it carefully to preserve the juices. Test for doneness by piercing the thigh with the tip of a sharp knife; if the juices run clear, it is done. If necessary, return the leg to the oven and bake about five minutes more.

To serve, undo each package and transfer the legs to a platter. Remove any garlic or basil that sticks to the foil and put them back on the chicken. Pour the collected juices from the foil packages over the legs.

SUGGESTED ACCOMPANIMENTS: *steamed carrots; romaine lettuce salad.*

Baked Chicken Breasts Stuffed with Tahini

SESAME PASTE, ALSO CALLED TAHINI, IS MADE FROM ROASTED OR UNROASTED GROUND SESAME SEEDS. IT IS AVAILABLE IN JARS OR CANS WHERE MIDDLE EASTERN FOODS ARE SOLD.

Serves 4
Working time: about 30 minutes
Total time: about 45 minutes

Calories **362**
Protein **32g.**
Cholesterol **73mg.**
Total fat **17g.**
Saturated fat **3g.**
Sodium **453mg.**

4 chicken breast halves, skinned and boned (about 1 lb.)
2 tbsp. sesame paste (tahini), or 2 tbsp. toasted sesame seeds, pulverized with a mortar and pestle
2 tbsp. chopped parsley
2 garlic cloves, finely chopped
1 tsp. fresh lemon juice
⅛ tsp. cayenne pepper
½ tsp. salt
freshly ground black pepper
2 tbsp. plain low-fat yogurt
2 tbsp. sesame seeds
½ cup dry bread crumbs
1½ tbsp. safflower oil
1 shallot, thinly sliced
¼ cup sherry
1 cup unsalted chicken stock
2 tsp. cornstarch, mixed with 1 tbsp. water
1 tomato, peeled, the outer flesh cut into strips

To make the tahini mixture, combine the sesame paste or pulverized sesame seeds, parsley, garlic, lemon juice and cayenne pepper in a small bowl. Cut a pocket in each breast half: Make a horizontal slit along the thicker long edge, beginning ½ inch from one end and stopping ½ inch from the other. Then slice horizontally into the breast, cutting to within ½ inch of the opposite edge to form a cavity bordered by ½ inch of uncut flesh. Stuff one fourth of the tahini mixture into each breast pocket. Sprinkle the chicken pieces with ¼ teaspoon of the salt and some pepper.

Preheat the oven to 350° F. To bread the pieces, first coat them with the yogurt. Mix the sesame seeds with the bread crumbs, and dredge the breasts in this mixture to coat them. Heat 1 tablespoon of the oil in a heavy-bottomed skillet over medium heat. Cook the chicken breasts until golden brown — about three minutes per side.

Place the skillet in the oven and bake the breasts, turning them once, until they feel firm but springy to the touch — about 15 minutes. Transfer the chicken to a serving platter and keep it warm.

For the sauce, heat the remaining ½ tablespoon of oil in a small saucepan over medium-high heat. Sauté the sliced shallot in the oil for one minute, then add the sherry and reduce the mixture to about 1 tablespoon. Pour in the stock and bring the liquid to a simmer. Stir in the cornstarch mixture and cook for two minutes more. Incorporate the tomato strips, the remaining ¼ teaspoon of salt and some pepper. Pour the sauce over the stuffed breasts and serve.

SUGGESTED ACCOMPANIMENT: *cucumber salad with fresh mint.*

Sesame Chicken Breasts

Serves 8
Working time: about 30 minutes
Total time: about 4 hours and 15 minutes
(includes chilling)

Calories **245**
Protein **21g.**
Cholesterol **50mg.**
Total fat **9g.**
Saturated fat **2g.**
Sodium **205mg.**

2½ cups dry white wine
2 tsp. sugar
1 tbsp. powdered gelatin
1 lb. cooked beets, peeled, sliced, and cut into 1½-inch-long batons
8 small chicken breast halves, skinned and boned (about ¼ lb. each)
6 tbsp. sesame seeds, toasted
½ tsp. ground cardamom
2 tsp. ground cumin
1½ tsp. chili powder
½ tsp. salt
freshly ground black pepper
1 egg white
8 tsp. sour cream for garnish

Put the wine and sugar into a nonreactive saucepan, and bring the wine just to a boil. Pour it into a flame-proof bowl and sprinkle on the gelatin, whisking well until the gelatin has dissolved. Let the gelatin solution cool slightly, then stir in the beets. Turn the mixture into a 1-quart container with a tightfitting lid. Refrigerate it, covered, for at least three hours, or overnight, until the gelatin has set.

Preheat the oven to 350° F., and lightly oil a shallow baking dish.

Wipe the chicken breasts on paper towels. Mix together the sesame seeds, cardamom, cumin, chili powder, salt, and some black pepper, and spread this mixture out on a plate. In a small bowl, lightly beat the egg white. Dip each chicken breast into the egg white, then coat it in the sesame-seed mixture, pressing the seeds and spices on with the back of a spoon. Place the breasts, skinned side up, in the baking dish and bake them until they are just cooked through—about 25 minutes. (The juices should run clear when a skewer is inserted in the thickest part of a breast.) Let them cool.

Cut each chicken breast into slices. Serve the chicken with the jellied beets, and garnish each portion of beets with a teaspoon of sour cream.

EDITOR'S NOTE: *To toast sesame seeds, warm them in a heavy-bottomed skillet over medium-low heat until they are golden—about three minutes.*

Jellied Chicken with Lemon and Dill

Serves 8
Working time: about 30 minutes
Total time: about 1 day

Calories **339**
Protein **43g.**
Cholesterol **125mg.**
Total fat **14g.**
Saturated fat **3g.**
Sodium **236mg.**

two 3 lb. chickens, skinned and cut into serving pieces
¼ tsp. salt
freshly ground black pepper
2 tbsp. virgin olive oil
1 large onion, finely chopped
⅓ cup chopped fresh dill
4 cups unsalted chicken stock
3 large carrots, thinly sliced
¾ cup green peas
⅓ cup fresh lemon juice

Sprinkle the chicken pieces with the salt and pepper. Heat the olive oil in a large, heavy-bottomed skillet and sauté as many pieces as will fit without crowding over medium-high heat until golden — about five minutes on each side. Arrange the pieces in a large casserole.

In the remaining oil, cook the onion over medium-low heat until translucent — about 10 minutes; stir in half of the dill. Spoon the onion mixture onto the chicken pieces. Pour the stock over all and bring to a simmer on top of the stove. After 20 minutes, turn the pieces, add the carrots and peas, and continue cooking until the juices run clear when a thigh is pierced with the tip of a sharp knife — about 10 minutes more.

Pour the lemon juice over the chicken and vegetables, and cool to room temperature. Sprinkle the remaining dill on top. Refrigerate for six hours or overnight to allow the natural gelatin to set. Serve cold.

SUGGESTED ACCOMPANIMENTS: *rice salad; sliced tomatoes.*

EDITOR'S NOTE: *If fresh dill is unavailable, parsley, tarragon or chervil may be substituted.*

Chicken Mole

THIS IS A VARIATION ON MOLE POBLANO, HERE MADE WITH
CHICKEN RATHER THAN TURKEY

Serves 6
Working time: about 1 hour
Total time: about 2 hours

Calories **294**
Protein **28g.**
Cholesterol **98mg.**
Total fat **17g.**
Saturated fat **4g.**
Sodium **242mg.**

12 chicken thighs, skinned and boned	
1 tsp. coriander seeds	
¼ tsp. anise seeds	
2 garlic cloves, coarsely chopped	
¼ tsp. cinnamon	
¼ tsp. salt	
¼ tsp. freshly ground black pepper	
2 tbsp. safflower oil	
2 jalapeño peppers or other hot chili peppers, halved lengthwise, seeded, and finely chopped	
1 onion, chopped	
2 small ripe tomatoes, peeled, seeded and chopped	
1¼ cups unsalted chicken stock	
½ oz. unsweetened chocolate, grated	
2 tsp. cornstarch, mixed with 2 tbsp. red wine	

In a small, heavy-bottomed saucepan, toast the coriander and anise seeds over medium heat for three to four minutes, shaking the pan frequently. Put the seeds along with the garlic, cinnamon, salt and pepper in a mortar; using a pestle, grind the seasonings to a paste.

Heat 1 tablespoon of the oil in a large, heavy-bottomed skillet over medium heat. Sauté the chilies in the oil, stirring constantly until they begin to brown — about three minutes. Then add the onion, tomatoes and seasoning paste. Cook until almost all the liquid evaporates — about 10 minutes. Transfer the mixture to a bowl and set aside.

Clean the pan and set it over medium-high heat. Add the remaining tablespoon of oil. Sauté the chicken thighs, in two batches if necessary, so that the pieces do not touch, until they are brown — about four minutes on each side. Pour off the fat. Add the stock, onion-and-tomato mixture, and chocolate. Bring the sauce to a boil and stir well to melt the chocolate. Reduce the heat to low, cover, and simmer until the juices run clear when a thigh is pierced with the tip of a sharp knife — about 20 minutes.

Transfer the pieces to a serving platter and keep them warm. Stir the cornstarch-and-wine mixture into the sauce and simmer, stirring frequently, until the sauce is reduced to approximately 1½ cups — about seven minutes. Pour the sauce over the chicken.

SUGGESTED ACCOMPANIMENTS: *yellow rice; black beans; orange and onion salad.*

Chicken Thighs Broiled with Sherry and Honey

Serves 4
Working time: about 20 minutes
Total time: about 25 minutes

Calories **338**
Protein **28g.**
Cholesterol **98mg.**
Total fat **11g.**
Saturated fat **3g.**
Sodium **384mg.**

8 chicken thighs, skinned
1 cup dry sherry
3 tbsp. honey
4 garlic cloves, finely chopped
3 tbsp. red wine vinegar
1 tbsp. low-sodium soy sauce
1 tbsp. cornstarch, mixed with 2 tbsp. dry sherry
¼ tsp. salt

Boil the sherry in a small saucepan until it is reduced by half — about seven minutes. Remove the pan from the stove and whisk in the honey, garlic, vinegar and soy sauce. Return the pan to the heat and whisk the cornstarch mixture into the sauce. Bring the sauce to a boil and cook for one minute, whisking constantly. Remove the pan from the heat and let the sauce cool.

Preheat the broiler. Sprinkle the salt on both sides of the thighs and lay them bone side up on a rack in a roasting pan. Brush the chicken pieces liberally with the sauce, then broil them 4 to 6 inches from the heat source for six to seven minutes. Turn them over and brush them again with the sauce. Broil the thighs for three or four minutes more, then brush them again with the remaining sauce. Continue broiling until the juices run clear when a thigh is pierced with the tip of a sharp knife — five to seven minutes more. Transfer the chicken pieces to a platter and trickle any remaining sauce from the roasting pan over them.

SUGGESTED ACCOMPANIMENT: *snow peas sautéed with water chestnuts and soy sauce.*

Curried Chicken with Chutney and Raisins

Serves 4
Working time: about 30 minutes
Total time: about 1 hour

Calories **476**
Protein **45g.**
Cholesterol **126mg.**
Total fat **22g.**
Saturated fat **4g.**
Sodium **437mg.**

one 3 lb. chicken, skinned and cut into serving pieces
½ tsp. salt
½ tsp. freshly ground black pepper
¼ cup cornmeal
3 tbsp. safflower oil
1 onion, finely chopped
1 carrot, finely chopped
½ small green pepper, finely chopped
3 garlic cloves, finely chopped
¾ lb. tomatoes, preferably the Italian plum variety, peeled, seeded and coarsely chopped, with juice reserved
1 ½ cups unsalted chicken stock

1 tbsp. curry powder
2 tsp. mango chutney
1 bay leaf
1 ½ tbsp. dark raisins
1 ½ tbsp. golden raisins
1 tbsp. sesame seeds

Sprinkle the chicken pieces with the salt and pepper, and dredge them lightly in the cornmeal. In a heavy-bottomed casserole large enough to hold the chicken in a single layer, heat 2 tablespoons of the oil over medium heat. Brown the chicken for two minutes on each side. Remove the chicken and set it aside. Preheat the oven to 350° F.

Put the remaining tablespoon of oil into the casserole. Add the onion, carrot and green pepper, and sauté lightly for about one minute. Add the garlic and sauté for 30 seconds more. Pour in the tomatoes, their reserved juice and the stock. Stir in the curry powder,

chutney, bay leaf, and 1 tablespoon of each type of raisin. Return the chicken to the casserole and bring the liquid to a simmer. Bake the casserole, covered, for 10 minutes. While it is baking, brown the sesame seeds in a piepan in the oven — about 10 minutes.

When the breasts feel firm but springy to the touch, remove them from the oven and set them aside on a plate, leaving the other chicken pieces in the casserole. Cover the breasts with aluminum foil to keep them warm. Bake the other pieces until the juices run clear when a thigh is pierced with the tip of a sharp knife — about five minutes more. Serve the chicken straight from the casserole or arranged on a platter, with the toasted sesame seeds and the remaining raisins scattered across the top.

SUGGESTED ACCOMPANIMENTS: *steamed rice; side dishes of yogurt, unsalted peanuts and chopped banana.*

Chicken Legs with Dark Rum, Papaya, Mango and Banana

Serves 4
Working time: about 30 minutes
Total time: about 50 minutes

Calories **538**
Protein **30g.**
Cholesterol **112mg.**
Total fat **18g.**
Saturated fat **6g.**
Sodium **397mg.**

4 whole chicken legs, skinned, cut into thighs and drumsticks
½ tsp. salt
freshly ground white pepper
1 tbsp. safflower oil
1 large onion, cut into eighths, layers separated
2 garlic cloves, finely chopped
2 tsp. finely chopped fresh ginger
1 cup dark rum
2 cups unsalted chicken stock
¼ cup heavy cream
1 large tomato, peeled, cored, seeded and cut into large chunks
1 medium papaya, scooped into balls with a melon-baller or cut into cubes, with the extra flesh chopped and reserved
1 small mango, peeled and cut into cubes
1 small banana, cut into ½-inch slices
⅛ tsp. freshly grated nutmeg

Sprinkle the chicken with ¼ teaspoon of the salt and some pepper. In a large, heavy-bottomed casserole, heat the oil over medium heat. Brown the chicken pieces lightly — about four minutes on each side.

Add the onion and cook it with the chicken, stirring frequently, until the onion is translucent — about five minutes. Add the garlic and ginger, and cook for one minute more. Remove the casserole from the heat and allow it to cool for one minute. Reserve 1 teaspoon of the rum and set it aside, and pour the rest into the casserole. Return the casserole to the heat and simmer until the liquid is reduced by half — about five minutes.

Add the stock to the casserole and bring it to a boil. Reduce the heat to low, and simmer until the juices run clear when a thigh is pierced with a sharp knife — about five minutes more. Transfer the chicken pieces to a heated serving platter and cover them with foil.

In a saucepan, bring the cream, tomato and extra papaya flesh to a simmer. Pour in the braising liquid from the casserole and simmer until the sauce thickens slightly — about three minutes. Purée the mixture in a food processor or blender, and return it to the pan.

Add the papaya balls or cubes, mango, banana, nutmeg, the reserved teaspoon of rum and the remaining ¼ teaspoon of salt, and cook just until the fruit is heated through — about one minute. Remove the foil from the chicken and pour the sauce over the pieces. Serve immediately.

SUGGESTED ACCOMPANIMENT: *yellow rice.*

Thai-Style Chicken Satay

SATAY, SKEWERS OF MEAT GRILLED OVER CHARCOAL, ARE
ENJOYED ALL OVER SOUTHEAST ASIA. THIS CHICKEN VERSION IS
DISTINGUISHED BY THE TYPICALLY
THAI SPICES GINGER, LEMON GRASS, AND CILANTRO.

Serves 6
Working time: about 1 hour
Total time: about 2 hours and 30 minutes
(includes marinating)

Calories **260**
Protein **22g.**
Cholesterol **80mg.**
Total fat **14g.**
Saturated fat **4g.**
Sodium **95mg.**

2 lb. chicken thighs, skinned and boned
1 tsp. tamarind concentrate, optional
2 garlic cloves, chopped
6 shallots, chopped
1-inch piece fresh ginger
1 tbsp. dark brown sugar
1 lime, juice only
1 tbsp. safflower oil
4 tsp. Asian fish sauce

Pineapple and cucumber relish

½ slightly underripe pineapple
½ cucumber, peeled
¼ tsp. salt
¼ to ½ tsp. sugar
2 limes, juice only
2 small red onions, sliced into rings
1 red chili pepper, seeded and thinly sliced into rings

Peanut and coconut dipping sauce

6 tbsp. unsalted dry-roasted peanuts, coarsely crushed
1 garlic clove, chopped
1 medium red onion, chopped
2 lemon grass bulbs, chopped
2 tbsp. cilantro
1 red chili pepper, seeded and chopped
1 tsp. safflower oil
1 cup unsweetened coconut milk
1 tbsp. Asian fish sauce
1 tsp. dark soy sauce
2 tsp. dark brown sugar
½ tsp. shrimp paste (optional)

Cut the chicken across the grain into long ribbons about ¼ inch thick and ¾ inch wide. Place the strips in a large, shallow, nonreactive dish.

Pound the tamarind concentrate, if you are using it, the garlic, the shallots, the ginger, and the sugar to a thick paste using a mortar and pestle. Add the lime juice, oil, and fish sauce, and stir them in. Pour this mixture over the chicken strips and turn them over to coat them thoroughly. Cover the dish and let the chicken marinate in the refrigerator for at least one hour, or overnight, stirring occasionally.

For the relish, remove the flesh from the pineapple half with a grapefruit knife, leaving a ½-inch-thick shell. Cover the shell with plastic wrap and put it into the refrigerator until it is needed. Remove any brown eyes from the flesh, and discard the central core if it is fibrous. Cut the flesh into ¾-inch chunks. Halve the cucumber lengthwise; remove the seeds with a spoon and discard them. Cut the cucumber into chunks. Mix the salt, ¼ teaspoon of the sugar, and the lime juice in a bowl. Add the pineapple, cucumber, red onion, and chili, and toss these ingredients well; add the remaining sugar if the pineapple is too sharp for your taste. Cover the dish with plastic wrap and place it in the refrigerator for at least one hour, or overnight, stirring the contents several times.

Soak twenty-four 10-inch bamboo skewers in water for 10 minutes. Remove the chicken strips from the marinade and thread each strip onto a skewer as if you were sewing with a needle, then gather up the strip slightly so that the meat on each skewer measures about 5 inches in length. Reserve the marinade.

Next, make the peanut and coconut sauce. Pound the peanuts, garlic, red onion, lemon grass, cilantro, and chili to a smooth paste using the mortar and pestle. Heat the oil in a wok or heavy-bottomed skillet and gently sauté the paste until it is light brown. Add the coconut milk, fish sauce, soy sauce, sugar, and shrimp paste, if you are using it, and bring the ingredients to a boil. Remove the pan from the heat and cover it with a lid.

Lightly oil the rack, and cook the satay over hot coals for 8 to 10 minutes, turning them once and brushing them several times with the marinade. Spoon the pineapple and cucumber relish into the chilled pineapple shell. Transfer the peanut and coconut sauce to serving bowls. Serve the satay immediately, with the dipping sauce and the relish.

SUGGESTED ACCOMPANIMENT: *triangles of toasted thin bread.*

Spit-Roasted Savory Chicken

Serves 8
Working time: about 35 minutes
Total time: about 7 hours (includes marinating)

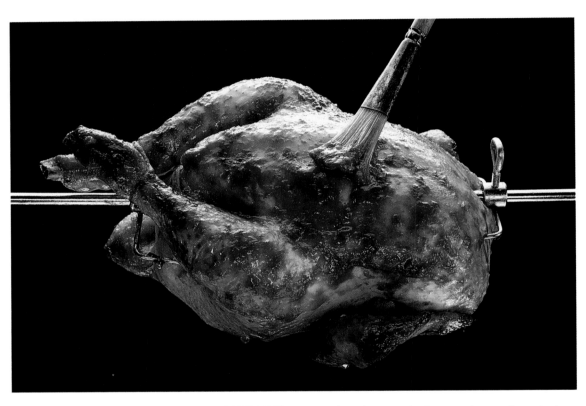

Calories **195**
Protein **24g.**
Cholesterol **90mg.**
Total fat **9g.**
Saturated fat **2g.**
Sodium **85mg.**

2 tbsp. safflower oil
1 small onion, grated
1 lb. tomatoes (3 medium), peeled, seeded, and chopped
½ lemon, strained juice only
2 tbsp. Worcestershire sauce
1 tsp. hot red-pepper sauce
1 tsp. dry mustard
2 tbsp. dark brown sugar
one 3½-lb. roasting chicken, giblets reserved for another use, rinsed and patted dry

First make the marinade. Heat the oil in a heavy, non-reactive saucepan over low heat. Add the onion and cook for two minutes, or until it is softened but not browned. Stir in the tomatoes, lemon juice, Worcestershire sauce, hot red-pepper sauce, mustard, and sugar. Cover the pan and simmer the ingredients for 15 minutes, stirring occasionally, until the tomatoes are reduced to a purée. Remove the pan from the heat and pour the marinade into a bowl, then set it aside until it is cool—about one hour.

Put the chicken in a large bowl and pour the cooled marinade over it. Cover the bowl and let the chicken marinate for at least four hours at room temperature, turning it several times.

Insert a rotisserie spit in the chicken by pushing it through the neck flap just above the breastbone and out just above the tail. Secure the spit with the holding forks, and attach the spit to the turning mechanism. Following the manufacturer's instructions, insert the drip tray immediately below the chicken to catch the cooking juices.

Cook the chicken until it is tender and the juices run clear when a thigh is pierced with a skewer—one and a quarter to one and a half hours. Baste the chicken frequently while it is cooking, first with the marinade, then with the cooking juices from the tray.

Chicken and Grapefruit Salad

Serves 6 as a main course
Working time: about 1 hour and 15 minutes
Total time: about 3 hours and 30 minutes
(includes marinating)

Calories **350**
Protein **26g.**
Cholesterol **80mg.**
Total fat **13g.**
Saturated fat **3g.**
Sodium **300mg.**

2 lb. chicken thighs, skinned and trimmed of fat
⅔ cup dry vermouth
½ tsp. salt
1 tbsp. chopped fresh oregano, or 1 tsp. dried oregano
1 tsp. anise seeds
2 garlic cloves, finely chopped
1 shallot, finely chopped
3 tbsp. honey
freshly ground black pepper
2 tbsp. virgin olive oil
4 carrots, quartered lengthwise and cut into 1-inch lengths
4 celery stalks, halved lengthwise and cut into 1-inch lengths
½ cup unsalted chicken stock
4 grapefruits
1 bunch of watercress, trimmed, washed and dried

Put the chicken thighs into a bowl with the vermouth, salt, oregano, anise seeds, garlic, shallot, 2 tablespoons of the honey and some pepper. Stir to combine the ingredients, then cover the bowl and let the chicken marinate in the refrigerator for two hours.

At the end of the marinating period, preheat the oven to 375° F. Drain the chicken and pat it dry with paper towels. Strain the marinade, reserving both liquid and solids. Heat the oil in a heavy-bottomed oven-proof pot over medium-high heat. Add the chicken thighs to the pot and sauté them until they are browned on all sides — about 10 minutes. Remove the thighs from the pot. Add the reserved solids to the pot and sauté them for one minute. Add the carrots and celery, then pour in the stock, and simmer the mixture for two minutes.

Set the chicken thighs atop the vegetables in the pot and transfer the pot, uncovered, to the oven. Bake the chicken and vegetables, stirring occasionally, until the juices run clear from a thigh pierced with a knife — about 25 minutes.

Remove the chicken from the pot and set it aside to cool. Then remove the vegetables and set them aside to cool as well.

While the chicken and vegetables are cooling, prepare the grapefruits and the dressing. Cut away the peel and pith from a grapefruit. To separate the segments from the inner membranes, slice down to the core on either side of each segment, working over a bowl to catch the juice. Discard the seeds and set the segments aside as you go. Squeeze the pulpy core of membranes over the bowl to extract every bit of juice. Repeat the process to segment the remaining three grapefruits.

Pour the reserved marinade into a small saucepan. Add the grapefruit juice and the remaining tablespoon of honey. Bring the liquid to a boil and cook it until it is reduced to about ⅔ cup — five to 10 minutes.

When the chicken is cool enough to handle, pull the meat from the bones and cut it into thin strips. Arrange the watercress on a platter. Top it with the vegetables, then with a layer of the grapefruit segments. Scatter the chicken on top of the grapefruit; just before serving the salad, pour the reduced marinade over all.

Yogurt Chicken Drumsticks

Serves 8
Working time: about 30 minutes
Total time: about 3 hours and 30 minutes
(includes marinating)

Calories **160**
Protein **26g.**
Cholesterol **90mg.**
Total fat **6g.**
Saturated fat **2g.**
Sodium **190mg.**

16 chicken drumsticks (about 3 lb.), skinned
½ tsp. salt
1 lemon, grated zest and juice
3 tbsp. paprika
½ tsp. hot red-pepper sauce
⅔ cup plain low-fat yogurt
freshly ground black pepper
crisp salad leaves for garnish

Cut two deep, diagonal slits in opposite sides of each drumstick. In a small bowl, stir the salt and the grated lemon zest into the lemon juice, then rub the mixture over each drumstick and into the slits. Lay the drumsticks on a wire rack set over a sheet pan, and sieve 1 tablespoon of the paprika evenly over the upper side of the drumsticks.

In another bowl, mix together the hot red-pepper sauce, the yogurt, and some black pepper. Using a brush, coat the paprika-sprinkled side of each drumstick with the yogurt mixture. Turn the drumsticks over, sieve another tablespoon of paprika over them, and coat them with the remaining yogurt mixture. Set the drumsticks aside in a cool place for three hours, or until the yogurt begins to dry.

Lightly oil the rack, and cook the drumsticks over hot coals for 15 to 20 minutes, turning them every five minutes. After the last turn, sprinkle the remaining paprika over the drumsticks. Serve the drumsticks immediately, garnished with crisp salad leaves.

SUGGESTED ACCOMPANIMENT: *sliced mushroom and sweet red-pepper salad.*

Grilled Cornish Hens with Peppered Fruit

Serves 4
Working time: about 1 hour and 15 minutes
Total time: about 15 hours (includes marinating)

Calories **450**
Protein **33g.**
Cholesterol **90mg.**
Total fat **13g.**
Saturated fat **3g.**
Sodium **105mg.**

2 Cornish hens (about ¾ lb. each)
¼ cup sweet white wine
1 tbsp. honey
1 tsp. Sichuan peppercorns
2 tsp. five-spice powder (glossary)
1 tsp. dry mustard
2 garlic cloves
1-inch piece fresh ginger, peeled
½ lime, juice only
1 tbsp. grape-seed or safflower oil
lime wedges for garnish
Peppered fruit
½ cup light brown sugar
1 lime, peel of whole cut into fine strips, and juice of half
2-inch piece fresh ginger, cut in half
½ tsp. green peppercorns, rinsed and crushed
1 chili pepper, seeded and cut into strips
½ small pineapple, peeled, cored, and cut into 8 chunks
1 small mango, peeled, pitted, and cut into 8 chunks
1 small banana, cut into 8 pieces
½ avocado, peeled, pitted, and cut into 12 pieces

Lay one Cornish hen on the work surface, breast down. Using a sharp knife, cut through the cartilage on each side of the backbone from the tail toward the neck; use a sawing motion to cut through the rib cage. Pull the backbone free and discard it. Turn the bird over and position it with its legs toward you. Place the heel of your hand on the breast and press down hard to break the breastbone, rib cage, collarbones, and wishbone, so that the bird lies flat. Slip your fingers under the skin at the neck and loosen the skin all over the bird, including the thigh. Repeat with the other bird.

In a small, nonreactive saucepan, warm the wine with the honey and the Sichuan peppercorns until the honey has dissolved. Stir in the five-spice powder and mustard, then remove the pan from the heat. Place the garlic in a press, and squeeze out the juice and a minimum of pulp into the wine mixture. Put the ginger into the garlic press, and squeeze as much ginger juice as possible into the saucepan. Add the lime juice and stir well. Place the birds in a large, shallow, nonreactive dish and pour the prepared wine marinade over them. Cover the dish and put the Cornish hens in the refrigerator to marinate for at least 12 hours, or up to 24 hours, turning them from time to time to coat them evenly in the marinade.

About one and a half hours before grilling the Cornish hens, remove the birds from the refrigerator and start preparing the peppered fruit. In a saucepan, dissolve the sugar in 1 cup of water. Add the strips of lime peel and the ginger. Bring the liquid to a boil and boil it for five minutes. Remove the pan from the heat, add the peppercorns and chili pepper, and let the syrup cool. Strain the cooled syrup into a dish. Add the lime juice and the pineapple and mango chunks, turning them to coat them with syrup. After 30 minutes, submerge the banana and avocado in the syrup, and set the fruit aside.

About 10 minutes before grilling the Cornish hens, put four wooden or bamboo skewers to soak in cold water. Pat the Cornish hens dry with paper towels and thread two lightly oiled metal skewers through each bird: one skewer through both wings and the second through both thighs. Drain the fruit and thread the pieces onto the soaked skewers. Boil the syrup rapidly until it is reduced to 2 to 3 tablespoons, and brush a little of the reduced syrup over the skewered fruit; reserve the remaining syrup.

Lightly oil the rack. Cook the Cornish hens for 20 minutes over medium-hot coals; start with the skin side down, and turn the birds once or twice during cooking. Brush the underside of the Cornish hens with a little of the grape-seed or safflower oil and the leftover marinade, as necessary, to keep them from drying out. About two minutes before the Cornish hens are cooked, glaze the skin side of each bird with the remaining reduced fruit syrup. Remove the Cornish hens from the heat and let them stand for three to five minutes before removing the skewers.

Meanwhile, grill the skewered fruit until the pieces are lightly caramelized—five to six minutes. Glaze the cooked fruit with a little more of the reduced syrup just before serving.

Serve the Cornish hens and peppered fruit hot, garnished with lime wedges.

SUGGESTED ACCOMPANIMENT: *brown rice.*

EDITOR'S NOTE: *For a slightly less spicy syrup in which to marinate the fruit, remove the strips of chili 10 minutes after the syrup has been set aside to cool.*

Cornish Hens with Rum

Serves 4
Working time: about 30 minutes
Total time: about 1 hour and 20 minutes
(includes marinating)

Calories **190**
Protein **27g.**
Cholesterol **90mg.**
Saturated fat **4g.**
Total fat **1g.**
Sodium **120mg.**

2 Cornish hens (about ¾ lb. each)
2 tbsp. dark rum
1 lime, juice only
1½ tbsp. honey
1 garlic clove, crushed
⅛ tsp. salt
1 tbsp. coriander seeds
½ tsp. black peppercorns

Using a pair of poultry shears or strong kitchen scissors, halve each Cornish hen lengthwise by cutting through the backbone and breastbone. Cut off and discard the leg tips and the tail. Wash the halves under running water and pat them dry.

In a small bowl, mix together the rum, lime juice, honey, garlic, and salt. Place the Cornish-hen halves in a shallow, nonreactive dish just large enough to accommodate them. Rub the rum mixture all over the Cornish hens, then set them aside in a cool place, covered, to marinate for 30 minutes.

Using a mortar and pestle or a coffee grinder, coarsely crush the coriander seeds and peppercorns. Remove the Cornish-hen halves from the marinade, and reserve the marinade.

Piercing the legs and wings as shown in the photograph below, thread two hen halves onto each of two long metal skewers. Brush the skewered Cornish hens with a little of the remaining marinade, then press the crushed coriander seeds and peppercorns all over the skin side of the birds.

Lightly oil the rack. Cook the Cornish-hen halves over hot coals for 20 to 25 minutes, turning them every five minutes, until the juices run clear when a skewer is inserted in a thigh.

SUGGESTED ACCOMPANIMENT: *a salad of mixed blanched vegetables, dressed with a vinaigrette.*

Minted Potato and Turkey Salad

Serves 4
Working time: about 30 minutes
Total time: about 40 minutes

Calories **275**
Protein **21g.**
Cholesterol **40mg.**
Total fat **9g.**
Saturated fat **2g.**
Sodium **55mg.**

1 lb. small new potatoes, scrubbed and cut into ½-inch chunks
6 oz. broccoli florets (about 2 cups)
1 red-skinned tart apple
10 oz. cooked skinless turkey breast, cut into ½-inch cubes
¼ lb. carrots (about 2 medium), julienned
3 scallions, trimmed and sliced diagonally into 1-inch pieces
mint sprigs for garnish
Lemon vinaigrette
2 tbsp. safflower oil
2 tbsp. fresh lemon juice
1 tbsp. white wine vinegar
½ lemon, grated zest only
½ tsp. grainy mustard
1 garlic clove, crushed
⅛ tsp. salt
freshly ground black pepper
½ tsp. sugar

Bring a large saucepan of water to a boil, and simmer the potatoes until they are tender but not too soft—about 10 minutes.

Meanwhile, prepare the vinaigrette. In a small, non-reactive bowl, whisk together the oil, 1 tablespoon of the lemon juice, the vinegar, lemon zest, mustard, garlic, salt, plenty of black pepper, and the sugar.

Drain the potatoes well and put them into a large mixing bowl. While the potatoes are still hot, add the dressing and toss them well. Let the potatoes cool.

Parboil the broccoli florets in boiling water for one to two minutes, then drain them, rinse them under cold running water, and drain them again very thoroughly. Quarter and core the apple, cut it into thin slices, and toss the slices in the remaining tablespoon of lemon juice. Add the broccoli florets, apple slices, turkey cubes, carrot sticks, and scallions to the cooled potatoes. Toss all the ingredients together.

Transfer the salad to a serving bowl. Use the scissors to cut one or two mint sprigs into strips over the salad. Finally, garnish the salad with a few whole mint sprigs.

Turkey Salad with Yogurt and Buttermilk Dressing

Serves 6
Working time: about 30 minutes
Total time: about 30 minutes

Calories **331**
Protein **27g.**
Cholesterol **53mg.**
Total fat **14g.**
Saturated fat **3g.**
Sodium **213mg.**

2¼ cups cooked turkey breast meat, skinned and cut into ½-inch cubes (about 1 lb.)
1¼ lb. small new potatoes
2 tbsp. virgin olive oil
1 cup medium mushrooms, quartered
⅛ tsp. salt
1 large green pepper, seeded, deribbed and cut into ½-inch chunks
2 tbsp. dry white wine
½ cup watercress leaves
½ cup chopped scallions
1 head Bibb lettuce, washed and trimmed
2 medium tomatoes
1 small cucumber, sliced
1 medium red onion, thinly sliced
Yogurt and buttermilk dressing
1 scallion, chopped
2 tbsp. red wine vinegar
1 tbsp. fresh lemon juice
½ tsp. celery seed
4 drops hot red pepper sauce
¼ tsp. salt
freshly ground black pepper
3 tbsp. virgin olive oil
¼ cup buttermilk
¼ cup plain low-fat yogurt
1 garlic clove, chopped

Turkey Salad with Feta Cheese

Serves 4
Working time: about 20 minutes
Total time: about 20 minutes

Calories **497**
Protein **42g.**
Cholesterol **103mg.**
Total fat **33g.**
Saturated fat **8g.**
Sodium **708mg.**

2¼ cups cooked turkey breast meat (about 1 lb.), skinned and cut into ½-inch cubes
1 small cucumber, peeled, halved, seeded and thinly cut on the diagonal
8 red radishes, diced
8 large Greek black olives, pitted and halved
4 oz. feta cheese, cut into cubes
1 lb. fresh spinach, stemmed, washed and dried
Basil vinaigrette
2 garlic cloves, finely chopped
2 tbsp. chopped fresh basil, or 2 tsp. dried basil
½ tsp. sugar
1 tbsp. grainy mustard
freshly ground black pepper
2 tbsp. fresh lemon juice
2 tbsp. red wine vinegar
2 tbsp. safflower oil
¼ cup virgin olive oil

To prepare the vinaigrette, place all the ingredients in a screw-top jar with a tight-fitting lid and shake vigorously until thoroughly blended — about 30 seconds.

To assemble the salad, combine the turkey, cucumber, radishes, olives and cheese in a large bowl, add the dressing, and toss. Arrange the spinach on salad plates and spoon the salad on top.

Drop the potatoes into boiling water, cover, and cook until tender, about 20 minutes. Drain. When they are cool enough to handle, cut the unskinned potatoes into ¾-inch cubes. Set aside in a warm place.

Heat the 2 tablespoons of olive oil in a small, heavy-bottomed, nonreactive saucepan over medium heat. Add the mushrooms and salt, and cook for about one minute. Add the green pepper and the wine and continue cooking for five minutes, stirring occasionally.

Meanwhile, in a large bowl, combine the turkey, warm potatoes, watercress and scallions. Toss in the mushroom-and-pepper mixture. Set aside.

To prepare the dressing, place all the ingredients in a screw-top jar with a tight-fitting lid and shake vigorously until thoroughly blended, about 30 seconds.

Add the dressing to the turkey mixture and toss lightly. Arrange lettuce on individual plates and place a generous portion of the salad on each. Garnish with slices of tomato, cucumber and red onion.

Turkey and Black Bean Salad

Serves 10
Working time: about 30 minutes
Total time: about 1 day

Calories **393**
Protein **30g.**
Cholesterol **47mg.**
Total fat **16g.**
Saturated fat **2g.**
Sodium **260mg.**

3½ cups cooked turkey breast meat (about 1½ lb.), cut into thin strips
1⅔ cups dried black beans, soaked for 8 hours and drained
1 medium onion, coarsely chopped
2 garlic cloves, chopped
3-inch cinnamon stick, broken in half
1½ tsp. fresh thyme or ½ tsp. dried thyme leaves
1 small dried hot red chili pepper with seeds removed or ¼ tsp. cayenne pepper
1 bay leaf
½ tsp. salt
½ lb. snow peas, with strings removed, sliced into thin strips
1 small cantaloupe, halved, seeded, and the flesh cut into small chunks
6 scallions, trimmed and finely sliced
3 medium tomatoes, peeled, seeded and coarsely chopped, placed in a strainer to drain
1 small green pepper, seeded, deribbed and chopped
1 head Bibb or red leaf lettuce
Cilantro dressing
¾ cup red wine vinegar
juice of 1 lemon or lime
2 tbsp. Dijon mustard
2 tbsp. honey
10 to 15 drops hot red pepper sauce
¼ tsp. salt
freshly ground black pepper
2 garlic cloves, chopped
5 tbsp. chopped cilantro
⅓ cup safflower oil
¼ cup virgin olive oil

Drain the soaked beans and put them into a heavy 4-quart casserole with the onion, garlic, cinnamon, thyme, chili pepper, bay leaf and salt. Add water to cover by 2 inches, bring to a boil, and boil for 10 minutes. Lower the heat and skim off the foam. Cover and simmer just until the beans are tender — one to one and a half hours. Drain the beans in a colander and rinse with cold water. Remove the chili pepper, cinnamon and bay leaf and allow the beans to drain further. (The beans can be prepared a day ahead.)

Blanch the snow peas in boiling water for 15 seconds and refresh them in cold water. Drain and place on paper towels to dry.

Put all the dressing ingredients, except the oils, in a food processor or blender and process for 15 seconds. Add the oil slowly and process until smooth, about 30 seconds more.

In a large bowl, combine the cantaloupe, scallions, tomatoes, green pepper and turkey. Add the snow peas and beans. Pour 1 cup of the dressing over the salad and toss lightly. To serve, mound the salad on lettuce leaves arranged on a platter or on individual plates and pass the remaining dressing.

Chilled Turkey with Creamy Tuna Sauce

THIS RECIPE WAS INSPIRED BY VITELLO TONNATO,
THE CLASSIC ITALIAN VEAL DISH

Serves 6
Working time: about 30 minutes
Total time: about 40 minutes

Calories **287**
Protein **31g.**
Cholesterol **70mg.**
Total fat **15g.**
Saturated fat **2g.**
Sodium **125mg.**

1½ lb. boneless turkey breast meat, skinned and cut into ¾-by-1-inch chunks
½ tsp. virgin olive oil
½ tsp. safflower oil
⅛ tsp. salt
½ cup unsalted turkey or chicken stock, warmed
4 fresh sage leaves, finely sliced for garnish (optional)

Tuna sauce

one 3½ oz. can white tuna, packed in water, drained
3 tbsp. virgin olive oil
2 tbsp. safflower oil
5 tbsp. buttermilk
1 tsp. fresh lime juice
1 tsp. capers, rinsed and patted dry

Heat the oils in a large heavy-bottomed skillet over medium heat. Sauté the turkey pieces for three minutes and turn them over. Sprinkle with the salt and cook for another three minutes. Add the stock, lower the heat, and simmer for two minutes more. Remove each piece as it whitens. Set aside to cool. Reduce the stock to about ¼ cup and reserve for the sauce.

To make the sauce, purée the tuna with the stock in a food processor or a blender. Scrape down the sides with a rubber spatula and process another 10 seconds. With the motor still running, pour in the oils slowly. Add the buttermilk, lime juice and capers, and process for one minute more or until smooth. (If you lack either appliance, you may pound the tuna to a paste in a mortar.) Transfer the sauce to a bowl and refrigerate.

To assemble the dish, pour a little sauce on individual plates. Put a portion of the turkey on each plate and dribble the remaining sauce over the turkey. Garnish with the sage or with chopped parsley.

SUGGESTED ACCOMPANIMENT: *julienned carrots; Italian bread.*

Turkey Scallops with Pine Nuts and Currants

Serves: 4
Working time: about 50 minutes
Total time: about 50 minutes

Calories **451**
Protein **33g.**
Cholesterol **59mg.**
Total fat **26g.**
Saturated fat **4g.**
Sodium **485mg.**

eight ¼-inch turkey breast cutlets (about 1 lb.), pounded to ⅛ inch thickness
3 egg whites
½ tsp. salt
freshly ground black pepper
3 tbsp. virgin olive oil
2 to 3 tbsp. finely chopped shallots
⅓ cup white wine vinegar
10 whole black peppercorns
3 bay leaves
3 tbsp. currants
⅓ cup safflower oil
⅔ cup dry bread crumbs
½ cup finely chopped fresh parsley
2 garlic cloves, finely chopped
zest of ½ orange, finely chopped or grated
3 tbsp. pine nuts, lightly toasted

In a shallow bowl, beat the egg whites with the salt and pepper. Add the cutlets one at a time, turning them to coat them with the mixture.

In a small heavy-bottomed saucepan, heat the olive oil. Add the shallots and sauté over medium heat until translucent — about five minutes. Add the vinegar, ⅔ cup of water, peppercorns and bay leaves, and simmer for 20 minutes. Stir in the currants and simmer for another 10 minutes, or until the liquid is reduced by half, to about ½ cup.

In the meantime, heat the safflower oil in a large heavy-bottomed skillet. Spread the bread crumbs in a plate. Dip the cutlets in the crumbs, then brown them in the hot oil over medium to high heat for one to two minutes on each side. Put the cooked cutlets on a heated platter and cover with foil to keep warm.

To assemble, combine the parsley, garlic and zest. Strain the reduced sauce, reserving the currants, and pour it evenly over the turkey cutlets. Sprinkle with the currants, the parsley mixture and the pine nuts. Serve warm or, if preferred, at room temperature.

SUGGESTED ACCOMPANIMENTS: *risotto; broccoli salad with julienned red pepper.*

3 *Fresh from the sea, lean fish—bass, red drum, flounder, red snapper, and tilefish, among others—shimmer on a bed of shaved ice.*

Fish and Shellfish

Whole Poached Salmon

Serves 8
Working (and total) time: about 30 minutes

Calories **280**
Protein **28g.**
Cholesterol **111mg.**
Total fat **17g.**
Saturated fat **4g.**
Sodium **90mg.**

one 4-lb. whole salmon, gutted
4 quarts court bouillon
Garnish
¼ lb. spinach, washed, stemmed and sliced thinly
½ lb. daikon radish, peeled and julienned
1 red plum, pitted and sliced

Pour the court bouillon into a fish poacher or pan large enough to accommodate the salmon.

Wash the salmon inside and out under cold running water. Wrap the salmon in a double thickness of cheesecloth that is about 10 inches longer than the fish. Knot each end of the cheesecloth and secure it by tying string around the fish in two or three places.

Holding the knotted ends of the cloth, gently lower the fish into the court bouillon. Bring the liquid to a simmer over medium heat. Cover the pan, reduce the heat to low, and cook the salmon for eight minutes per inch of thickness (measured at its thickest point).

Let the fish cool in the court bouillon, then carefully transfer it to a work surface. Cut away the strings, untie the knots, and unwrap the cheesecloth, leaving the fish on the cloth. Cut out all but the pectoral fins of the fish. Make a long cut down the back and down the belly of the salmon. Cut through the skin at the base of the tail. Then, working from the base of the tail toward the head, gently pull off the skin in strips. Discard the skin.

Carefully transfer the fish to a long platter, placing it skinned side down. Make another cut at the base of the tail and remove the skin from the second side.

Combine the sliced spinach and julienned radish and arrange them around the salmon. Garnish with the plum slices. Serve the salmon warm or cold, accompanied by any number of the sauces that follow.

Each of the sauce recipes below yields one third of the amount of sauce necessary to accompany the salmon. If you decide to make only one, remember to triple the ingredients.

Spinach-and-Garlic Sauce

Makes about 1 cup
Working (and total) time: about 15 minutes

Calories **20**
Protein **1g.**
Cholesterol **0mg.**
Total fat **2g.**
Saturated fat **0g.**
Sodium **85mg.**

1 lb. spinach, washed and stemmed
1 tbsp. safflower oil
2 garlic cloves, finely chopped
⅔ cup fish stock
¼ tsp. salt
⅛ tsp. white pepper
pinch of nutmeg

Place the spinach, with just the water that clings to its leaves, in a large saucepan over high heat. Cover the pan and steam the spinach until it is wilted — one to two minutes. Drain it well. Squeeze the spinach with your hands to rid it of excess liquid, then chop the spinach coarsely and set it aside.

Heat the oil in a small saucepan over medium heat. Add the garlic and cook it for about 30 seconds. Add the spinach, stock, salt, pepper and nutmeg, and simmer the mixture for three minutes. Transfer the mixture to a food processor or blender and purée it. Pour the sauce into a serving bowl. Serve the sauce warm with the poached salmon.

Radish-and-Ginger Sauce

Makes about 1 cup
Working time: about 15 minutes
Total time: about 25 minutes

Calories **40**
Protein **1g.**
Cholesterol **3mg.**
Total fat **3g.**
Saturated fat **1g.**
Sodium **80mg.**

1 tbsp. safflower oil
1 small onion, finely chopped
2 tbsp. finely chopped fresh ginger
½ lb. daikon radish, peeled and thinly sliced
½ cup fish stock
¼ tsp. salt
⅛ tsp. white pepper
¼ cup sour cream
¼ cup plain low-fat yogurt

Heat the oil in a small saucepan over medium heat. Add the onion and cook it, stirring occasionally, until it is transparent — three to four minutes. Stir in the ginger and cook for one minute more. Add the daikon radish and the stock; simmer the mixture, partially covered, until the radish is tender — about 10 minutes.

Transfer the mixture to a food processor or blender and purée it. Add an additional tablespoon of stock or water, if necessary, to achieve a smooth consistency. Transfer the purée to a bowl and stir in the salt and pepper, then fold in the sour cream and the yogurt. Spoon the sauce into a serving bowl and serve it with the poached salmon.

Plum Sauce with Chutney

Makes about 1 cup
Working (and total) time: about 15 minutes

Calories **50**
Protein **0g.**
Cholesterol **0mg.**
Total fat **0g.**
Saturated fat **0g.**
Sodium **20mg.**

¾ lb. red plums, halved and pitted
¼ cup mango chutney
¼ cup dry white wine

Combine the plums, chutney and wine in a small saucepan over medium-low heat, and bring the liquid to a simmer. Cover the pan and cook the mixture until the plums have softened — about seven minutes. Transfer the mixture to a food processor or blender and purée it. Pour the sauce into a serving bowl. Serve the sauce with the poached salmon.

Pickled Salmon and Red Potatoes

Serves 6 as a first course
Working time: about 25 minutes
Total time: 24 hours

Calories **250**
Protein **24g.**
Cholesterol **40mg.**
Total fat **11g.**
Saturated fat **2g.**
Sodium **115mg.**

1½ lb. red or silver salmon fillets, skinned
1 cup lightly packed fresh dill sprigs
2 tbsp. virgin olive oil
1¼ cups red wine vinegar or white wine vinegar
juice of 1 lemon
juice of 1 orange
1 bunch scallions, trimmed and sliced diagonally into ½-inch pieces
1 tbsp. mustard seeds
1 tsp. black peppercorns, cracked
3 bay leaves
½ tsp. salt
1 tsp. whole cloves
1 lb. red potatoes, the skin left on

Rinse the fillets under cold running water and pat them dry with paper towels. Cut the fish into chunks about ¾ inch thick.

In a large glass bowl, combine the salmon chunks, ¾ cup of the dill sprigs and the oil. Put the vinegar, lemon juice, orange juice, scallions, mustard seeds, pepper, bay leaves, salt and cloves in a large, nonreactive saucepan. Bring the mixture to a boil, then pour it over the salmon chunks. Gently stir the marinade and salmon to coat the pieces. Allow the marinade to cool, then cover the bowl and refrigerate it for at least 24 hours.

At the end of the marinating time, strain ¾ cup of the marinade into a second glass bowl. Add the remaining ¼ cup of dill sprigs to the strained marinade. Cut the potatoes into 1-inch pieces and place them in a steamer. Fill a saucepan about 1 inch deep with water. Put the steamer in the saucepan, cover the pan and bring the water to a simmer. Steam the potatoes until they are soft — 10 to 15 minutes. Immediately transfer the potatoes to the strained marinade; stir gently to coat the potatoes.

Serve the hot potatoes at once with the cold salmon.

SUGGESTED ACCOMPANIMENT: *pumpernickel bread.*

Flounder with Lemon and Parsley

MICROWAVING FISH FILLETS ON A BED OF HERBS AND
AROMATIC VEGETABLES RETAINS THE MOISTURE AND ENHANCES
THE FLAVOR OF ANY LEAN, WHITE-FLESHED SPECIES.

Serves 8
Working (and total) time: 30 minutes

Calories **65**	8 flounder fillets (about 4 oz. each), skinned
Protein **11g.**	⅛ tsp. salt
Cholesterol **35mg.**	freshly ground black pepper
Total fat **2g.**	1 small onion, very finely chopped
Saturated fat **0g.**	2 tbsp. finely chopped parsley
Sodium **125mg.**	3 tbsp. lemon juice
	4 tbsp. white wine
	8 thin slices of lemon

Lay the fillets flat on a work surface, skinned side up.
Season them with the salt and some pepper.

In the base of a shallow serving dish, spread out the
onion and parsley, and sprinkle them with the lemon
juice and white wine. Double over each fillet, with the
skinned side innermost, and arrange the fillets in the
dish in two overlapping rows. Tuck slices of lemon
between the fillets.

Cover the dish loosely with plastic wrap, then microwave on high until the fish is opaque—three to four
minutes. Rotate the dish once during the cooking time.

Let the fish stand, still covered with plastic wrap, for
three minutes. Remove the wrap and ·serve the fish
straight from the dish, spooning a little of the cooking
liquid over each fillet.

EDITOR'S NOTE: *The fish and its cooking liquid may also be
served cold, garnished with a salad of radicchio leaves.*

White Sea Bass with 20 Cloves of Garlic

Serves 4
Working time: about 20 minutes
Total time: about 1 hour

Calories **200**
Protein **23g.**
Cholesterol **47mg.**
Total fat **10g.**
Saturated fat **1g.**
Sodium **210mg.**

1¼ lb. Pacific white sea bass steaks (or halibut)
2 tbsp. safflower oil
2 red peppers, diced
20 garlic cloves, very thinly sliced
1 jalapeño pepper, seeded and finely chopped
6 tbsp. finely chopped cilantro, plus several whole sprigs for garnish
¼ tsp. salt
freshly ground black pepper
1 tsp. paprika, preferably Hungarian
2 cups fish stock or dry white wine

Rinse the fish under cold running water and pat it dry with paper towels. Remove any scales from the skin; if the steaks are large, cut them in half lengthwise.

Heat the oil over medium heat in a heavy-bottomed skillet large enough to hold the fish in one layer. Add the red pepper and sauté it lightly for two minutes. Add the garlic, jalapeño pepper and chopped cilantro; reduce the heat to low and cook, stirring frequently, for one minute. Place the fish on top of the vegetables and sprinkle it with the salt, some pepper and the paprika. Pour in the stock or wine and bring the liquid to a simmer, basting the fish occasionally. Cover the skillet and reduce the heat to low. Cook the fish until it is opaque — about eight minutes.

With a slotted spoon, transfer the fish to a deep platter. Remove the skin from the steaks. Cover the platter with aluminum foil to keep the fish from drying out while you finish the sauce.

Boil the liquid in the skillet, stirring occasionally, until only about ½ cup remains — five to 10 minutes. Pour the sauce over the fish. Serve the fish at room temperature or cold, garnished with the cilantro sprigs.

SUGGESTED ACCOMPANIMENTS: *green salad; sourdough rolls.*

Striped Bass on a Bed of Mushrooms and Spinach

Serves 4
Working (and total) time: about 35 minutes

Calories **185**
Protein **24g.**
Cholesterol **91mg.**
Total fat **6g.**
Saturated fat **1g.**
Sodium **260mg.**

1 lb. striped bass fillets (or black sea bass, red snapper or rockfish), skin left on
12 oz. mushrooms, wiped clean and sliced
juice of 1 lemon
freshly ground black pepper
1 lb. fresh spinach, washed and stemmed, or 10 oz. frozen spinach, thawed
1 tbsp. safflower oil
1 onion, finely chopped
⅛ tsp. grated nutmeg
¼ tsp. salt

Put the mushrooms in a saucepan with the lemon juice and a generous grinding of pepper. Pour in enough water to cover them, then bring the liquid to a boil. Reduce the heat to medium and simmer the mixture until the mushrooms are tender — about five minutes. Set the pan aside.

Put the fresh spinach, with water still clinging to its leaves, in a large pot over medium heat. Cover the pot and steam the spinach until the leaves are wilted — two to three minutes. (Frozen spinach needs no cooking.) Squeeze the moisture from the spinach and chop it coarsely.

Heat the oil in a large, heavy-bottomed skillet over medium heat. Add the onion and cook it until it is translucent — about four minutes. Drain the mushrooms and add them to the skillet, then stir in the spinach and cook for two minutes. Season the mixture with the nutmeg, salt and some additional pepper, then spread it evenly in the bottom of a flameproof baking dish.

Preheat the broiler. Rinse the fillets under cold running water and pat them dry with paper towels. Lay the fillets skin side up on the vegetable mixture. Broil the fish until the flesh feels firm to the touch and the skin is crisp — about five minutes. Serve immediately.

SUGGESTED ACCOMPANIMENT: *sautéed sliced turnips.*

Grilled Swordfish with Ancho Chili Sauce

Serves 6
Working time: about 30 minutes
Total time: about 1 hour

Calories **265**
Protein **28g.**
Cholesterol **56mg.**
Total fat **9g.**
Saturated fat **1g.**
Sodium **325mg.**

6 small swordfish steaks (about 5 oz. each), ½ to ¾ inch thick
2 tbsp. fresh thyme, or 2 tsp. dried thyme leaves
3 garlic cloves, finely chopped
juice of 2 lemons
4 dried ancho chili peppers, stemmed and seeded
1 oz. sun-dried tomatoes (3 or 4)
¾ cup fish stock
½ cup tawny port
2 tsp. safflower oil

Rinse the steaks under cold running water and pat them dry with paper towels. In a shallow dish large enough to hold the steaks in a single layer, combine the thyme, two thirds of the garlic and the lemon juice. Put the steaks in the dish and marinate them in the refrigerator for one hour, turning them once or twice.

Start the coals in an outdoor grill about 40 minutes before serving time. While the coals are heating, cover the chilies with 1 quart of boiling water and soak them for 20 minutes.

Drain the chilies and transfer them to a blender or food processor. Add the tomatoes and stock, and purée the mixture.

Pour the port into a nonreactive saucepan over medium-high heat; bring the port to a boil and cook it until it is reduced by half — three to four minutes. Stir in the chili-tomato purée and the remaining third of the garlic. Reduce the heat to medium and cook the sauce, stirring occasionally, for five minutes. Strain the sauce through a fine sieve into the bottom of a warmed serving platter.

When the coals are hot, remove the steaks from the marinade and brush them with the oil. Grill the steaks for only two or three minutes per side — the flesh should be barely opaque. Set the steaks on top of the sauce and serve immediately.

SUGGESTED ACCOMPANIMENTS: *green salad; corn bread.*
EDITOR'S NOTE: *If you wish to broil rather than grill the steaks, cook them for just two to three minutes per side.*

Grilled Swordfish in Apple-Tarragon Sauce

Serves 4
Working time: about 15 minutes
Total time: about 25 minutes

Calories **304**
Protein **30g.**
Cholesterol **59mg.**
Total fat **10g.**
Saturated fat **2g.**
Sodium **290mg.**

1½ lb. swordfish steak (or shark or tuna), trimmed and cut into quarters
2 tbsp. safflower oil
2 tbsp. finely chopped shallot
2 tbsp. chopped fresh tarragon, or 2 tsp. dried tarragon
½ cup fish stock
¼ cup unsweetened apple juice
1½ tsp. cornstarch, mixed with 1 tbsp. cold water
¼ tsp. salt
freshly ground black pepper
1 red apple, quartered, cored and cut into thin wedges
1 yellow apple, quartered, cored and cut into thin wedges

Preheat the grill or broiler.

To prepare the sauce, pour 1 tablespoon of the oil into a saucepan over medium heat. Add the shallot and cook it until it is translucent — one to two minutes. Add the tarragon, stock, apple juice, cornstarch mixture, ⅛ teaspoon of the salt and some pepper. Whisking constantly, bring the mixture to a boil and let it thicken. Reduce the heat to low and simmer the sauce for two or three minutes. Set the pan aside.

Rinse the fish steaks under cold running water and pat them dry with paper towels. Season the steaks with the remaining ⅛ teaspoon of salt and a generous grinding of pepper, then brush them with the remaining tablespoon of oil. Grill or broil the steaks until their flesh is opaque and feels firm to the touch — three to four minutes per side.

When the fish is nearly done, reheat the sauce over low heat. Serve the steaks immediately, topped with the warm sauce and garnished with the apple slices.

SUGGESTED ACCOMPANIMENT: *sautéed yellow squash.*

Scandinavian-Style Bluefish Salad

Serves 6 as a main course
Working time: about 40 minutes
Total time: about 3 hours and 15 minutes
(includes marinating)

Calories **535**
Protein **36g.**
Cholesterol **90mg.**
Total fat **14g.**
Saturated fat **4g.**
Sodium **430mg.**

1 cup sugar
2 cups white wine vinegar
2 small red onions, thinly sliced
freshly ground black pepper
½ tsp. mustard seeds
2 bay leaves
one 3½-lb. bluefish, dressed and cut into 1-inch-thick steaks
4 boiling potatoes (about 1½ lbs.), peeled and sliced
3 carrots, sliced into thin rounds
2 tbsp. chopped fresh dill, or 2 tsp. dried dill
1 cucumber, preferably unwaxed
6 radishes, thinly sliced
1 head of Boston lettuce, or 2 heads of Bibb lettuce, washed and dried
Pumpernickel toast
2 tbsp. unsalted butter
2 tbsp. grated red onion
½ tsp. caraway seeds
12 slices dark pumpernickel bread

Put the sugar, vinegar, half of the onions, some pepper, the mustard seeds and the bay leaves into a small, nonreactive saucepan. Bring the liquid to a boil, reduce the heat, and simmer the marinade for 10 minutes.

Set the bluefish steaks in a nonreactive heatproof dish large enough to hold them in a single layer. Strain the marinade over them, discarding the solids. Simmer the fish over medium heat for two minutes. Remove the dish from the heat and allow it to cool to room temperature — about 30 minutes.

Pour enough water into a saucepan to fill it about 1 inch deep. Set a vegetable steamer in the pan and bring the water to a boil. Put the potatoes into the steamer, cover the pan tightly, and steam the potatoes until they are tender — about six minutes. Add the potatoes to the fish. Steam the carrots in the same way, but for only three minutes. Add the carrots to the fish and potatoes. Sprinkle the dill over the fish and vegetables, cover the dish, and refrigerate the mixture for at least two hours.

Shortly before serving the salad, score the cucumber lengthwise with a channel knife or a paring knife. Slice the cucumber into thin rounds and add them to the fish along with the radishes and the remaining onion.

To make the toast, first preheat the oven to 450° F. Mix together the butter, grated onion, caraway seeds and some pepper. Spread this mixture on the pumpernickel slices, then toast them in the oven for about four minutes.

Using a slotted spoon, transfer the salad to a serving dish lined with the lettuce leaves. Pour about half the marinade over the salad; discard the remainder. Serve the salad accompanied by the pumpernickel toast.

Seviche Salad

THIS RECIPE CALLS FOR ¼ CUP OF SUGAR; IT IS ADDED TO THE WATER USED FOR BLANCHING ORANGE ZEST, THEN DISCARDED.

Serves 8 as a main course
Working time: about 45 minutes
Total time: about one day (includes marinating time)

Calories **210**
Protein **22g.**
Cholesterol **47mg.**
Total fat **7g.**
Saturated fat **1g.**
Sodium **380mg.**

4 oranges
¼ cup sugar
3 limes
3 lemons
3 celery stalks, thinly sliced
1 green pepper, seeded, deribbed and julienned
1 yellow pepper, seeded, deribbed and julienned
1 small red onion, thinly sliced
1 garlic clove, finely chopped
2 tbsp. chopped cilantro
1 tsp. salt
½ tsp. black pepper
hot red-pepper sauce
½ tsp. ground cumin
¼ tsp. cumin seeds
1 lb. bay scallops, the bright, white connective tissue removed, the scallops rinsed and patted dry
1 lb. halibut fillets, rinsed, patted dry and cut into ½ inch cubes
¼ lb. spinach, washed, stemmed and dried, or 1 head of oakleaf lettuce, washed and dried
2 tbsp. chopped parsley, preferably Italian
2 tbsp. virgin olive oil

Using a vegetable peeler, remove the zest from one orange, leaving behind as much of the pith as possible. Cut the zest into fine julienne, then put it into a small saucepan with 1½ cups of water and the sugar. Bring the water to a boil and cook the zest for 2 minutes. Drain the zest and transfer it to a large, nonreactive bowl. Into another bowl, squeeze the juice from the oranges, limes and lemons, strain it and set it aside.

Add the celery, green and yellow peppers, onion, garlic, cilantro, salt, pepper, a few drops of red-pepper sauce, the ground cumin and cumin seeds to the bowl. Gently toss the contents of the bowl with the scallops and the halibut cubes. Pour the citrus juices over all and toss again. Press down on the solid ingredients so that they are completely submerged. Cover the bowl and let the seviche marinate in the refrigerator for 8 hours.

Use a slotted spoon to transfer the seviche to a platter or individual plates lined with the spinach or lettuce. Pour ½ cup of the marinade into a small bowl. Add the parsley; then, whisking constantly, pour in the oil in a slow, steady stream. Spoon the dressing over the salad and serve immediately.

Orzo and Mussels

Serves 4
Working time: about 30 minutes
Total time: about 40 minutes

Calories **398**
Protein **17g.**
Cholesterol **19mg.**
Total fat **9g.**
Saturated fat **1g.**
Sodium **391mg.**

8 oz. orzo (or other small pasta)
1 orange
2 tbsp. virgin olive oil
1 onion, finely chopped
4 garlic cloves, finely chopped
2 lb. tomatoes, peeled, seeded and finely chopped (about 2½ cups)
2 tsp. fennel seeds
1½ tbsp. tomato paste
½ cup dry vermouth
¼ tsp. salt
3 tbsp. chopped fresh parsley, or 1 tbsp. dried parsley
1 tsp. fresh thyme, or ¼ tsp. dried thyme leaves
1½ lb. mussels, scrubbed and debearded

With a sharp knife, pare the zest from the orange and cut it into tiny julienne. Put the strips in a small saucepan with 1 cup of cold water. Bring the water to a boil, then remove the pan from the heat. Rinse the zest under cold running water and set it aside. Squeeze the juice from the orange and reserve it as well.

Heat the oil in a large casserole over medium heat. Add the onion and cook it for three minutes, stirring constantly. Add the garlic and cook, stirring, until the onion is translucent — about two minutes more.

Push the onion-garlic mixture to one side of the casserole. Add the tomatoes and the fennel seeds, and raise the heat to high. Cook the tomatoes just enough to soften them without destroying their texture — approximately one minute. Stir the onion-garlic mixture in with the tomatoes. Add the tomato paste, orange juice, vermouth and salt to the casserole, and stir well. Reduce the heat to medium and simmer the sauce for five minutes. Add the parsley, thyme and orange zest.

Place the mussels on top of the sauce. Cover the casserole and steam the mussels until they open — three to five minutes. If any mussels remain closed, discard them. Remove the casserole from the heat and set it aside with its lid on to keep the contents warm.

Add the orzo to three quarts of boiling water with 1½ teaspoons of salt. Start testing after 10 minutes and cook it until it is *al dente*. Drain the orzo and divide it among four deep plates. Ladle the mussels and sauce over each serving.

Clams and Rice Yucatan Style

Serves 4
Working time: about 30 minutes
Total time: about 1 hour

Calories **470**
Protein **16g.**
Cholesterol **34mg.**
Total fat **8g.**
Saturated fat **1g.**
Sodium **200mg.**

36 littleneck clams, scrubbed
3 ripe tomatoes, peeled, seeded and coarsely chopped
1 large onion, coarsely chopped
3 garlic cloves, coarsely chopped
3 jalapeño peppers, seeded and coarsely chopped
2¼ cups fish stock or water
2 tbsp. safflower oil
1½ cups rice
¼ tsp. salt
freshly ground black pepper
½ cup peas, blanched for 1 minute if fresh
juice of 1 lime
several fresh cilantro sprigs

Purée the tomatoes, onion, garlic, jalapeño peppers and ½ cup of the fish stock or water in a food processor or blender. Preheat the oven to 400° F.

Heat the oil in a large ovenproof skillet or casserole over medium heat. Add the rice and sauté it in the oil, stirring constantly, until it is lightly browned — three to four minutes. Stir in the tomato purée, the remaining 1¾ cups of stock or water, the salt and some black pepper. Bring the mixture to a simmer, reduce the heat to medium low and cook the rice, covered, until most of the liquid has been absorbed — about 15 minutes. Stir in the peas.

Tap the clams and discard any that do not close. Set the clams on top of the rice, cover the dish with aluminum foil and transfer it to the oven. Bake the clams until they open — about 10 minutes. Drizzle the lime juice over the clams and garnish the dish with the cilantro sprigs. Serve immediately.

SUGGESTED ACCOMPANIMENTS: *warm tortillas; raw jícama and orange salad or chopped avocado salad.*

Steamed, Spiced Crabs

Serves 4
Working time: about 20 minutes
Total time: about 45 minutes

Calories **115**
Protein **17g.**
Cholesterol **78mg.**
Total fat **1g.**
Saturated fat **0g.**
Sodium **135mg.**

12 live blue crabs
¼ cup finely chopped fresh ginger
1 whole garlic bulb, the cloves peeled and finely chopped
1 tbsp. mustard seeds
½ tsp. ground allspice
2 tsp. hot red-pepper flakes, crushed
6 bay leaves, crushed
1 tbsp. fennel seeds
2 onions, finely chopped
1 cup cider vinegar
1 cup dry white wine

If the crabs are sandy, wash each one under cold running water, holding it with kitchen tongs.

Combine the ginger, garlic, mustard seeds, allspice, red pepper, bay leaves, fennel seeds and onions in a bowl. Set a steamer in a tall stockpot and pour in the vinegar, wine and 2 cups of water. Bring the liquid to a boil, then remove the pot from the heat.

Put three crabs in the steamer and scatter a quarter of the spice-and-onion mixture over them. Layer the remaining crabs on top, with three crabs and a quarter of the spice mixture in each layer. Cover the pot tightly and set it over high heat.

Steam the crabs for 20 minutes, timing from the moment when steam first escapes from the pot. At the end of the steaming period, turn off the heat and let the pot stand, still covered, while the steam subsides — about three minutes.

Serve the crabs hot, providing a mallet for cracking the claws, nutpicks for extracting the meat, and plenty of napkins.

SUGGESTED ACCOMPANIMENTS: *corn on the cob; potato salad.*

Batter-Dipped Soft-Shell Crabs with Ham and Scallions

Serves 6
Working time: about 50 minutes
Total time: about 1 hour

Calories **285**
Protein **35g.**
Cholesterol **154mg.**
Total fat **8g.**
Saturated fat **1g.**
Sodium **560mg.**

12 soft-shell crabs, cleaned and trimmed
¾ cup light beer
¾ cup flour
3 tbsp. grainy mustard
2 tbsp. safflower oil
freshly ground black pepper
1 oz. lean ham, diced
2 scallions, trimmed and thinly sliced
1 lemon, cut into 6 wedges

Preheat the oven to 375° F. Lightly oil a baking sheet large enough to hold the crabs in one layer, and set the baking sheet aside.

Pour the beer into a large bowl. Gradually whisk the flour into the beer until a smooth batter results. Stir in the mustard and set the batter aside.

Heat 1 tablespoon of the oil in a large nonstick or heavy-bottomed skillet over medium-high heat. Sprinkle the crabs with some pepper. Dip six of the crabs in the batter, lightly shaking off any excess, and place them in the skillet. Cook the crabs on the first side until they are browned — about 45 seconds — then carefully turn them over and brown them on the second side for 45 seconds. Transfer the crabs to the baking sheet.

Wipe the skillet clean and return it to the heat. Pour in the remaining tablespoon of oil. Dip the remaining six crabs in the batter and brown them in the skillet the same way you cooked the first batch. Transfer the second batch to the baking sheet.

Bake the crabs for eight minutes. Remove the crabs from the oven and scatter the ham and scallions over them, then return them to the oven and bake for two minutes more. Serve the crabs immediately, with the lemon wedges alongside.

SUGGESTED ACCOMPANIMENT: *green bean salad.*

Shrimp and Artichoke Salad

Serves 6 as a main course at lunch
Working (and total) time: about 1 hour and 15 minutes

Calories **140**
Protein **13g.**
Cholesterol **87mg.**
Total fat **5g.**
Saturated fat **1g.**
Sodium **70mg.**

4 artichokes
1 lemon, cut in half
1 lb. medium shrimp, peeled, and deveined if necessary
¼ lb. green beans, trimmed and cut into ½-inch lengths
4 large ripe tomatoes (about 2 lb.), peeled, seeded and cut into ½-inch chunks
2 tbsp. finely cut chives
6 basil leaves, thinly sliced
1 garlic clove, finely chopped
4 tbsp. sherry vinegar or red wine vinegar
1 tsp. grainy mustard
3 tbsp. grated onion
2 tbsp. virgin olive oil

Cut the stems off the artichokes. Rub the cut surfaces with one of the lemon halves to prevent discoloration.

Bring 4 quarts of water to a boil in a large, nonreactive saucepan. Squeeze the juice of the lemon half into the water, then add the half itself. Put the artichokes into the water; reduce the heat to maintain a strong simmer, and cook the artichokes until they are tender — about 20 minutes. Remove the artichokes from the water with a slotted spoon and set them aside.

Bring 2 quarts of water to a boil in a nonreactive saucepan. Add the juice from the second lemon half, and drop in the rind as well. Add the shrimp and cook them until they are opaque — 30 seconds to one minute. Drain the shrimp, refresh them under cold running water, and drain them again. Reserve six of the shrimp for garnish; cut the remainder into ¾-inch pieces. Put the shrimp pieces in a large bowl.

When the artichokes are cool enough to handle, pull off their leaves. Discard the dark green outer leaves but save the inner ones for garnish. With a teaspoon, scoop the furry choke from each bottom and discard it. Cut the bottoms into ½-inch-long pieces and add them to the shrimp.

Blanch the beans in 1 quart of boiling water until they turn bright green and are tender yet still somewhat crisp — one to two minutes. Drain the beans, refresh them under cold running water, and drain them again. Transfer the beans to the bowl containing the shrimp; add the tomatoes, chives, basil and garlic.

In a small bowl, whisk together the vinegar, mustard, onion and oil. Pour this dressing over the shrimp and beans, and toss well. Spoon the salad onto individual plates, garnishing each serving with the remaining artichoke leaves and one of the reserved whole shrimp.

Shrimp Salad on Fresh Pineapple-Mango Relish

Serves 8 as a main course at lunch
Working time: about 30 minutes
Total time: about 1 hour

Calories **160**
Protein **13g.**
Cholesterol **104mg.**
Total fat **4g.**
Saturated fat **1g.**
Sodium **200mg.**

2 large ripe mangoes
1 pineapple, peeled and cut into ¼-inch cubes
¼ cup fresh lime juice
½ cup finely chopped fresh cilantro
1½ lb. medium shrimp, peeled, and deveined if necessary
2 sweet red peppers, halved, seeded and deribbed
¼ cup mayonnaise (recipe, page 172)
4 scallions, trimmed and thinly sliced
2 tbsp. very finely chopped fresh ginger
½ tsp. salt
1 cilantro sprig for garnish

To prepare the relish, first peel the mangoes and remove the flesh in pieces. Purée one quarter of the flesh in a food processor or a blender, then pass it through a sieve set over a bowl. Refrigerate the purée. Cut the remaining mango pieces into ¼-inch cubes and place them in a bowl. Add the pineapple, lime juice and chopped cilantro; stir the relish and refrigerate it.

Bring 2 quarts of water to a boil in a large saucepan. Add the shrimp and cook them until they are opaque — about one minute. Drain the shrimp and refresh them under cold running water. Transfer the shrimp to a bowl.

Dice one of the pepper halves and add the dice to the bowl containing the shrimp. Julienne the remaining pepper halves and set the julienne aside. Stir the mayonnaise, mango purée, scallions, ginger and salt into the shrimp-and-pepper mixture. Chill the salad for at least 30 minutes.

To serve, spoon some of the pineapple-mango relish onto a large platter and surround it with some of the shrimp salad. Top the relish with the remaining shrimp salad; garnish the dish with the pepper julienne and the cilantro sprig.

Broccoli-Studded Shrimp

Serves 4
Working (and total) time: about 30 minutes

Calories **160**
Protein **17g.**
Cholesterol **130mg.**
Total fat **8g.**
Saturated fat **1g.**
Sodium **155mg.**

24 large shrimp (about 1¼ lb.), peeled, the tails left on
24 broccoli florets, each stem trimmed to 1 inch long and tapered to a point, blanched for 1 minute
2 scallions, trimmed and finely chopped
1 garlic clove, finely chopped
2 tsp. finely chopped fresh ginger
2 tbsp. rice vinegar
2 tbsp. rice wine or dry sherry
1 tsp. chili paste with garlic
1 tsp. tomato paste
1 tsp. cornstarch, mixed with 2 tbsp. water
2 tbsp. safflower oil

Using a skewer, make a ¼-inch-diameter hole through a shrimp from front to back, about one third of the way from its larger end. Insert a broccoli stem into the hole so that the floret nestles within the curve of the shrimp, as shown. Repeat the process with the remaining shrimp and broccoli. Carefully transfer the shrimp to a bowl with the scallions, garlic and ginger; toss the mixture gently and let it stand for 10 minutes.

While the shrimp are marinating, combine the vinegar, rice wine or sherry, chili paste, tomato paste and the cornstarch mixture in a small bowl. Stir the mixture well and set it aside.

Heat a wok or heavy-bottomed skillet over medium-high heat, then pour in the oil. Add half of the shrimp and gently stir fry them until they are opaque and firm — about two minutes. Remove the shrimp and keep them warm. Stir fry the second batch of shrimp.

Return the first batch of shrimp to the wok and pour in the sauce. Stirring gently to coat the shrimp, cook until the sauce thickens — about one minute.

SUGGESTED ACCOMPANIMENT: *rice with peppers and scallions.*

Gingered Shrimp on Black Beans

Serves 6
Working time: about 1 hour
Total time: about 9 hours

Calories **425**
Protein **30g.**
Cholesterol **108mg.**
Total fat **6g.**
Saturated fat **1g.**
Sodium **345mg.**

1¼ lb. medium shrimp, peeled and deveined, the shells reserved
1-inch piece of fresh ginger, peeled and thinly sliced, plus 1 tbsp. chopped fresh ginger
1½ cups dry white wine
1 lb. dried black beans, soaked for at least 8 hours and drained
2 onions, chopped
4 garlic cloves, 2 crushed and 2 very thinly sliced
1 cinnamon stick, broken into 3 or 4 pieces
freshly ground black pepper
¼ tsp. salt
1 tbsp. grated lemon zest
2 tbsp. virgin olive oil
½ tsp. ground cinnamon
1 tsp. fresh lemon juice
3 scallions, trimmed and thinly sliced

Put the shrimp shells in a large saucepan. Add the ginger slices, 1 cup of the wine and 2 cups of water, and bring the mixture to a boil. Reduce the heat to medium and cook until the liquid is reduced by half — about 30 minutes. Strain the stock into a bowl, pressing down on the shells to extract any liquid, and set the bowl aside.

While the shells are cooking, put the drained beans in a large, heavy-bottomed saucepan along with the onions, crushed garlic cloves, the pieces of cinnamon stick and some pepper. Pour in enough water to cover the beans by about 1½ inches and boil the beans for 10 minutes. Skim off the foam and reduce the heat to low. Add the shrimp stock, salt and lemon zest, and simmer the mixture until the beans are tender but not mushy and a thick sauce results — one and a half to two hours. Remove the cinnamon-stick pieces and discard them.

About five minutes before the beans finish cooking, pour the oil into a large, heavy-bottomed skillet over medium-high heat. When the oil is hot, add the shrimp and sprinkle them with some pepper. Add the chopped ginger, the thinly sliced garlic and the ground cinnamon, and sauté the shrimp, stirring frequently, for three minutes. Pour the lemon juice and the remaining ½ cup of wine into the skillet; continue cooking the mixture, stirring frequently, until the shrimp are opaque and the liquid is reduced to a glaze — two to three minutes more. Stir in the scallions.

Pour the beans onto a serving platter and top them with the shrimp mixture. Serve immediately.

SUGGESTED ACCOMPANIMENT: *crisp green salad.*

4 *Tropical fruit provides a refreshing garnish for spicy pan-fried sirloin steaks (recipe, page 109).*

Beef, Veal, Lamb, and Pork

Grilled Sirloin Stuffed with Summer Vegetables

Serves 8
Working time: about 1 hour
Total time: about 2 hours (includes marinating)

Calories **210**
Protein **27g.**
Cholesterol **76mg.**
Total fat **9g.**
Saturated fat **3g.**
Sodium **190mg.**

one 2½-lb. sirloin steak, about 2 inches thick, trimmed of fat	
1 tsp. Dijon mustard	
freshly ground black pepper	
1 garlic clove, crushed	
⅛ tsp. salt	
¼ cup red wine	
thyme sprigs for garnish (optional)	

Vegetable stuffing
1 tbsp. virgin olive oil
⅓ cup chopped onion
1 sweet green pepper, seeded, deribbed, and diced
1 sweet red pepper, seeded, deribbed, and diced
¼ cup diced zucchini
¼ cup diced yellow squash
2 garlic cloves, finely chopped
1½ tsp. chopped fresh thyme, or ½ tsp. dried thyme leaves
1½ tsp. chopped fresh oregano, or ½ tsp. dried oregano
¼ tsp. hot red-pepper flakes
¼ tsp. salt
freshly ground black pepper
¾ cup fresh breadcrumbs

Using the technique shown below, cut a pocket in the beef. Combine the mustard, pepper, garlic, salt, and wine in a shallow, nonreactive dish. Add the steak to the dish and turn the meat in the marinade once to coat it evenly. Marinate the steak, covered, for one hour at room temperature, turning it several times.

Meanwhile, make the stuffing. Heat the oil in a large, heavy-bottomed skillet over low heat. Add the onion, green and red peppers, zucchini, yellow squash, and garlic. Partially cover the skillet and cook the vegetables, stirring frequently, until they begin to soften—about seven minutes. Add the thyme, oregano, red-pepper flakes, salt, and some black pepper. Stir the mixture well and remove it from the heat. Add the breadcrumbs and toss them with the vegetables. Allow the mixture to cool.

About 30 minutes before cooking the meat, prepare the coals for grilling. When the coals are nearly ready,

remove the meat from the dish, reserving the marinade. Stuff the beef with the cooled vegetable mixture and tie it as demonstrated below.

When the coals are hot, bank them against the sides of the grill. Place a foil drip pan in the center of the coal grate and set the rack in place. Lay the meat in the center of the rack. Grill the meat, basting it occasionally with the reserved marinade, for 20 minutes on the first side. Turn the meat over and continue cooking it for 10 to 20 minutes longer for medium-rare meat.

Remove the meat from the grill and let it stand for 30 minutes. Discard the strings and slice the meat across the grain. Arrange the slices on a platter and serve immediately, garnished with thyme, if you wish. This dish can also be served cold.

SUGGESTED ACCOMPANIMENTS: *grilled sliced potatoes; spinach salad.*

Cutting and Stuffing a Pocket in a Sirloin Steak

1 *CUTTING A POCKET. Insert the tip of a knife (here, a boning knife) in the side of a 2-inch-thick boneless sirloin steak. Cut in as deeply as possible without piercing the outer edge of the meat to form a pocket.*

2 *STUFFING THE POCKET. Using your hands, stuff the prepared filling (recipe, pages 24-25) into the pocket. Be sure to push the filling in as deeply as possible.*

3 *MAKING THE FIRST LOOP. To keep the pocket from opening during cooking, tie the steak as you would a roast. First, loop butcher's twine around one end of the steak and knot the string, leaving several inches of twine loose at the end.*

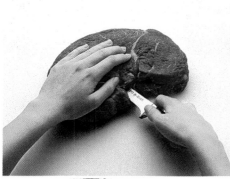

4 *MAKING SUCCESSIVE LOOPS. With the string still attached to the ball of twine, form a loose loop and twist the string around itself twice. Bring the loop over and under the other end of the meat.*

5 *TIGHTENING THE STRING. Slide the loop forward so that it rests about 1½ to 2 inches in front of the first loop, and tighten it by pulling both ends of the twine at once. Repeat the process, making three or more loops around the meat and tightening the string after each loop.*

6 *TYING THE ROAST TOGETHER. Finally, draw the string under the entire length of the meat and back to the first loop you made. Knot the string to the loose length at that end, then sever the string from the ball of twine.*

Mustard Steaks with Yogurt Sauce and Belgian Endive Salad

Serves 4
Working time: about 20 minutes
Total time: about 45 minutes

Calories **325**
Protein **45g.**
Cholesterol **100mg.**
Total fat **14g.**
Saturated fat **6g.**
Sodium **125mg.**

4 sirloin steaks (about 5 oz. each), trimmed of fat
2 tbsp. grainy mustard, tarragon flavored if possible
2 garlic cloves, crushed
⅔ cup plain low-fat yogurt
freshly ground black pepper
Belgian endive salad
3 oz. mushrooms, wiped clean and trimmed
2 tbsp. fresh lemon juice
6 oz. Belgian endive, trimmed and thinly sliced
¼ cup radish sprouts (glossary)
4 scallions, trimmed and sliced
½ sweet red or orange pepper, sliced and blanched

Starting at the untrimmed side of each steak, cut a pocket almost through to the opposite side. Coat the insides of the pockets with half of the grainy mustard, then rub the steaks all over with half of the crushed garlic. Place the steaks in a dish and set them aside, covered, in a cool place for 30 minutes to marinate.

Meanwhile, make the sauce. Put the yogurt, the remaining mustard and garlic, and plenty of freshly ground black pepper into a bowl, and mix them together thoroughly.

For the salad, slice the mushrooms and put them into a bowl with the lemon juice. Toss the mushrooms well and let them stand for 10 minutes. Add the Belgian endive, radish sprouts, scallions, and sweet pepper, and mix the ingredients together well. Cover the salad and chill it until it is needed.

Brush the rack with oil and cook the steaks over hot coals for three to five minutes on each side. Serve the steaks with the salad and sauce.

Peppercorn-Crusted Tenderloin with Three Sauces

Serves 16
Working time: about 1 hour and 30 minutes
Total time: about 2 hours and 15 minutes

Calories **290**
Protein **33g.**
Cholesterol **72mg.**
Total fat **16g.**
Saturated fat **6g.**
Sodium **480mg.**

3 garlic cloves, crushed
4½ lb. beef tenderloin in one piece, trimmed of fat
½ cup black peppercorns, crushed
2 tbsp. virgin olive oil

Spinach sauce

1 tbsp. polyunsaturated margarine
1 leek, trimmed, washed thoroughly, and sliced
1 shallot, chopped
2 garlic cloves, coarsely chopped
1 lb. fresh spinach, washed and stemmed
1 tbsp. fresh lemon juice
½ tsp. salt
3 tbsp. crème fraîche or sour cream

Pumpkin sauce

1 lb. pumpkin, peeled, seeds removed, flesh cubed
1¼ cups unsalted chicken stock
1 tsp. molasses
¾ oz. Parmesan cheese, grated
1 tbsp. cut chives
¼ small nutmeg, grated, or ¼ tsp. ground nutmeg
1 tsp. salt
¼ cup sour cream

Parsnip and apple sauce

14 oz. parsnips, trimmed and cubed
3 baking apples, peeled, cored, and coarsely chopped, placed in acidulated water
1 cinnamon stick
½ lemon, peel only, cut into wide strips
2 tbsp. polyunsaturated margarine
1 tsp. salt
1 tbsp. finely chopped fresh chervil

Rub the garlic all over the beef tenderloin. Put the peppercorns on a plate and roll the beef in them, pressing them firmly and evenly into the surface to form a compact crust. Place the meat on a platter, then cover it and set it aside while you prepare the sauces.

For the spinach sauce, melt the margarine in a large saucepan over medium heat. Add the leek, shallot, and garlic, and cook the vegetables until they are just softened—about five minutes. Add the spinach with water still clinging to its leaves, then cook the vegetables for one minute more, turning the spinach continuously to prevent it from sticking and to coat it in the cooking juices. Cover the saucepan and cook the vegetables gently, stirring occcasionally, until they are tender—about five minutes. Remove the pan from the heat and let the spinach mixture cool slightly, then transfer it to a food processor or blender with all the cooking juices, and process it to a purée. Add the lemon juice and the salt, and process the sauce for 10 seconds before adding the crème fraîche or sour cream. Process the sauce very briefly, then pour it into a small, nonreactive saucepan, ready to be reheated before serving.

For the pumpkin sauce, put the pumpkin into a large saucepan and add the chicken stock. Bring the stock to the simmering point, then simmer the pumpkin until it is soft—15 to 20 minutes. Remove the pan from the heat, allow the pumpkin to cool slightly, then transfer it to a food processor or blender, pouring in all the cooking liquid. Add the molasses, Parmesan cheese, chives, nutmeg, and salt, and process the mixture until it forms a smooth purée. Add the sour cream to the sauce and process it for a few seconds more. Press the sauce through a fine sieve into a small saucepan, then set it aside, ready to be reheated.

To make the third sauce, place the parsnips and apples in a large saucepan. Add the cinnamon stick and lemon peel. Pour in 1 cup of water, and bring it to a simmer over medium heat. Simmer the parsnips and apples for 10 to 15 minutes, or until they are soft. Discard the cinnamon stick and all but a 1-inch strip of the lemon peel. Transfer the parsnips and apples and the reserved lemon peel with all the cooking liquid to a food processor or blender. Add the margarine and salt, then process the mixture until it forms a smooth purée. Press the sauce through a fine sieve into a saucepan. Stir in the chervil and set the sauce aside.

Brush the olive oil over the beef's peppercorn crust, reserving any excess to baste the meat as it cooks. Set the rack close to medium-hot coals, and cook the meat for 15 minutes to seal it, turning it frequently and basting it with any remaining oil. Raise the rack and continue to cook the meat for 15 minutes more for rare beef, or 20 minutes for rare to medium meat. During the latter stage of the cooking, keep the thin end of the tenderloin away from the hottest part of the fire to prevent it from overcooking.

While the beef is cooking, gently reheat the sauces without letting them boil. Transfer the peppercorn-crusted tenderloin to a board or serving platter, and carve it into thick slices. Serve the sauces separately.

Grilled Top Loin Steaks with Glazed Shallots and Mushrooms

Serves 4
Working time: about 20 minutes
Total time: about 40 minutes

Calories **290**
Protein **26g.**
Cholesterol **61mg.**
Total fat **9g.**
Saturated fat **3g.**
Sodium **210mg.**

2 top loin steaks (about 10 oz. each), trimmed of fat and cut into 2 pieces
2 tsp. safflower oil
½ lb. mushrooms, wiped clean
½ lb. shallots, peeled
2 tbsp. honey
1 tsp. chopped fresh tarragon, or ½ tsp. dried tarragon
½ cup Madeira or port
½ cup unsalted brown stock or unsalted chicken stock
2 tsp. cornstarch mixed with 1 tbsp. of the stock
¼ tsp. salt
freshly ground black pepper

If you plan to grill the steaks, prepare the coals about 30 minutes before cooking time; to broil, preheat the broiler for 10 minutes.

Heat the oil in a nonstick skillet over medium heat; add the mushrooms and sauté them until they are lightly browned — about four minutes. Using a slotted spoon, transfer the mushrooms to a bowl. Pour 1 cup of water into the skillet and add the shallots, honey and tarragon. Partially cover the skillet; bring the liquid to a simmer and cook the mixture until the shallots are translucent and only ¼ cup of liquid remains — eight to 10 minutes.

Return the mushrooms to the skillet and toss them with the shallots and the liquid until all are coated with a syrupy glaze — about two minutes longer. Keep the glazed shallots and mushrooms warm.

In a small saucepan, reduce the Madeira or port by half over medium-high heat. Add the stock and bring the mixture to a simmer. Whisk the cornstarch mixture into the simmering liquid. Continue cooking the sauce until it thickens, and add ⅛ teaspoon of the salt and some pepper. Keep the sauce warm while you prepare the steaks.

Grill or broil the steaks for three minutes. Turn the steaks over and season them with the remaining ⅛ teaspoon of salt and some more pepper. Cook the steaks for three minutes longer for medium-rare meat. Serve the steaks with the glazed shallots and mushrooms on the side and the sauce poured on top.

SUGGESTED ACCOMPANIMENT: *steamed green beans.*

Low-Fat Hamburgers with Spicy Pumpkin Ketchup

THE RECIPE FOR PUMPKIN KETCHUP YIELDS MORE THAN ENOUGH FOR EIGHT HAMBURGERS; THE EXCESS MAY BE STORED IN THE REFRIGERATOR FOR UP TO ONE WEEK.

Serves 8
Working time: about 15 minutes
Total time: about 1 hour and 15 minutes

Calories **275**
Protein **21g.**
Cholesterol **47mg.**
Total fat **5g.**
Saturated fat **2g.**
Sodium **155mg.**

1¾ lb. beef round, trimmed of fat and ground
1⅓ cups bulgur
2 garlic cloves, very finely chopped
⅓ cup finely chopped fresh parsley
2 tbsp. grainy mustard
Spicy pumpkin ketchup
16 oz. canned pumpkin (1½ cups)
1 onion, finely chopped
1 apple or pear, peeled, cored and chopped
½ cup cider vinegar
2 tbsp. sugar
1 tbsp. honey
½ tsp. ground cloves
½ tsp. curry powder
¼ tsp. ground allspice
¼ tsp. cayenne pepper
¼ tsp. salt
freshly ground black pepper

Combine the ketchup ingredients in a nonreactive saucepan. Stir in 1 cup of water and simmer the mixture over medium-low heat for one hour. Purée the ketchup in a food processor or a blender, then work it through a sieve with a wooden spoon. Transfer the ketchup to a serving bowl and set it aside.

While the ketchup is simmering, put the bulgur into a heatproof bowl and pour 1⅔ cups of boiling water ▶

over it. Cover the bowl and set it aside for 30 minutes.

If you plan to grill the hamburgers, prepare the coals about 30 minutes before cooking time; to broil, pre-heat the broiler for 10 minutes.

Put the ground beef, soaked bulgur, garlic, parsley and mustard into a bowl, and combine them thoroughly by hand. Form the mixture into eight patties. Grill or broil the hamburgers for three to four minutes on each side for medium-rare meat. Serve the hamburgers hot with the ketchup alongside.

SUGGESTED ACCOMPANIMENTS: *poppy-seed rolls; sliced tomatoes; lettuce leaves.*

Sirloin Grilled in Garlic Smoke

Serves 6
Working time: about 30 minutes
Total time: about 45 minutes

Calories **220**
Protein **26g.**
Cholesterol **76mg.**
Total fat **11g.**
Saturated fat **3g.**
Sodium **105mg.**

one 2-lb. boneless sirloin steak, about 1½ inches thick, trimmed of fat
10 unpeeled garlic cloves, crushed
Onion-pepper relish
2 tbsp. safflower oil
1 small red onion, thinly sliced
1 garlic clove, finely chopped
1 tsp. finely chopped fresh ginger
1 green pepper, seeded, deribbed and julienned
2 scallions, trimmed and thinly sliced
2 tbsp. rice vinegar or distilled white vinegar
¼ tsp. sugar
⅛ tsp. salt

About 30 minutes before cooking time, prepare the coals in an outdoor grill. Put the crushed garlic cloves in 1 cup of cold water and let them soak while you make the relish.

Heat the oil in a heavy-bottomed or nonstick skillet over medium heat. Add the red-onion slices and cook them, stirring frequently, until they have softened without losing their color — three to four minutes. Add the chopped garlic and ginger, and cook the mixture for 30 seconds longer; transfer it to a bowl. Add the green pepper, scallions, vinegar, sugar and salt; stir the relish and set it aside.

When the coals are hot, grill the steak for seven minutes on the first side. Drain the water from the garlic cloves. Remove the steak from the grill and toss the soaked garlic cloves directly onto the coals; a garlicky smoke will curl up. Return the steak to the grill and cook it on the second side for five to seven minutes longer for medium-rare meat.

Transfer the steak to a platter and let it rest for five minutes. Carve the steak into thin slices; spread the onion-pepper relish over each portion just before serving, or present the relish on the side.

SUGGESTED ACCOMPANIMENT: *baked potatoes.*

Steaks Creole

Serves 4
Working time: about 45 minutes
Total time: about 5 hours (includes marinating)

Calories **320**
Protein **29g.**
Cholesterol **60mg.**
Total fat **11g.**
Saturated fat **3g.**
Sodium **120mg.**

1 lb. sirloin or top loin steaks, trimmed of fat, cut into four ¾-inch-thick pieces
¾ lb. fresh pineapple, peeled and sliced crosswise
¾ lb. watermelon, peeled and sliced
1 papaya, peeled, halved, seeded, and sliced
1 mango, peeled, pitted, and sliced
1 tbsp. virgin olive oil
2 tbsp. lime juice
2 tsp. chopped fresh mint
⅛ tsp. salt
Rum marinade
2 tbsp. dark rum
½ tbsp. virgin olive oil
2 garlic cloves, crushed
12 whole allspice, crushed
1 tsp. cayenne pepper

freshly ground black pepper

To make the marinade, mix together the rum, oil, garlic, whole allspice, cayenne pepper, and some black pepper. Put the beef into a shallow, nonreactive dish and brush the marinade over both sides of each steak. Cover the steaks loosely and let them marinate in a cold place or the refrigerator for at least four hours, preferably overnight.

Before cooking, let the steaks stand at room temperature for 30 minutes. Meanwhile, arrange the sliced fruit on individual plates. Whisk together the oil, lime juice, mint, and salt, and set aside.

Place the steaks in a heavy, nonstick skillet over high heat. Cook them for four minutes on each side for rare steaks, or longer if you prefer them well done. Arrange the steaks on the plates with the sliced fruit. Drizzle the dressing over the fruit or serve it separately. Serve the steaks at once.

EDITOR'S NOTE: *This dish is best served without additional accompaniments, which would mar the complementary flavors of meat and fruit.*

Veal Chops Dijonnaise

Serves 4
Working time: about 15 minutes
Total time: about 2 hours and 15 minutes
(includes marinating)

Calories **255**
Protein **23g.**
Cholesterol **120mg.**
Total fat **16g.**
Saturated fat **5g.**
Sodium **120mg.**

4 veal chops (6 to 7 oz. each), trimmed of fat
3 tbsp. capers, drained and crushed
2 tbsp. virgin olive oil
2 tbsp. fresh lemon juice
2 tsp. Dijon mustard
2 tsp. chopped fresh tarragon, or 1 tsp. dried tarragon
freshly ground black pepper
tarragon sprigs for garnish (optional)

Place the chops side by side in a shallow, nonreactive dish. In a mixing bowl, whisk together the capers, oil, lemon juice, mustard, tarragon, and some black pepper. Brush the mixture over both sides of the chops. Cover the chops and let them marinate in the refrigerator for two hours.

Preheat the broiler. Place the chops on the broiler rack and broil for four minutes, basting frequently with the marinade. Turn the chops over and broil for another four minutes, again basting them with the marinade. Pour the cooking juices from the broiler pan over the chops and garnish them with the tarragon sprigs, if desired. Serve hot.

SUGGESTED ACCOMPANIMENTS: *green salad; mushrooms cooked in lemon juice.*

Grilled Veal Cutlets

Serves 4
Working time: about 25 minutes
Total time: about 4 hours and 25 minutes
(includes marinating)

Calories **150**
Protein **53g.**
Cholesterol **30mg.**
Total fat **7g.**
Saturated fat **5g.**
Sodium **220mg.**

8 small thick-cut veal cutlets (about 1½ oz. each), trimmed of fat
¼ cup plain low-fat yogurt
1 tbsp. virgin olive oil
1 tbsp. balsamic vinegar
1 tbsp. grainy mustard
ground white pepper
8 fresh sage leaves, finely chopped
¼ tsp. salt
coarsely crushed white peppercorns (optional)

Lay a cutlet on the work surface between two sheets of plastic wrap. Using the smooth side of a meat mallet or a rolling pin, pound it until it is about ¹⁄₁₆ inch thick. Repeat this process with the other cutlets. In a small bowl, whisk together the yogurt, oil, vinegar, mustard, pepper, and chopped sage leaves. Brush the cutlets with the marinade and place them in a shallow, non-reactive dish; reserve any remaining marinade. Cover the dish, and let the cutlets marinate for four to six hours at room temperature, or for 12 to 24 hours in the refrigerator. (Remove the chilled cutlets from the refrigerator about one hour before cooking to allow them to reach room temperature.)

Cook the veal cutlets over hot coals for 45 seconds on each side, basting them with any remaining marinade. Sprinkle the cooked cutlets with the salt and, if you like, with crushed white peppercorns. Serve the cutlets immediately.

SUGGESTED ACCOMPANIMENTS: *a salad of pink grapefruit and young spinach leaves; radicchio hearts dressed with a balsamic vinaigrette; crusty rolls.*

Veal Cutlets in Tarragon and Mushroom Sauce

Serves 4
Working time: about 15 minutes
Total time: about 1 hour and 15 minutes
(includes marinating)

Calories **240**
Protein **22g.**
Cholesterol **100mg.**
Total fat **11g.**
Saturated fat **3g.**
Sodium **215mg.**

4 thin veal cutlets (about 4 oz. each)
2 tbsp. virgin olive oil
2 tbsp. finely shredded fresh tarragon leaves
freshly ground black pepper
Mushroom sauce
¼ cup Marsala
6 oz. mushrooms, trimmed and very thinly sliced
2 tbsp. unbleached all-purpose flour
2 tbsp. sour cream mixed with enough skim milk to make ⅔ cup
¼ tsp. salt

Blend the oil with 1 tablespoon of the tarragon and some pepper in a shallow dish. Add the cutlets and turn them in the oil until they are evenly coated. Cover the dish and let the veal marinate at room temperature for at least one hour.

Heat a browning dish on high for the maximum time allowed in the instruction manual. Brown the cutlets on each side in the hot dish, then cover the dish with plastic wrap pulled back at one edge and microwave on high for one and a half minutes. Transfer the cutlets to a plate, cover them, and set them aside.

To make the sauce, stir the Marsala into the browning dish, add the mushrooms, and microwave on high for two minutes. Blend the flour with the sour-cream mixture, the remaining tarragon, the salt, and a little black pepper until smooth. Stir into the mushrooms and microwave on high for one minute. Return the veal to the dish, coat well with the sauce, and microwave for two and a half to three minutes, repositioning the cutlets halfway through cooking. Serve at once.

SUGGESTED ACCOMPANIMENTS: *rice with peas, scallions, and sweet peppers; French bread.*

Veal Chops with Spinach and Ricotta

Serves 4
Working time: about 45 minutes
Total time: about 1 hour and 15 minutes

Calories **310**
Protein **33g.**
Cholesterol **120mg.**
Total fat **17g.**
Saturated fat **5g.**
Sodium **290mg.**

4 veal loin chops (about ½ lb. each), trimmed of fat
1½ lb. ripe tomatoes (about 4), peeled, seeded, and chopped, or 14 oz. canned tomatoes, chopped
2 large sprigs fresh rosemary, or 1 tsp. dried rosemary, crumbled
2 tbsp. virgin olive oil
1 onion, finely chopped
3 cups spinach leaves, washed, drained, and chopped
⅓ cup low-fat ricotta cheese
⅛ tsp. freshly grated or ground nutmeg
¼ tsp. salt
freshly ground black pepper
1 garlic clove, crushed
small rosemary sprigs for garnish (optional)

Cut a pocket in the meaty part of each chop, through to the bone (or ask the butcher to do this for you). Set the chops aside. Put the tomatoes into a heavy-bottomed, nonreactive saucepan with the rosemary, adding a little water if you are using fresh tomatoes. Simmer for 10 minutes, stirring occasionally.

Meanwhile, heat 1 tablespoon of the oil in a large, nonstick skillet over low heat. Add the onion and cook gently, stirring occasionally, until it is softened—about five minutes. Add the chopped spinach and cook, stirring, until it has wilted and the excess moisture has evaporated—three to four minutes.

Transfer the spinach mixture to a bowl. Add half of the ricotta, all of the nutmeg, the salt, and some pepper to the spinach, mix well, and set aside.

Preheat the oven to 350° F. Combine the garlic with the remaining ricotta; divide the mixture into four portions and use it to stuff the pockets in the chops. Close the openings with wooden toothpicks.

Heat the remaining oil in a large, nonstick skillet over medium-high heat and brown the chops on both sides—about five minutes in all. Transfer the chops to a baking dish in which they fit comfortably side by side (above). Spread the spinach and ricotta mixture over them. Discard the rosemary sprigs, if you are using them, from the tomatoes, and spoon the tomatoes over the chops to cover the cheese mixture. Bake for 30 minutes. Remove the toothpicks and serve the chops hot, garnished, if you like, with rosemary sprigs.

SUGGESTED ACCOMPANIMENT: *risotto with eggplant and sweet red pepper.*

Aromatic Leg of Lamb

TURNING THE LAMB AND BASTING IT AT REGULAR INTERVALS
DURING COOKING KEEPS THE JUICES WITHIN THE MEAT
AND ENSURES SUCCULENCE.

Serves 12
Working time: about 1 hour
Total time: about 27 hours (includes marinating)

Calories **250**
Protein **31g.**
Cholesterol **80mg.**
Total fat **12g.**
Saturated fat **5g.**
Sodium **170mg.**

⅔ cup plain low-fat yogurt
1 tbsp. fresh lemon juice
1 tbsp. ground coriander
2 tsp. ground cinnamon
1 tsp. ground cardamom
1 tsp. ground ginger
½ tsp. ground cloves
freshly ground black pepper
1 tbsp. virgin olive oil
5 lb. leg of lamb, boned, trimmed of fat, and opened out flat
½ tsp. salt
1 tbsp. poppy seeds
1 tbsp. sesame seeds
1 large pita bread (optional)
Citrus-yogurt sauce
1 lemon, finely grated zest only
1 cup sour cream
½ cup plain low-fat yogurt
2 tbsp. fresh lemon balm finely chopped

In a small bowl, stir together ⅔ cup yogurt, lemon juice, coriander, cinnamon, cardamom, ginger, cloves, and some black pepper to form a light paste. Spread the paste all over the lamb. Place the lamb in a large, flat dish, cover it, and let the meat marinate in the refrigerator for at least 24 hours, or up to three days. Remove the meat from the refrigerator at least two hours before you plan to cook it.

Open up the meat to form a rough rectangle. Thread two metal skewers through the meat, each about 3 inches from the edge of a long side; this will keep the meat flat while it is cooking. Set the rack at its lowest position and brush it lightly with oil. Sear each side of the lamb over hot coals for five to eight minutes, or until the surface is caramelized and lightly charred. Remove the meat from the rack and adjust the rack to its highest position. Return the meat to the rack. Brush one side with a little oil, sprinkle on ¼ teaspoon of the salt and 1½ teaspoons each of the poppy and sesame seeds, and cook the lamb for three minutes more. Turn the meat over, brush it with oil, sprinkle on the remaining salt and poppy and sesame seeds, and grill it for three minutes. Turn the lamb four more times, brushing it each time with any remaining marinade or with a little oil and grilling it for three minutes after each turn. The meat should be crisp and dark on the outside but still tender and pink inside. For meat that is more well done, cook it for four to six minutes more, turning it once and brushing on more oil as necessary

to prevent it from drying out. If you like, place the cooked leg on a round of pita bread set on a carving surface: The bread will catch the meat juices and may be served in chunks with the meat. Remove the skewers, cover the meat lightly with foil, and allow it to rest for 5 to 10 minutes before carving.

Meanwhile, prepare the sauce. Set 1 teaspoon of the lemon zest aside. Mix together the remaining lemon zest, the sour cream, the yogurt, and, the lemon balm. Sprinkle the reserved lemon zest over the sauce. Serve the meat accompanied by the sauce.

SUGGESTED ACCOMPANIMENT: *a salad of crisp mixed lettuce leaves with blanched sliced zucchini and snow peas.*

EDITOR'S NOTE: *Throwing cinnamon sticks and bay leaves onto the coals for the last 5 to 10 minutes of grilling will enhance the flavor of the meat.*

Loin on a Bed of Spring Greens

ASK YOUR BUTCHER TO SAW THROUGH THE CHINE BONE OF THE ROASTS SO YOU CAN CARVE THE MEAT.

Serves 8
Working time: about 40 minutes
Total time: about 1 hour and 30 minutes

Calories **225**
Protein **24g.**
Cholesterol **68mg.**
Total fat **11g.**
Saturated fat **3g.**
Sodium **195mg.**

two 2½-lb. lamb loin roasts, trimmed of fat
1 tbsp. olive oil
1 tbsp. grainy mustard
⅛ tsp. salt
freshly ground black pepper
2 garlic cloves, finely chopped
½ cup fresh whole-wheat breadcrumbs
1 tbsp. chopped fresh parsley
1 tsp. chopped fresh thyme, or ¼ tsp. dried thyme leaves
1 tsp. chopped fresh rosemary, or ¼ tsp. dried rosemary, crumbled
Wilted spring-greens salad
1 tbsp. olive oil
2 scallions, trimmed and chopped
1 lb. dandelion greens, mustard greens, or spinach, stemmed, washed, and dried
1 bunch watercress, trimmed, washed, and dried
16 cherry tomatoes, cut in half
1 tbsp. red wine vinegar
⅛ tsp. salt
freshly ground black pepper

Set the lamb roasts in a roasting pan with their bone sides down. In a small bowl, combine 1 teaspoon of the oil, the mustard, salt, some pepper, and half of the garlic. Rub this mixture over the lamb and let it stand at room temperature for one hour.

Preheat the oven to 450° F. Roast the lamb until it has browned—about 15 minutes. In the meantime, mix together the breadcrumbs, parsley, thyme, rosemary, the remaining garlic, and some pepper.

Sprinkle the breadcrumb mixture over the top of the lamb roasts; drizzle the remaining 2 teaspoons of oil over the breadcrumbs. Continue roasting the lamb until the breadcrumbs have browned and the meat is medium rare—about 10 minutes more, or until a meat thermometer inserted in the center registers 140° F. Keep the lamb warm while you make the salad.

For the salad, heat the tablespoon of olive oil in a skillet over medium-high heat. Add the scallions and sauté them for 45 seconds. Add the greens or spinach, along with the watercress, tomatoes, and vinegar. Toss the vegetables in the skillet until the greens are slightly wilted—about 30 seconds. Remove the pan from the heat, and season the salad with the salt and some freshly ground black pepper.

Carve the lamb roasts into 16 pieces and serve them atop the salad.

SUGGESTED ACCOMPANIMENTS: *parslied potatoes; rolls.*

Roast Shoulder with Rosemary

Serves 12
Working time: about 40 minutes
Total time: about 3 hours (includes marinating)

Calories **310**
Protein **20g.**
Cholesterol **75mg.**
Total fat **12g.**
Saturated fat **5g.**
Sodium **130mg.**

one 5-lb. shoulder of lamb, trimmed of fat
1 tbsp. virgin olive oil
2 tsp. mixed dried herbs
½ tsp. salt
4 long sprigs rosemary
1½ tsp. all-purpose flour
2½ cups unsalted chicken or brown stock
freshly ground black pepper

Make four diagonal incisions with a sharp knife across the shoulder, almost down to the bone. Rub the virgin olive oil, mixed dried herbs, and salt all over the lamb, then insert the rosemary sprigs in the diagonal cuts. Place the lamb shoulder in a roasting pan and set it aside in a cool place to marinate for one hour. Preheat the oven to 425° F.

Roast the shoulder for 15 minutes, then lower the oven temperature to 375° F. and continue to roast for 45 minutes to one hour for rare to medium meat, basting frequently with the juices in the pan. Transfer the shoulder to a serving dish, cover it loosely with aluminum foil, and set it aside in a warm place while you make the gravy.

To make the gravy, tip the roasting pan slightly so that the juices run to one corner, then skim off any fat. Sprinkle the flour over the juices left in the pan and stir with a wooden spoon until the mixture is well blended. Gradually stir in the stock. Place the pan over medium heat and bring the gravy to a boil, stirring all the time until it thickens; season with some freshly ground black pepper. Reduce the heat to low and simmer for six to eight minutes, stirring occasionally. Strain the gravy through a sieve into a hot gravy boat and serve with the shoulder.

SUGGESTED ACCOMPANIMENTS: *steamed rutabaga and parsnips; green salad.*

Shoulder of Lamb with Anchovy Stuffing

Serves 10
Working time: about 45 minutes
Total time: about 12 hours (includes marinating)

Calories **185**
Protein **24g.**
Cholesterol **65mg.**
Total fat **9g.**
Saturated fat **3g.**
Sodium **290mg.**

½ oz. rosemary sprigs, woody stems trimmed
½ cup loosely packed fresh parsley
3 garlic cloves
½ lemon, grated zest and juice
2 oz. canned anchovy fillets in oil
freshly ground black pepper
one 2½-lb. shoulder of lamb, skinned and boned, trimmed of all fat

Lemon sauce

1 tbsp. virgin olive oil
1 small onion, finely chopped
1 tbsp. unbleached all-purpose flour
2 cups unsalted chicken or vegetable stock
1 lemon, finely grated zest and juice
2 tbsp. chopped fresh parsley

Place the rosemary sprigs in a food processor with the parsley, garlic, lemon zest and juice, anchovies with their oil, and some freshly ground black pepper. Process the ingredients until they form a smooth paste.

Wipe the lamb with paper towels to remove any watery juices. Lay the meat out flat on the work surface, boned side up, and spread the herb and anchovy paste over the meat as evenly as possible. Fold the two opposite sides of the meat over the filling so that they meet in the center; secure them in place with long metal skewers to prevent the paste from running out of the cavity. Cover the lamb and let it marinate in the refrigerator for at least eight hours, or up to 24 hours. Remove the meat from the refrigerator about two hours before you plan to cook it, to allow it to reach room temperature.

Lightly oil the rack, and cook the stuffed lamb over medium-hot coals for about two hours, turning it frequently. Test the meat by inserting a skewer in the center—the juices will run clear when the lamb is well cooked. (For meat that is slightly pink in the middle, reduce the cooking time to one and a quarter to one and a half hours.)

About 20 minutes before the lamb is ready, prepare the sauce. Heat the oil in a small, heavy-bottomed, nonreactive saucepan. Add the onion and cook it over medium heat until it is transparent—about five minutes. Stir in the flour and cook for one minute, stirring constantly. Gradually pour in the stock, stirring continuously, and bring the sauce to a boil. Lower the heat and simmer the sauce for 10 minutes, then stir in the lemon zest and juice, and simmer the sauce for five minutes more. Remove the pan from the heat. Stir the parsley into the sauce just before serving.

Carve the lamb into thick slices, and pour a little of the sauce over each serving.

SUGGESTED ACCOMPANIMENTS: *small new potatoes, parboiled for 10 to 15 minutes until they are just tender, then skewered, brushed with honey, and heated on the grill for three to four minutes; oakleaf lettuce.*

Lamb Noisettes with Tomato and Olive Relish

Serves 4
Working time: about 30 minutes
Total time: about 5 hours and 30 minutes
(includes marinating)

Calories **225**
Protein **28g.**
Cholesterol **70mg.**
Total fat **10g.**
Saturated fat **4g.**
Sodium **180mg.**

4 long, thick rosemary sprigs, plus rosemary sprigs for garnish (optional)
4 lean noisettes of lamb, trimmed of fat (about 3½ oz. each)
1 onion, thinly sliced
2 garlic cloves, chopped
1 tsp. chopped fresh oregano, or ¼ tsp. dried oregano
¼ tsp. salt
freshly ground black pepper
⅔ cup dry white wine
Tomato and olive relish
1 tsp. virgin olive oil
1 small onion, finely chopped
8 black olives, pitted and finely chopped
2 tsp. white wine vinegar
½ tsp. sugar
2 tsp. chopped fresh thyme, or ½ tsp. dried thyme leaves
2 tbsp. dry white wine or water
5 tomatoes, peeled, seeded coarsely chopped, and strained

Push a rosemary sprig through each noisette, then place the noisettes in a shallow, nonreactive dish large enough to hold them in a single layer. Sprinkle the onion, garlic, oregano, salt, and some pepper evenly over the lamb, then pour on the wine. Cover the dish and put the lamb in the refrigerator to marinate for about four hours; turn the noisettes several times during this period. Remove the lamb from the refrigerator about one hour before cooking, to allow it to reach room temperature.

To make the tomato and olive relish, heat the oil in a small, nonreactive saucepan. Add the onion and cook it over very low heat for about eight minutes, stirring occasionally, until it is softened but not browned. Stir in the olives, vinegar, sugar, thyme, wine or water, and tomatoes. Remove the pan from the heat and set it aside.

Lightly oil the rack, and cook the noisettes over hot coals for six to eight minutes on each side, until they are firm to the touch and browned. Meanwhile, reheat the relish for about two minutes, and transfer it to a serving bowl. Remove the strings from the noisettes, and serve them accompanied by the relish and, if you wish, garnished with rosemary.

EDITOR'S NOTE: *If the rosemary sprigs are too soft to push through the noisettes, make a hole in the noisettes first with a metal skewer.*

Mexican Pork

Serves 4
Working time: about 20 minutes
Total time: about 8 hours (includes soaking)

Calories **250**
Protein **25g.**
Cholesterol **80mg.**
Total fat **11g.**
Saturated fat **4g.**
Sodium **290mg.**

1 lb. pork tenderloin, trimmed of fat and cut into 1-inch cubes
⅓ cup dried kidney beans, soaked in cold water for 7 to 8 hours, or overnight
1 tbsp. virgin olive oil
1 onion, finely chopped
1 garlic clove, crushed
1 tsp. chili powder
¼ tsp. ground allspice
1½ tbsp. tomato paste
1¼ cups unsalted chicken stock
2 tsp. arrowroot
½ tsp. salt
2 tbsp. sour cream
2 tbsp. plain low-fat yogurt

Drain the beans, place them in a pan, cover with water, and bring to a boil. Boil rapidly for at least 10 minutes, then lower the heat, cover, and simmer until the beans are tender—25 to 30 minutes. Drain well.

Heat the oil in a large, heavy-bottomed pan on medium high; add the pork, onion, and garlic; cook for about five minutes, stirring frequently to brown the meat all over. Stir in the chili powder, allspice, and tomato paste; add the stock. Bring to a boil, then lower the heat, cover, and simmer for 20 minutes.

Add the cooked kidney beans to the pan. In a small bowl, mix the arrowroot with 2 tablespoons of cold water. Add the arrowroot mixture to the pan and stir well, until the juices thicken. Season with the salt.

Mix together the sour cream and yogurt. Spoon one-quarter of the mixture onto each serving.

Skewers of Spiced Pork, Eggplant, and Pepper

Serves 12
Working time: about 30 minutes
Total time: about 2 hours and 30 minutes
(includes marinating)

Calories **155**
Protein **22g.**
Cholesterol **50mg.**
Total fat **6g.**
Saturated fat **2g.**
Sodium **100mg.**

2 lb. lean pork loin, trimmed of all fat, cut into ½-inch slices
3 medium eggplants, quartered and cut into 1-inch slices
3 sweet green peppers, seeded, deribbed, and cut into 1-inch squares
1 tbsp. safflower oil
Garlic and cumin marinade
2 green chili peppers, seeded and finely chopped
1 small onion, thinly sliced
1-inch piece fresh ginger, finely chopped
4 garlic cloves, crushed
3 bay leaves
1 lime, grated zest and juice
2 cinnamon sticks, halved
1 tbsp. whole cloves
2 tsp. ground cumin
¼ tsp. ground turmeric

1 tbsp. garam masala
½ tsp. salt
freshly ground black pepper
⅔ cup plain low-fat yogurt

In a bowl, mix together the marinade ingredients. Add the pork slices, tossing them in the marinade to coat them well. Cover the bowl and let the meat chill in the refrigerator for two to four hours.

Remove the pork from the marinade and discard the bay leaves, cloves, and pieces of cinnamon stick. Thread the pork onto 12 metal skewers, pushing the skewers through the circumference of each slice. Thread the pieces of eggplant and sweet green pepper alternately onto 12 more skewers. Brush the vegetable kabobs with the safflower oil.

Oil the rack lightly and cook the pork and vegetable kabobs over hot coals for three to four minutes on each side, until the meat is lightly browned and cooked through and the peppers and eggplant are tender. Serve the kabobs immediately.

Lemon Pork

Serves 4
Working time: about 30 minutes
Total time: about 5 hours and 30 minutes
(includes marinating)

Calories **250**
Protein **33g.**
Cholesterol **70mg.**
Total fat **11g.**
Saturated fat **4g.**
Sodium **85mg.**

1 lb. boned pork loin, trimmed of fat
1 lemon
ground white pepper
½ cup basil leaves
1 garlic clove, crushed
3 tbsp. dry white wine

Using a vegetable peeler, remove the zest from the lemon in long strips, working from top to bottom. Put the strips into a pan of cold water, bring to a boil, drain, and refresh the zest under cold running water. Drain well. Cut the strips into threads that can be inserted into a larding needle. Weave some of the threads into the outer surface of the pork, then press the remainder of the threads onto the inner surface. Season the pork inside and out with some white pepper. Roll up the pork and secure with string.

Squeeze the juice from the lemon. Tear the basil leaves into small pieces and place them in a nonreactive dish with the garlic. Place the pork on top, pour the lemon juice over it, cover, and set it aside to marinate in a cool place for four hours, turning the pork occasionally.

Heat the oven to 350° F. Lift the pork from the marinade and place it on a piece of foil. Fold the sides of the foil up, then pour in the marinade and the wine. Fold the foil loosely over the pork and seal the edges together firmly. Place the parcel on a baking sheet and cook it in the oven until the pork is tender—approximately 40 minutes.

Transfer the pork to a warmed plate, cover, and let it rest. In a saucepan, boil the cooking juices until they are slightly thickened.

Slice the pork, divide the slices among four warmed plates, and spoon the juices around the meat.

SUGGESTED ACCOMPANIMENT: *steamed sliced zucchini.*

5 *One of the earliest (and best) of convenience foods, dried pasta fills glass storage jars in a kitchen reminiscent of pasta's Mediterranean homeland.*

Pasta

Chilled Rotini with Arugula Pesto

Serves 4
Working time: about 25 minutes
Total time: about 2 hours

Calories **536**
Protein **17g.**
Cholesterol **8mg.**
Total fat **22g.**
Saturated fat **4g.**
Sodium **397mg.**

12 oz. rotini
2 cups arugula, washed, cleaned and stemmed
1 small garlic clove, coarsely chopped
¼ cup pine nuts
3 tbsp. virgin olive oil
1 tbsp. safflower oil
½ cup freshly grated Parmesan cheese
¼ tsp. salt
freshly ground black pepper
1 red pepper, seeded, deribbed and finely diced
2 tbsp. balsamic vinegar, or 1 tbsp. red wine vinegar

Add the rotini to 4 quarts of boiling water with 2 teaspoons of salt. Start testing the pasta after eight minutes and cook it until it is *al dente*.

Meanwhile, prepare the pesto: Put the arugula, garlic, pine nuts, olive oil and safflower oil in a blender or food processor. Blend for two minutes, stopping two or three times to scrape down the sides. Add the cheese and the ¼ teaspoon of salt; blend the mixture briefly to form a purée.

Drain the pasta, transfer it to a large bowl, and season it with some black pepper. Add the diced red pepper, the vinegar and pesto, and toss well. Chill the pasta salad in the refrigerator for an hour or two before serving it.

Ziti with Italian Sausage and Red Peppers

Serves 4
Working time: about 30 minutes
Total time: about 40 minutes

Calories **298**
Protein **11g.**
Cholesterol **12mg.**
Total fat **7g.**
Saturated fat **2g.**
Sodium **332mg.**

8 oz. ziti (or other fancy tubular pasta)
3 red peppers
2 spicy Italian sausage links (about 4 oz.)
2 garlic cloves, finely chopped
2 tsp. fresh thyme, or ½ tsp. dried thyme leaves
1 large tomato, peeled, seeded and puréed
1 tbsp. red wine vinegar
⅛ tsp. salt

Preheat the broiler. Broil the peppers about two inches below the heat source, turning them from time to time, until they are blackened all over — 15 to 18 minutes. Put the peppers in a bowl and cover it with plastic wrap. The trapped steam will loosen their skins.

Squeeze the sausages out of their casings and break the meat into small pieces; sauté the pieces over medium-high heat until they are browned — about three minutes. Remove the pan from the heat and stir in the garlic and the thyme.

Add the pasta to 3 quarts of boiling water with 1½ teaspoons of salt; start testing it after 10 minutes and cook it until it is *al dente*.

While the pasta is cooking, peel the peppers, working over a bowl to catch the juices. Remove and discard the stems, seeds and ribs from the peppers; strain the juices and reserve them. Slice the peppers lengthwise into thin strips.

Set the skillet containing the sausage mixture over medium heat. Add the pepper strips and their reserved juices, the puréed tomato, the vinegar and the ⅛ teaspoon of salt. Simmer the sauce until it thickens and is reduced by about one third — five to seven minutes.

Drain the pasta, return it to the pot, and combine it with the sauce. Cover the pot and let the pasta stand for five minutes to allow the flavors to blend.

Rigatoni with Red Potatoes and Radicchio

Serves 6 as an appetizer
Working (and total) time: about 45 minutes

Calories **273**
Protein **7g.**
Cholesterol **0mg.**
Total fat **10g.**
Saturated fat **1g.**
Sodium **98mg.**

8 oz. rigatoni (or medium shells)
3 large unpeeled red potatoes (about ½ lb.), each cut into 8 pieces
4 tbsp. virgin olive oil
½ lb. spinach, washed, stemmed, and squeezed into a ball to remove excess water
2 garlic cloves, finely chopped
1 small head radicchio (about 4 oz.), torn into 1½-inch pieces
2 tbsp. Dijon mustard
2 tbsp. red wine vinegar
¼ cup chopped fresh basil
2 bunches scallions, trimmed and cut into 1-inch pieces
freshly ground black pepper

In a large, covered pot, bring 3 quarts of water and 1½ teaspoons of salt to a boil; add the rigatoni to the boiling water. Start testing the pasta after 13 minutes and cook it until it is *al dente.*

While the pasta is cooking, pour enough water into a saucepan to fill it about 1 inch deep. Add ½ teaspoon of salt and set a vegetable steamer in the bottom of the pan. Bring the water to a boil. Add the potatoes, cover the pot, and steam the potatoes until they are tender when pierced with the tip of a thin knife — about eight minutes. Transfer the potatoes to a large bowl.

When the pasta is cooked, drain it and transfer it to the bowl with the potatoes. Pour in 1 tablespoon of the oil and toss well to coat the pasta and the potatoes.

Heat another tablespoon of the oil in a large, heavy-bottomed skillet over medium-high heat. When it is hot, add the spinach and garlic, and sauté them for 30 seconds, stirring constantly. Add the radicchio and cook until the spinach has wilted — about 30 seconds more. Scrape the contents of the skillet into the bowl containing the pasta and the potatoes.

In a small bowl, whisk together the mustard and vinegar. Whisk in the remaining 2 tablespoons of oil, then pour this mixture over the pasta. Add the basil, scallions and some pepper to the bowl, toss well to combine, and serve.

EDITOR'S NOTE: *This dish may be served warm, at room temperature, or chilled.*

Capellini with Chilled Tomatoes, Black Olives and Garlic

Serves 6 as an appetizer
Working time: about 20 minutes
Total time: about 1 hour

Calories **190**
Protein **6g.**
Cholesterol **0mg.**
Total fat **4g.**
Saturated fat **0g.**
Sodium **191mg.**

8 oz. capellini (or other thin spaghetti)
3 large, ripe tomatoes, peeled, seeded and chopped (about 2 cups)
4 garlic cloves, finely chopped
5 oil-cured black olives, pitted and finely chopped
1 small hot chili pepper, seeded, deribbed and finely chopped
1 tbsp. virgin olive oil
juice of 1 lime
1 tbsp. chopped cilantro
⅛ tsp. salt
freshly ground black pepper

Put the chopped tomatoes in a strainer set over a large bowl; place the bowl in the refrigerator and let the tomatoes drain for at least 30 minutes.

Put 3 quarts of water on to boil with 1½ teaspoons of salt. In a separate bowl, combine the garlic, olives, chili pepper, oil, lime juice, cilantro, salt and pepper. Refrigerate the mixture.

Drop the capellini into the boiling water. Begin testing the pasta after three minutes and continue to cook it until it is *al dente.*

While the pasta is cooking, combine the garlic mixture with the drained tomatoes; discard the juice. Drain the pasta, put it in a bowl and toss it immediately with the sauce.

Gemelli with Sun-Dried Tomatoes, Rosemary and Thyme

Serves 8 as an appetizer
Working time: about 25 minutes
Total time: about 30 minutes

Calories **176**
Protein **5g.**
Cholesterol **2mg.**
Total fat **6g.**
Saturated fat **1g.**
Sodium **248mg.**

8 oz. gemelli (or other short tubular pasta)
2 oz. sun-dried tomatoes packed in oil, drained and thinly sliced
4 small leeks, trimmed, cleaned and cut into ¾-inch slices
2 shallots, finely chopped
1 tsp. fresh rosemary, or ¼ tsp. dried rosemary
1½ tbsp. fresh lemon juice
2 tbsp. virgin olive oil
½ tsp. salt
freshly ground black pepper
1 tsp. fresh thyme, or ¼ tsp. dried thyme leaves
¼ cup dry white wine
¼ cup freshly grated Parmesan cheese

Precook the gemelli in 3 quarts of unsalted boiling water for two minutes — the pasta will be underdone. Drain it and put it in a large casserole. Stir in the toma-toes, 1 cup of water, ½ cup of the white part of the leeks, the shallots, rosemary, lemon juice, 1 table-spoon of the oil, ¼ teaspoon of the salt and some pepper. Cover the casserole and cook the mixture over low heat, stirring occasionally, until all the liquid has been absorbed — about eight minutes.

Meanwhile, in a large, heavy-bottomed skillet, heat the remaining tablespoon of oil over medium heat. Add the remaining leek slices, the remaining ¼ tea-spoon of salt, some pepper and the thyme. Cook the mixture for three minutes, stirring from time to time. Raise the heat to high and cook the mixture for one minute more, then pour in the wine. Cook until the liquid has evaporated — about four minutes.

Add the leek mixture to the casserole, then stir in the cheese. To infuse the pasta with the flavors of the herbs and sun-dried tomatoes, cover the casserole and let it stand for five minutes before serving it.

EDITOR'S NOTE: *Two tablespoons of the oil in which the sun-dried tomatoes are packed may be substituted for the virgin olive oil called for here.*

Penne with Provençal Vegetables

Serves 4
Working (and total) time: about 40 minutes

Calories **336**
Protein **11g.**
Cholesterol **1mg.**
Total fat **7g.**
Saturated fat **1g.**
Sodium **185mg.**

8 oz. penne (or other short, tubular pasta)
1 small eggplant (about ½ lb.)
2 zucchini
2 red peppers, seeded, deribbed and cut into ½-inch squares
3 garlic cloves, peeled and thinly sliced
2 tbsp. chopped fresh parsley
¼ tsp. fresh oregano, or ⅛ tsp. dried oregano
¼ tsp. finely chopped fresh rosemary, or ⅛ tsp. dried rosemary, crushed
¼ tsp. fresh thyme, or ⅛ tsp. dried thyme leaves
⅛ tsp. fennel seeds
¼ tsp. salt
freshly ground black pepper
2 tbsp. virgin olive oil
2 cups unsalted chicken stock
1 cup unsalted tomato juice

Halve the eggplant and the zucchini lengthwise, then cut them lengthwise again into wedges about ½ inch wide. Slice the wedges into 1-inch-long pieces. Put the pieces in a baking dish along with the red pepper, garlic, parsley, oregano, rosemary, thyme, fennel seeds, salt and some pepper. Cover the dish and microwave it on high for two minutes. Rotate the dish half a turn and microwave it on high until the vegetables are barely tender — about two minutes more. Stir in the oil and set the mixture aside while you cook the pasta.

In a deep bowl, combine the penne, stock and tomato juice. If necessary, add just enough water to immerse the pasta in liquid. Cover the bowl and microwave it on high, rotating the bowl a quarter turn and stirring the pasta every two minutes, until it is *al dente* — about 15 minutes in all. With a slotted spoon, transfer the pasta to the baking dish with the vegetable mixture and stir to combine. Pour about half of the pasta-cooking liquid into the dish, then cover the dish and microwave it on high for two minutes more to heat it through. Serve at once.

Rotini with Lemon Sauce and Dill

Serves 4
Working (and total) time: about 20 minutes

Calories **288**
Protein **9g.**
Cholesterol **8mg.**
Total fat **3g.**
Saturated fat **1g.**
Sodium **99mg.**

8 oz. rotini
1 cup milk
⅛ tsp. salt
¼ cup aquavit, or ¼ cup vodka and 1 tsp. caraway seeds
3 tbsp. fresh lemon juice
2-inch strip of lemon zest
2 tbsp. finely cut fresh dill, or 2 tsp. dried dill

Put the milk, salt, aquavit or vodka and caraway seeds, lemon juice and lemon zest in a large nonstick or heavy-bottomed skillet. Bring the liquid to a boil, reduce the heat and simmer gently for three minutes. Add the rotini and enough water to almost cover them. Cover the skillet and cook over low heat, removing the lid and stirring occasionally, until the rotini are *al dente* and about ¼ cup of sauce remains — approximately 15 minutes. (If necessary, add more water to keep the rotini from sticking.) Remove the lemon zest and discard it. Stir in the chopped dill and serve the dish immediately.

Spaghetti with Smoked Salmon and Watercress

Serves 4
Working (and total) time: about 15 minutes

Calories **243**
Protein **10g.**
Cholesterol **3mg.**
Total fat **3g.**
Saturated fat **0g.**
Sodium **216mg.**

8 oz. spaghetti
1½ tsp. virgin olive oil
1 garlic clove, finely chopped
2 oz. smoked salmon, julienned
1 bunch watercress, washed and stemmed
freshly ground black pepper

Cook the spaghetti in 3 quarts of boiling water with 1½ teaspoons of salt. Start testing the pasta after eight minutes and cook it until it is *al dente*.

Just before the spaghetti finishes cooking, heat the oil in a large skillet over medium heat. Cook the garlic in the oil for 30 seconds, stirring constantly. Add the salmon, watercress and pepper, and cook for 30 seconds more before removing the skillet from the heat.

Drain the spaghetti and add it to the skillet. Toss the spaghetti to distribute the sauce and serve at once.

Rotini with Spring Vegetables

Serves 8 as a first course
Working time: about 40 minutes
Total time: about 1 hour

Calories **170**
Protein **5g.**
Cholesterol **0mg.**
Total fat **4g.**
Saturated fat **1g.**
Sodium **175mg.**

1 cup unsalted veal, chicken or vegetable stock
½ lb. fresh shiitake mushrooms, wiped clean and cut into ½-inch pieces
1 large onion (about ½ lb.), halved, each half quartered
½ tsp. salt
2 tbsp. virgin olive oil
¼ cup red wine vinegar
3 carrots
2 tbsp. fresh lemon juice
½ lb. asparagus, trimmed and sliced diagonally into 1-inch lengths
½ lb. rotini or other fancy pasta
¼ cup thinly sliced fresh basil leaves
freshly ground black pepper

Heat ¾ cup of the stock in a large, nonreactive skillet over medium heat. Add the mushrooms, onion chunks and ¼ teaspoon of the salt. Bring the mixture to a simmer, reduce the heat to low, and cover the pan. Cook the vegetables for five minutes. Remove the lid and continue cooking the vegetables, stirring frequently, until all the stock has evaporated. Stir in 1 tablespoon of the olive oil and cook the mixture for three minutes more.

Transfer the contents of the skillet to a large bowl and return the skillet to the stove over low heat. Pour the vinegar and the remaining ¼ cup of stock into the skillet. Simmer the liquid, scraping the bottom of the pan with a wooden spoon to dislodge any pan deposits, until only 2 tablespoons of liquid remain. Stir the reduced liquid into the mushrooms and onions in the bowl; set the bowl aside.

Bring 2 quarts of water to a boil in a saucepan. While the water heats, prepare the carrots: Cut off the tip of each one at an oblique angle. Roll the carrot a quarter or third turn, and with the knife still at the same angle, cut again. Continue rolling and cutting until you near the end of the carrot.

Add to the boiling water 1 tablespoon of the lemon juice, ¼ teaspoon of salt and the roll-cut carrots. Boil the carrots until they are barely tender — about six minutes. Add the asparagus pieces and boil them for 30 seconds. With a slotted spoon, transfer the vegetables to a colander; do not discard the cooking liquid. Refresh the carrots and asparagus under cold running water; when they are thoroughly cooled, drain them well and toss them with the mushrooms and onions.

Refrigerate the vegetables while you finish the salad.

Return the water in the saucepan to a full boil; add the pasta and the remaining tablespoon of lemon juice. Start testing the pasta for doneness after 10 minutes and cook it until it is *al dente*. Drain the pasta and rinse it under cold running water. Drain it again.

Add the pasta to the vegetables along with the remaining tablespoon of olive oil, the basil, the remaining ¼ teaspoon of salt and a generous grinding of pepper. Toss the salad well and chill it for 10 minutes before serving.

Chilled Rice Noodle Salad

Serves 4 as a main course at lunch
Working time: about 15 minutes
Total time: about 1 hour (includes chilling)

Calories **375**
Protein **14g.**
Cholesterol **25mg.**
Total fat **10g.**
Saturated fat **3g.**
Sodium **210mg.**

6 oz. boneless pork loin, julienned
¼ cup rice vinegar
1 tbsp. finely chopped garlic
1 tbsp. finely chopped fresh ginger
2 tsp. Chinese five-spice powder
¼ cup cream sherry
½ lb. sugar snap peas or snow peas, stems and strings removed
1 tbsp. safflower oil
½ lb. dried rice noodles
¼ tsp. salt
freshly ground black pepper
½ tsp. dark sesame oil

Put the pork in a small heatproof bowl and set it aside. Combine the vinegar, garlic, ginger, five-spice powder and sherry in a small saucepan, and bring the mixture to a simmer. Pour the marinade over the pork and let it cool to room temperature — about 15 minutes.

Meanwhile, if you are using sugar-snap peas, blanch them in boiling water until they are just tender — about four minutes; if you are using snow peas, blanch them for only 30 seconds. Refresh the peas under cold running water, then drain them well and transfer them to a large bowl.

Drain the pork, reserving the marinade for the dressing. Heat the safflower oil in a heavy-bottomed skillet over medium-high heat. Add the pork and sauté it until it loses its pink hue — three to four minutes. With a slotted spoon, transfer the pork to the bowl containing the peas. Pour the reserved marinade into the skillet and bring it to a boil; cook the marinade for one minute. Remove the skillet from the heat and set it aside. ▶

Add the noodles to 3 quarts of boiling water with 1 teaspoon of salt. Start testing the noodles for doneness after four minutes and cook them until they are *al dente*. Drain the noodles and rinse them under cold running water; drain them again and add them to the pork and peas. Pour the reserved marinade over the noodle mixture, then add the ¼ teaspoon of salt, some pepper and the sesame oil. Toss the salad well and refrigerate it for at least 20 minutes before serving it.

EDITOR'S NOTE: *A variation of Chinese five-spice powder may be made at home by chopping in a blender equal parts of Sichuan peppercorns, fennel seeds, ground cloves and ground cinnamon.*

Wagon-Wheel Pasta Salad

Serves 12 as a first course
Working (and total) time: about 35 minutes

Calories **210**
Protein **7g.**
Cholesterol **0mg.**
Total fat **4g.**
Saturated fat **1g.**
Sodium **170mg.**

8 sun-dried tomatoes
1 lb. wagon wheels (or other fancy pasta)
2 cups fresh lima beans, or 10 oz. frozen baby lima beans
2 garlic cloves, peeled
¼ cup red wine vinegar
¼ tsp. salt
freshly ground black pepper
2 tbsp. cut chives
4 cherry tomatoes, cut into quarters
1 tbsp. virgin olive oil

Put the sun-dried tomatoes into a small heatproof bowl and pour ½ cup of boiling water over them. Let the tomatoes soak for 20 minutes.

While the tomatoes are soaking, cook the pasta and lima beans: Add the pasta to 4 quarts of boiling water with 1 teaspoon of salt. Begin testing the pasta for doneness after five minutes and cook it until it is *al dente*. Drain the pasta and rinse it under cold running water; drain it once more and transfer the pasta to a large bowl. Add the fresh lima beans to 1 quart of boiling water and cook them until they are barely tender — eight to 10 minutes. Drain the beans and set them aside. (If you are using frozen limas, cook them in ¼ cup of boiling water for five minutes.)

In a blender or food processor, purée the sun-dried tomatoes along with their soaking liquid, the garlic, vinegar, salt and some pepper. Add the lima beans, chives, cherry tomatoes, oil and tomato-garlic purée to the pasta; toss well and serve the salad immediately.

Pasta Salad with Black Bean Sauce

Serves 8 as a main course at lunch
Working time: about 15 minutes
Total time: about 1 hour and 30 minutes
(includes chilling)

Calories **290**
Protein **12g.**
Cholesterol **0mg.**
Total fat **7g.**
Saturated fat **1g.**
Sodium **495mg.**

1 lb. vermicelli (or other thin pasta)
2 tbsp. peanut oil
2 small dried hot red chili peppers, coarsely chopped
3 scallions, trimmed and sliced diagonally
2 garlic cloves, finely chopped
½ cup fermented black beans, rinsed (about 1 oz.)
½ lb. firm tofu, cut into ¾-inch cubes
½ cup unsalted chicken stock
2 celery stalks, sliced diagonally
¼ tsp. salt
4 tsp. rice vinegar

Add the vermicelli with 1 teaspoon of salt to 4 quarts of boiling water. Start testing the pasta after five minutes and cook it until it is *al dente*. Drain the pasta, transfer

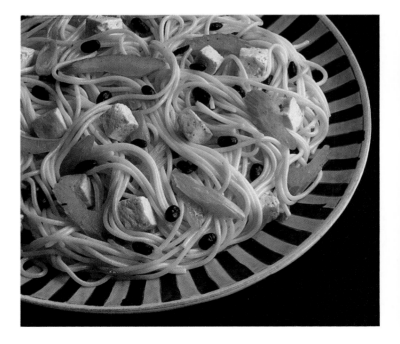

it to a large bowl of cold water, and set it aside while you make the sauce.

To begin the sauce, heat the peanut oil and chili peppers in a small saucepan; when the oil begins to smoke, remove the pan from the heat and set it aside to cool for about five minutes. Strain the oil into a heavy-bottomed skillet. Discard the chili peppers.

Put the scallions and garlic into the skillet containing the peanut oil; cook them over medium heat for two minutes. Add the black beans, tofu and stock, and simmer the mixture for five minutes. Stir in the celery and salt, and continue cooking the mixture until the celery is barely tender — about two minutes more.

While the sauce is simmering, drain the noodles well. Transfer the noodles to a large bowl and toss them with the vinegar. Pour the hot sauce over all and mix thoroughly. Refrigerate the salad for at least one hour before serving.

Buckwheat Noodle Salad

Serves 8 as a first course
Working (and total) time: about 25 minutes

Calories **130**
Protein **3g.**
Cholesterol **0mg.**
Total fat **3g.**
Saturated fat **0g.**
Sodium **135mg.**

½ lb. dried buckwheat noodles (soba)
1 sweet red pepper, seeded, deribbed and julienned
3 Nappa cabbage leaves, torn into small pieces
Ginger-lime dressing
1-inch piece of fresh ginger, peeled and coarsely chopped
1 lime, the zest grated and the juice reserved
¼ tsp. salt
½ tsp. honey
1 small shallot, finely chopped
1 ½ tbsp. safflower oil
½ tsp. dark sesame oil

Add the noodles to 8 cups of boiling water in a large saucepan. Start testing them for doneness after five minutes and cook them until they are *al dente*. Drain the noodles and rinse them well; then cover them with cold water and set them aside.

To make the dressing, place the ginger, lime zest and salt in a mortar; mash them with a pestle until the ginger is reduced to very small pieces. Stir in the lime juice, honey, shallot, safflower oil and sesame oil.

Drain the noodles thoroughly and transfer them to a serving platter. Pour the dressing over the noodles and toss them with the pepper strips. Serve the salad immediately, surrounded by the cabbage.

Ditalini Salad with Smoked Salmon

Serves 8 as a first course or side dish
Working time: about 20 minutes
Total time: about 30 minutes

Calories **130**
Protein **5g.**
Cholesterol **3mg.**
Total fat **1g.**
Saturated fat **0g.**
Sodium **110mg.**

½ lb. ditalini or elbow macaroni
½ cup plain low-fat yogurt
1 tbsp. brown sugar
¾ tsp. dry mustard
2 tbsp. cut fresh dill
2 tbsp. fresh lemon juice
¼ tsp. salt
freshly ground black pepper
1 oz. smoked salmon, cut into ¼-inch cubes

Add the pasta to 4 quarts of boiling water with 1½ teaspoons of salt. Begin testing the pasta after five minutes and cook it until it is *al dente*. Drain the pasta and rinse it under cold running water; drain it once more and transfer it to a large bowl.

To prepare the dressing, whisk together the yogurt, brown sugar, mustard, dill, lemon juice, salt and some pepper in a small bowl.

Add the salmon to the pasta, pour the dressing over all, and toss well; serve the salad immediately.

EDITOR'S NOTE: *Both the dressing and pasta may be prepared an hour before serving time; they should be refrigerated separately and assembled at the last possible moment.*

Pasta Salad with Tomato-Anchovy Sauce

Serves 6 as a side dish
Working time: about 1 hour and 15 minutes
Total time: about 2 hours and 15 minutes

Calories **135**
Protein **4g.**
Cholesterol **0mg.**
Total fat **3g.**
Saturated fat **0g.**
Sodium **45mg.**

1 tbsp. virgin olive oil
¼ cup finely chopped red onion
1 garlic clove, finely chopped
½ tsp. paprika, preferably Hungarian
¼ tsp. cinnamon
¼ tsp. ground cumin
cayenne pepper
freshly ground black pepper
4 ripe tomatoes (about 1½ lb.), peeled, seeded and chopped
2 anchovies, rinsed, patted dry with paper towels and cut into pieces
1 tsp. red wine vinegar
4 small carrots (about ¼ lb.), peeled and cut into bâtonnets
¼ lb. green beans, trimmed and cut into 1½-inch lengths
2 yellow or sweet red peppers
¼ lb. penne or ziti
2 tbsp. chopped fresh basil

To prepare the tomato sauce, heat the oil in a large, heavy-bottomed skillet over medium heat. Add the onion and garlic and sauté them, stirring frequently, until the onion is translucent — about five minutes. Add the paprika, cinnamon, cumin, a pinch of cayenne pepper and some black pepper; continue sautéing, stirring constantly, for 30 seconds. Stir in the tomatoes and anchovy pieces, and raise the heat to medium high. Bring the sauce to a simmer and cook it, stirring frequently, until it is thickened — about 12 minutes. Remove the skillet from the heat and stir in the vinegar. Set the sauce aside and let it cool thoroughly.

While the sauce is thickening, cook the vegetables: Pour enough water into a saucepan to fill it about 1 inch deep. Set a vegetable steamer in the pan and bring the water to a boil. Put the carrots and green beans into the steamer, cover the pan, and steam the vegetables until they are tender — two to three minutes. Refresh the vegetables under cold running water; drain them and set them aside.

Roast the yellow or red peppers about 2 inches below a preheated broiler, turning them until they are blistered on all sides. Place the peppers in a bowl and cover the bowl with plastic wrap; the trapped steam will loosen their skins. Peel and seed the peppers, then cut them into ½-inch squares.

Add the pasta to 2 quarts of boiling water with ½ teaspoon of salt. Start testing the pasta after eight minutes and cook it until it is *al dente*. Drain the pasta and rinse it under cold running water, then drain it again. Transfer the pasta to a large bowl. Add the tomato sauce along with the carrots, beans, pepper pieces and basil; toss the salad well. Let the salad stand at room temperature for one hour before serving it.

Green Fettuccine with Flounder

Serves 4
Working (and total) time: about 25 minutes

Calories **329**
Protein **19g.**
Cholesterol **30mg.**
Total fat **6g.**
Saturated fat **1g.**
Sodium **327mg.**

8 oz. green fettuccine
4 tsp. virgin olive oil
2 garlic cloves, peeled and finely chopped
1 tbsp. chopped fresh oregano
14 oz. unsalted canned whole tomatoes, drained and coarsely chopped
½ cup clam juice
½ lb. fillet of flounder, cut into bite-size pieces
¼ tsp. salt
freshly ground black pepper
2 tbsp. freshly grated Parmesan cheese

Pour 5 cups of hot water into a 2-quart glass bowl. Cover the bowl with a lid or plastic wrap and micro-wave it on high until the water comes to a boil — about six minutes. Stir in ½ teaspoon of salt and add the fettuccine; cover the bowl again and microwave it on high, stirring once after three minutes, until the pasta is *al dente* — about six minutes in all. Drain the fettuc-cine, then toss it with 2 teaspoons of the oil and set it aside in a microwave-safe serving dish.

In a shallow 1-quart dish, combine the remaining 2 teaspoons of oil with the garlic, oregano and toma-toes. Cover the bowl with a lid or plastic wrap and microwave the mixture on medium high (70 percent power) until it is heated through — about 90 seconds. Uncover the dish and stir in the clam juice and the flounder; cover the dish again and microwave it on high until the flounder is cooked through and can be easily flaked with a fork — two to three minutes.

Pour the fish mixture over the fettuccine, season with the ¼ teaspoon of salt and some pepper, and toss well. Cover the dish and microwave it on high until it is heated through — about one minute. Sprinkle the cheese over the top and serve immediately.

Spaghetti with Garlic, Oregano and Parsley

Serves 4
Working (and total) time: about 30 minutes

Calories **290**
Protein **8g.**
Cholesterol **0mg.**
Total fat **8g.**
Saturated fat **1g.**
Sodium **240mg.**

8 oz. spaghetti
2 whole garlic bulbs, the cloves separated and peeled
¼ tsp. chopped fresh oregano, or ⅛ tsp. dried oregano
2 tbsp. chopped fresh parsley, preferably Italian
¼ tsp. salt
⅛ tsp. cayenne pepper
2 tbsp. virgin olive oil
1 lemon, cut into 8 wedges

In a baking dish, combine the garlic, oregano, parsley, salt, cayenne pepper and ½ cup of water. Cover with a lid or plastic wrap, and microwave the mixture on high for six minutes, rotating the dish every two minutes. Remove the dish from the oven and let it stand for two minutes. Purée the mixture and set it aside.

Cook the spaghetti in the conventional manner: Add it to 3 quarts of boiling water with 1½ teaspoons of salt. Start testing after 10 minutes and cook the spaghetti until it is *al dente*. Drain the pasta and return it to the pot. Pour in the oil and toss well. Add the garlic sauce and toss again. Garnish with the lemon wedges.

Couscous Salad with Snow Peas and Wild Mushrooms

Serves 6 as a first course or side dish
Working time: about 20 minutes
Total time: about 35 minutes

Calories **135**
Protein **5g.**
Cholesterol **0mg.**
Total fat **4g.**
Saturated fat **1g.**
Sodium **150mg.**

1½ cups unsalted chicken stock
¼ cup chopped shallot
2½ tbsp. fresh lemon juice
freshly ground black pepper
1 cup couscous
⅓ cup coarsely chopped cilantro
1½ tbsp. virgin olive oil
¼ lb. fresh cepes, chanterelles or other wild mushrooms, wiped clean and sliced
1 tsp. fresh thyme, or ¼ tsp. dried thyme leaves
¼ lb. snow peas, stems and strings removed, each cut diagonally into 3 pieces
¼ tsp. salt
1 tsp. red wine vinegar
1 head of oakleaf lettuce or red-leaf lettuce, washed and dried

Pour the stock into a large saucepan; add 2 tablespoons of the shallot, 2 tablespoons of the lemon juice and some pepper. Bring the stock to a boil, then stir in the couscous and half of the cilantro. Cover the pan tightly and remove it from the heat; let it stand while you complete the salad.

Meanwhile, heat 1 tablespoon of the oil in a large, heavy-bottomed skillet over medium-high heat. When the oil is hot, add the mushrooms, thyme and the remaining 2 tablespoons of shallot. Sauté the mushrooms until they begin to brown — about four minutes. Stir in the snow peas, the salt and some pepper. Cook the mixture, stirring frequently, for two minutes more. Remove the skillet from the heat.

Transfer the couscous to a large bowl and fluff it with a fork. In a small bowl, combine the vinegar, the remaining ½ tablespoon of oil, the remaining ½ tablespoon of lemon juice and the remaining cilantro. Drizzle this vinaigrette over the couscous and fluff the couscous once again to distribute the dressing evenly. Add the contents of the skillet to the bowl, using a rubber spatula to scrape out the flavor-rich juices. Toss the salad well and chill it for at least 15 minutes.

To serve, arrange the lettuce on a serving platter and mound the salad atop the leaves.

Chilled Spinach Spirals with Shrimp, Eggplant and Yellow Squash

Serves 6 as a main course
Working time: about 35 minutes
Total time: about 45 minutes

Calories **260**
Protein **16g.**
Cholesterol **79mg.**
Total fat **6g.**
Saturated fat **1g.**
Sodium **250mg.**

2 tbsp. virgin olive oil
2½ tbsp. fresh lime juice
1 medium eggplant (about 6 oz.), halved lengthwise, the halves cut crosswise into ½-inch-thick slices
½ lb. spinach rotini (corkscrew pasta) or other fancy spinach pasta
2 ripe plum tomatoes (about ½ lb.)
1 large yellow squash (about ¼ lb.), halved lengthwise, the halves cut diagonally into ½-inch-thick slices
2 shallots, finely chopped
¾ lb. medium shrimp, peeled, and deveined if necessary
1 tsp. fresh thyme, or ¼ tsp. dried thyme leaves
¼ tsp. salt
freshly ground black pepper
2 oz. goat cheese
¼ cup plain low-fat yogurt
2 tbsp. whole milk

Preheat the broiler. Bring 3 quarts of water to a boil in a large saucepan.

Meanwhile, mix 1 tablespoon of the oil with 1 tablespoon of the lime juice and brush the mixture over both sides of the eggplant slices. Set the slices on a baking sheet and broil them on one side until they are lightly browned — three to four minutes. Turn the slices over and broil them on the second side. Let the slices cool somewhat before transferring them to a large bowl. Put the bowl into the refrigerator.

Add the spinach rotini to the boiling water with 1½ teaspoons of salt. Start testing the pasta for doneness after 10 minutes and cook it until it is *al dente*. Drain the pasta, rinse it under cold running water, and drain it again. Add the pasta to the bowl with the eggplant.

While the pasta is cooking, cut the tomatoes into strips: Place a tomato, stem end down, on a clean work surface. With a small, sharp knife, cut the flesh from the tomato in wide, flat sections; discard the pulpy core and seeds. Slice the sections of flesh lengthwise into strips about ¼ inch wide and set them aside. Repeat the process to cut up the other tomato.

Heat the remaining tablespoon of oil in a large, heavy-bottomed skillet over medium-high heat. When the oil is hot, add the squash and shallots. Cook the vegetables, stirring frequently, for one minute. Add ▶

the shrimp, thyme, salt, some pepper and the remaining 1½ tablespoons of lime juice, and sauté the mixture until the shrimp are just cooked through — about two minutes. Stir in the tomato strips and cook the mixture for 30 seconds more. Transfer the contents of the skillet to the bowl with the pasta and eggplant, and toss the mixture well; return the bowl to the refrigerator.

To prepare the dressing, put the cheese, yogurt, milk and a liberal grinding of black pepper into a blender or food processor. Purée the mixture, scraping down the sides at least once. Add the dressing to the salad; toss the salad well and chill it briefly before serving.

Orzo with Pistachio Pesto

Serves 8 as a side dish
Working time: about 15 minutes
Total time: about 35 minutes

Calories **160**
Protein **6g.**
Cholesterol **3mg.**
Total fat **5g.**
Saturated fat **1g.**
Sodium **140mg.**

½ lb. orzo or farfalline
1 yellow pepper, seeded, deribbed and cut into small dice
2 tbsp. white wine vinegar
Pistachio pesto
1½ cups celery leaves, several leaves reserved for garnish
3 tbsp. coarsely chopped pistachio nuts (about ¾ oz.)
1 tbsp. virgin olive oil
1 garlic clove, finely chopped
½ cup unsalted chicken stock
⅓ cup freshly grated Parmesan cheese (about 1 oz.)

Add the pasta with ½ teaspoon of salt to 1 quart of boiling water. Start testing the pasta for doneness af-

ter 8 minutes and cook it until it is *al dente*.

Meanwhile, combine the yellow pepper and the vinegar in a large bowl. Drain the cooked pasta and rinse it well under cold running water. Drain the pasta again and toss it with the pepper and vinegar.

To prepare the pesto, purée the celery leaves, 2 tablespoons of the pistachios, the oil, garlic and stock in a blender or food processor, scraping down the sides from time to time. Add the Parmesan and blend the mixture just enough to incorporate the cheese.

Pour the pesto over the pasta and toss well. Garnish the salad with the reserved celery leaves and the remaining 1 tablespoon of pistachios. Serve cold.

Chinese Pasta and Long Bean Salad

Serves 8 as a side dish
Working (and total) time: about 30 minutes

Calories **150**
Protein **5g.**
Cholesterol **0mg.**
Total fat **3g.**
Saturated fat **0g.**
Sodium **20mg.**

½ lb. dried Chinese wheat noodles or dried vermicelli
½ lb. long beans or green beans, trimmed and cut into 2½-inch lengths
3 scallions, trimmed and finely chopped
1 tbsp. finely chopped cilantro
1 tbsp. roasted, unsalted peanuts, chopped
Celery-sesame dressing
½ cup chopped celery
¼ cup chopped onion
2 tbsp. rice vinegar
1 tbsp. safflower oil
1 tbsp. low-sodium soy sauce
1 tbsp. finely chopped fresh ginger
1 tsp. dark sesame oil
1 clove garlic, finely chopped
2 tbsp. fresh lemon juice
¼ tsp. chili paste

Bring 4 quarts of water to a boil in a large pot. Add the pasta and cook it until it is *al dente* — about three minutes for fresh noodles, or five minutes for dried vermicelli. Drain the pasta and rinse it under cold running water. Transfer it to a large bowl of cold water and set it aside.

Bring 2 quarts of water to a boil in a large saucepan. Add the beans and blanch them until they are just tender — about three minutes. Drain the beans and refresh them under cold running water. Drain them again and set them aside.

To make the dressing, put the celery, onion, vinegar, safflower oil, soy sauce, ginger, sesame oil, garlic, lemon juice and chili paste into a blender or food processor. Purée the dressing until it is smooth.

Drain the pasta well and transfer it to a bowl. Pour in the dressing, scallions and cilantro, and toss. Heap the dressed noodles or vermicelli in the center of a round platter or serving dish, then poke the beans one at a time into the mound to form a sunburst pattern. Sprinkle on the peanuts. Serve the salad at once.

6 *Cooked ahead of time to allow its flavors to mingle, this fragrant mélange of vegetables contains only 3 grams of fat per serving (recipe, page 169).*

Vermicelli Salad with Sliced Pork

Serves 6
Working (and total) time: about 30 minutes

Calories **206**
Protein **9g.**
Cholesterol **14mg.**
Total fat **3g.**
Saturated fat **1g.**
Sodium **235mg.**

8 oz. vermicelli (or other long, thin pasta)
½ tbsp. safflower oil
4 oz. pork loin, fat trimmed, meat pounded flat and sliced into thin strips
2 garlic cloves, finely chopped
3 carrots, peeled and julienned (about 2 cups)
4 celery stalks, trimmed and julienned (about 2 cups)
2 tsp. dark sesame oil
¼ tsp. salt
freshly ground black pepper
6 drops hot red-pepper sauce
2 tbsp. rice vinegar
1 tsp. cream sherry

Break the vermicelli into thirds and drop it into 3 quarts of boiling water with 1½ teaspoons of salt. Start testing the pasta after five minutes and continue to cook it until it is *al dente*.

While the pasta is cooking, heat the safflower oil in a wok or a large skillet over medium-high heat. Stir fry the pork strips in the oil for two minutes. Add the garlic and cook for 30 seconds, stirring constantly to keep it from burning. Add the carrot and celery, and stir fry the mixture for two minutes more.

Drain the pasta and toss it in a large bowl with the pork-and-vegetable mixture. Drizzle the sesame oil over the pasta, then sprinkle it with the ¼ teaspoon of salt, the black pepper and the hot-pepper sauce, and toss thoroughly. Pour the vinegar and sherry over the salad and toss it once more. Serve the salad at room temperature or chilled.

Penne with Canadian Bacon and Mushroom Sauce

Serves 8
Working time: about 15 minutes
Total time: about 45 minutes

Calories **317**
Protein **11g.**
Cholesterol **7mg.**
Total fat **6g.**
Saturated fat **2g.**
Sodium **214mg.**

1 lb. penne (or other short, tubular pasta)
2½ lb. Italian plum tomatoes, quartered, or 28 oz. unsalted canned whole tomatoes, drained
4 whole dried red chili peppers
2 tbsp. virgin olive oil
1 onion, finely chopped
1 lb. mushrooms, wiped clean and sliced
2 oz. Canadian bacon, julienned
4 garlic cloves, finely chopped
½ cup dry white wine
2 tbsp. chopped fresh parsley, preferably Italian
1 tbsp. unsalted butter

In a large saucepan, combine the tomatoes, chili peppers and ¼ cup of water. Cook over medium heat until the tomatoes have rendered their juice and most of the liquid has evaporated — about 20 minutes. Work the mixture through a food mill or sieve and set it aside.

Add the penne to 3 quarts of boiling water with 1½ teaspoons of salt. Begin testing the pasta after 10 minutes and cook it until it is *al dente*.

While the pasta is cooking, heat the oil in a large skillet over medium-high heat. Add the onion and sauté it, stirring constantly, until it turns translucent — about three minutes. Add the mushrooms and sauté them for two minutes, then add the bacon and garlic and sauté for two minutes more. Pour in the wine and cook the mixture until the liquid is reduced by half — about three minutes. Stir in the reserved tomato mixture and the parsley, and keep the sauce warm.

When the penne finishes cooking, transfer it to a platter or bowl. Toss it with the butter and the sauce and serve immediately.

Chicken Couscous with Raisins and Almonds

Serves 6
Working (and total) time: about 1 hour

Calories **336**
Protein **31g.**
Cholesterol **90mg.**
Total fat **13g.**
Saturated fat **3g.**
Sodium **188mg.**

1 cup couscous
6 chicken drumsticks, skinned and boned, the meat cut into 1-inch pieces
⅛ tsp. cayenne pepper
¼ tsp. ground cloves
¼ tsp. ground cinnamon
¼ tsp. ground cardamom
½ tsp. ground cumin
1 tsp. turmeric
¼ cup raisins
1 tbsp. safflower oil
1 onion, finely chopped
4 garlic cloves, finely chopped
¼ tsp. salt
2 cups unsalted chicken stock
2 tbsp. slivered almonds

Put the chicken pieces in a bowl and sprinkle them with the cayenne pepper, cloves, cinnamon, cardamom, cumin and turmeric. Toss the pieces to coat them with the spices. Let them stand at room temperature for at least 30 minutes.

To prepare the couscous, combine it with the raisins in a bowl and pour in 1 cup of boiling water. Cover the bowl and let it stand for at least five minutes.

Heat the oil in a large, heavy-bottomed skillet over medium heat, tilting the pan to coat it evenly. Add the onion and garlic and sauté them, stirring constantly, until the onion is translucent — about three minutes. Sprinkle the salt over the chicken and add the pieces to the skillet. Sauté, stirring frequently, until the chicken feels firm but springy to the touch — about five minutes. Pour the stock over the chicken and bring the liquid to a boil. Immediately drain the chicken and onions, reserving the liquid and the solids separately, and set them aside.

Fluff up the couscous-and-raisin mixture with a fork

and transfer it to a serving platter, hollowing out the center to form the couscous into the shape of a wreath. Mound the chicken mixture in the center of the wreath. Drizzle the stock over all and top the dish with the slivered almonds.

Spinach-Shell Salad with Chunks of Chicken

Serves 4
Working (and total) time: about 40 minutes

Calories **319**
Protein **22g.**
Cholesterol **36mg.**
Total fat **3g.**
Saturated fat **1g.**
Sodium **272mg.**

8 oz. medium spinach shells
2 chicken breast halves, skinned and boned (about ½ lb.), cut into pieces about 1 inch square
¼ tsp. salt
freshly ground black pepper
2 large shallots, thinly sliced
½ tsp. ground cinnamon
3 ripe tomatoes (about 1½ lb.), peeled, seeded and chopped
zest of 1 orange, cut into thin strips

Arrange the chicken pieces in a single layer in a deep, heatproof dish or a pie pan about 10 inches in diameter. Sprinkle the chicken with the salt and pepper. Scatter the shallot slices evenly over the chicken and top them with the cinnamon and tomatoes. Strew the orange zest over all. Cover the dish tightly with foil.

Pour enough water into a saucepan approximately 8 inches in diameter to fill it about one third full. Bring the water to a rolling boil. Set the covered dish on top of the saucepan like a lid and cook the chicken over the boiling water. After five minutes, test the chicken: If the meat is still pink at the center, cover the dish again and continue to steam the chicken until all trace of pink has disappeared and the meat feels firm but springy to the touch. Remove the dish from the saucepan and uncover it.

While the chicken is cooking, add the shells to 3 quarts of boiling water with 1½ teaspoons of salt. Start testing the shells after 12 minutes and cook them until they are *al dente*.

Drain the shells and transfer them to a heated bowl. Add the chicken-and-tomato sauce and toss it with the shells. Serve hot or at room temperature.

6 *Cooked ahead of time to allow its flavors to mingle, this fragrant mélange of vegetables contains only 3 grams of fat per serving (recipe, page 169).*

Vegetables

Cold Asparagus with Grainy Mustard Vinaigrette

Serves 4
Working time: about 20 minutes
Total time: about 40 minutes

Calories **129**
Protein **3mg.**
Cholesterol **0mg.**
Total fat **11g.**
Saturated fat **1g.**
Sodium **96mg.**

20 medium asparagus stalks, trimmed and peeled
1 tbsp. chopped shallot
2 tbsp. balsamic vinegar, or 1½ tbsp. red wine vinegar mixed with ½ tsp. honey
2 tbsp. grainy mustard
3 tbsp. safflower oil
4 large fresh basil leaves, sliced into thin strips, or ½ tsp. dried basil

In a small bowl, mix together the chopped shallot and the balsamic vinegar or vinegar and honey. Let steep for about 15 minutes. Stir in the mustard. Pour in the oil in a slow, thin stream, whisking vigorously. Add the basil, and set aside.

Pour enough water into a large skillet to fill it 1 inch deep, and bring to a boil. Line up the asparagus on the bottom, with the tips facing in one direction. Position the skillet so that the thicker ends of the stalks are over the center of the burner, and cook the asparagus until they are tender but still crisp — about five minutes. Drain the asparagus and then refresh them under cold running water to arrest their cooking and to preserve their color. Remove them from the water when cool, dry them on paper towels and refrigerate them until ready to serve.

At serving time, arrange the asparagus on individual plates or on a large serving plate. Whisk the vinaigrette again and pour it over the stalks.

Cold Asparagus with Orange Vinaigrette

Serves 4
Working time: about 25 minutes
Total time: about 40 minutes

Calories **91**
Protein **2g.**
Cholesterol **0mg.**
Total fat **7g.**
Saturated fat **1g.**
Sodium **2mg.**

20 medium asparagus stalks, trimmed and peeled
⅓ cup fresh orange juice
1 tsp. fresh lime juice
1 tbsp. finely chopped shallot
1 tsp. finely chopped garlic
1 tbsp. orange zest, cut into thin strips and blanched in boiling water for 30 seconds
2 tbsp. virgin olive oil
1 tbsp. red wine vinegar

In a small bowl, mix together the orange and lime juices, the chopped shallot and garlic, and the zest. Let steep for at least 10 minutes. Whisk in the oil and vinegar, and set aside.

Pour enough water into a skillet to fill it 1 inch deep, and bring to a boil. Line up the asparagus on the bottom, with the tips facing in one direction. Position the skillet so that the thicker ends of the stalks are over the center of the burner, and cook the asparagus until they are tender but still crisp — about five minutes. Drain the asparagus and then refresh them under cold running water to arrest their cooking and to preserve their color. Remove them from the water when cool, dry them on paper towels and refrigerate until you are ready to serve them.

At serving time, arrange the stalks on individual plates or on a large serving plate. Whisk the vinaigrette again and pour it over the asparagus.

Stir-Fried Asparagus with Soy Sauce

Serves 4
Working time: about 25 minutes
Total time: about 30 minutes

Calories **86**
Protein **4g.**
Cholesterol **0mg.**
Total fat **6g.**
Saturated fat **1g.**
Sodium **311mg.**

1 lb. asparagus, trimmed and cut diagonally into ½-inch-thick pieces
2 tbsp. low-sodium soy sauce
1½ tsp. finely chopped fresh ginger
1 garlic clove, finely chopped
1½ tbsp. dark sesame oil
1 tbsp. sesame seeds

In a small bowl, combine the soy sauce, ginger and garlic, and set aside.

In a wok or a large, heavy-bottomed skillet, heat the oil over medium-high heat. Add the soy mixture and the asparagus, and stir fry for three minutes. Cover and allow the asparagus to steam until just tender — about two minutes. Stir in the sesame seeds and serve immediately.

Baked Asparagus with Pine Nuts and Gruyère

Serves 4
Working time: about 20 minutes
Total time: about 25 minutes

Calories **145**
Protein **7g.**
Cholesterol **18mg.**
Total fat **13g.**
Saturated fat **4g.**
Sodium **48mg.**

1 lb. medium asparagus, trimmed and peeled
1 tsp. unsalted butter
½ cup grated Gruyère cheese
3 tbsp. pine nuts
1 tbsp. virgin olive oil
freshly ground black pepper

Preheat the oven to 350° F.

In a large, ovenproof skillet, melt the butter over medium heat. Line up the asparagus on the bottom, with the tips facing in one direction. Add three tablespoons of water and cover the skillet. Position it so that the thicker ends of the stalks are over the center of the burner, and steam the asparagus for two minutes. Remove the skillet from the heat, and sprinkle the cheese on the stems, but not the tips. Strew the pine nuts on the cheese, then dribble the oil on top. Sprinkle the asparagus with pepper.

Place the skillet in the oven, and bake, uncovered, until the cheese has melted — about five minutes. Serve bubbling hot.

Chilled Beans with Yogurt and Mint

Serves 6
Working time: about 20 minutes
Total time: about 45 minutes

Calories **38**
Protein **2g.**
Cholesterol **0mg.**
Total fat **1g.**
Saturated fat **0g.**
Sodium **101mg.**

1 lb. green beans, trimmed
¼ tsp. salt
1½ tsp. dry mustard
1 tbsp. fresh lime or lemon juice
2 tbsp. chopped fresh mint
1 small garlic clove, very finely chopped
½ tsp. sugar
freshly ground black pepper
⅓ cup plain low-fat yogurt
1 tomato, cut into wedges

Pour enough water into a large saucepan to fill it about 1 inch deep. Set a vegetable steamer in the pan and bring the water to a boil. Add the beans, cover the pan tightly, and steam the beans until they are tender — about six minutes. Remove the beans from the pan, and refresh them under cold running water to arrest their cooking and preserve their color. When the beans are cool, drain them thoroughly and place them in a bowl. Sprinkle the salt over the beans and toss well.

In a bowl, stir together the dry mustard and the lime or lemon juice until a smooth paste is formed. Add the mint, garlic, sugar, pepper and yogurt, and blend well. Add the beans and toss to coat them. Refrigerate for at least 30 minutes. At serving time, garnish with the tomato wedges.

Green Beans with Creamy Horseradish Dressing

Serves 8 as a first course
Working time: about 40 minutes
Total time: about 1 hour and 15 minutes

Calories **55**
Protein **3g.**
Cholesterol **1mg.**
Total fat **1g.**
Saturated fat **0g.**
Sodium **115mg.**

2 sweet red peppers
8 artichokes
1 lemon, halved
½ lb. green beans, trimmed
½ lb. okra, trimmed
Horseradish dressing
½ cup plain low-fat yogurt
¼ cup prepared horseradish, drained
1 tsp. celery seeds
1 tsp. fresh lemon juice
¼ tsp. salt
1 tbsp. chopped fresh thyme, or 1 tsp. dried thyme leaves
3 tbsp. chopped fresh parsley
⅛ tsp. cayenne pepper
freshly ground black pepper

Roast the peppers about 2 inches below a preheated broiler, turning them until their skin has blistered on all sides. Transfer the peppers to a bowl and cover it with plastic wrap; the trapped steam will loosen their skins. When the peppers are cool enough to handle, peel, seed and derib them, and cut them into ¼-inch cubes.

To prepare each artichoke bottom, first break or cut off the stem. Snap off and discard the outer leaves, starting at the base and continuing until you reach the pale yellow leaves at the core. Cut the top two thirds off the artichoke. Trim away any dark green leaf bases that remain on the artichoke bottom. Rub the artichoke all over with one of the lemon halves.

Fill a large, nonreactive saucepan with water and bring it to a boil. Squeeze the juice of both lemon halves into the water, then add the lemon halves themselves. Add the artichoke bottoms to the boiling water and cook them until they can be easily pierced with the tip of a sharp knife — about 15 minutes. Drain the artichoke bottoms and refresh them under cold running water. Using a teaspoon, scrape the furry choke from each artichoke bottom. Rinse and drain the bottoms, and cut each one into eight pieces.

Pour enough water into a large saucepan to fill it about 1 inch deep. Set a vegetable steamer in the pan and bring the water to a boil. Put the green beans into the steamer, cover the pan tightly, and steam the beans until they are tender — about six minutes. Lift out the steamer; refresh the beans under cold running water, then drain them well, and set them aside.

Return the steamer to the pan and bring the water to a boil. Set the okra in the steamer, cover the pan tightly, and steam the okra until it is barely tender — about three minutes. Remove the okra from the pan and refresh it under cold running water. Cut each okra in half lengthwise and set it aside.

To prepare the dressing, whisk together the yogurt, horseradish, celery seeds, lemon juice, salt, thyme, parsley, cayenne pepper and some black pepper in a large bowl. Add the beans, artichoke bottoms, okra and all but 2 tablespoons of the red peppers to the dressing. Toss well and serve the salad with the reserved red pepper cubes sprinkled on top.

EDITOR'S NOTE: *Provided it is stored in the refrigerator, the dressing may be made a day in advance.*

Carrot and Orange Salad with Dill

Serves 4 as a side dish
Working time: about 10 minutes
Total time: about 25 minutes

Calories **90**
Protein **2g.**
Cholesterol **0mg.**
Total fat **0g.**
Saturated fat **0g.**
Sodium **50mg.**

1 navel orange
6 carrots (about 1¼ lb.), finely grated
1 tbsp. red wine vinegar
½ cup fresh orange juice
½ tsp. grated orange zest
2 tbsp. fresh dill

Working over a bowl to catch the juice, cut away the peel, white pith and outer membrane from the orange. To separate the segments from the inner membranes, slice down to the core with a sharp knife on either side of each segment and set the segments aside.

Combine the carrots, vinegar, orange juice and zest in the bowl. Add the orange segments and 1 tablespoon of the dill; gently toss the ingredients. Refrigerate the salad for at least 15 minutes. Shortly before serving, garnish the top with the remaining dill.

Broiled Eggplant with Mint

Serves 6 as a side dish
Working time: about 25 minutes
Total time: about 50 minutes

Calories **70**
Protein **2g.**
Cholesterol **0mg.**
Total fat **3g.**
Saturated fat **0g.**
Sodium **190mg.**

1 lb. eggplant, cut into 1-inch cubes
½ tsp. salt
2 tbsp. balsamic vinegar, or 1 ½ tbsp. red wine vinegar mixed with ½ tsp. honey
¼ lb. mushrooms, wiped clean and quartered
juice of ½ lemon
2 ripe tomatoes, peeled, seeded and cut into strips
1 tbsp. sliced fresh mint leaves
Peppery orange dressing
juice of 1 orange
juice of 1 lemon
1 garlic clove, finely chopped
⅛ tsp. crushed hot red-pepper flakes
¼ tsp. salt
1 tbsp. virgin olive oil

Toss the eggplant cubes with the salt and let them stand for 30 minutes to make them less bitter. Rinse the cubes and pat them dry with paper towels.

Preheat the broiler. Put the eggplant cubes into a flameproof dish and broil them, stirring often, until they are browned — about five minutes. Transfer the eggplant cubes to a bowl and mix in the vinegar. Set the bowl aside.

Put the mushrooms into a nonreactive saucepan with the lemon juice; pour in enough water to cover the mushrooms and simmer them over medium heat for about five minutes. Set the saucepan aside.

To make the dressing, combine the orange juice, lemon juice, garlic, red-pepper flakes and salt in a small saucepan. Bring the mixture to a boil and cook it until the liquid is reduced by half — about five minutes. Remove the pan from the heat and whisk in the oil.

Arrange the eggplant and tomatoes on a large plate. Drain the mushrooms and scatter them over the tomatoes. Pour the dressing over the vegetables, then sprinkle the fresh mint on top. Serve the salad at room temperature.

Fava Bean Salad

Serves 6 as a first course or side dish
Working time: about 40 minutes
Total time: about 50 minutes

Calories **125**
Protein **6g.**
Cholesterol **3mg.**
Total fat **3g.**
Saturated fat **1g.**
Sodium **95mg.**

2 tsp. virgin olive oil
1 large onion, thinly sliced
1 large garlic clove, finely chopped
2½ lb. fresh fava beans, shelled and peeled (about 2 cups), or 2 cups frozen lima beans, defrosted
2 paper-thin slices of prosciutto (about 1 oz.), julienned
1½ lb. ripe tomatoes, peeled, seeded and coarsely chopped, or 14 oz. canned unsalted tomatoes, chopped, with their juice
1 cup unsalted chicken stock, or ½ cup unsalted chicken stock if canned tomatoes are used
1 tbsp. chopped fresh oregano, or 1 tsp. dried oregano
½ tsp. cracked black peppercorns
2 tbsp. balsamic vinegar, or 1½ tbsp. red wine vinegar mixed with ½ tsp. honey

Heat the oil in a heavy-bottomed skillet over medium heat. Add the onion slices and cook them until they are translucent — four to five minutes. Stir in the garlic and cook the mixture for one minute more. Add the beans, prosciutto, tomatoes, stock, oregano and peppercorns. Bring the liquid to a simmer and cook the mixture until the beans are just tender — eight to 10 minutes. Transfer the salad to a bowl and refrigerate it.

When the salad is cool, pour in the vinegar, toss well, and serve at once.

Green Bean Salad with Gruyère and Grainy Mustard

Serves 6 as a first course or side dish
Working time: about 15 minutes
Total time: about 30 minutes

Calories **70**
Protein **3g.**
Cholesterol **8mg.**
Total fat **5g.**
Saturated fat **2g.**
Sodium **120mg.**

¾ lb. thin green beans, trimmed and cut in half diagonally
1 shallot, finely chopped
1½ tbsp. grainy mustard, or 1 tbsp. Dijon mustard
3 tbsp. red wine vinegar
1 tbsp. virgin olive oil
⅛ tsp. salt
freshly ground black pepper
1½ oz. Gruyère cheese, julienned (about ⅓ cup)

Pour enough water into a large saucepan to fill it about 1 inch deep. Set a vegetable steamer in the pan and bring the water to a boil. Put the beans into the steamer, cover the pan, and cook the beans until they are just tender — seven to eight minutes. Refresh the beans under cold running water; when they are cool, drain them on paper towels.

Mix the shallot, mustard, vinegar, oil, salt and some pepper in a large bowl. Add the cheese and green beans, and toss the beans well. Refrigerate the salad for 10 minutes. Toss it once again just before serving.

Wax Beans and Cherry Tomatoes

Serves 6
Working time: about 25 minutes
Total time: about 30 minutes

Calories **71**
Protein **2g.**
Cholesterol **0mg.**
Total fat **5g.**
Saturated fat **1g.**
Sodium **94mg.**

1 lb. wax beans, trimmed
2 tbsp. virgin olive oil
1 small onion, thinly sliced
1 garlic clove, finely chopped
1 cup cherry tomatoes, halved
2 tbsp. chopped fresh basil, plus several whole leaves for garnish
¼ tsp. salt
freshly ground black pepper

Pour enough water into a saucepan to fill it about 1 inch deep. Set a vegetable steamer in the pan and bring the water to a boil. Put the beans in the steamer, cover the pan, and steam the beans until they are tender but still crisp — five to seven minutes.

Pour the oil into a large skillet over medium heat. Cook the onion and garlic in the oil until the onions are soft — two to three minutes. Add the beans and cook, stirring from time to time, for two minutes. Add the tomatoes, chopped basil, salt and pepper. Stir well and continue cooking until the tomatoes are heated through — about two minutes. Transfer the vegetables to a serving dish and garnish them with the whole basil leaves. Serve immediately.

Zucchini Sautéed with Shallots and Tomato Strips

Serves 6
Working (and total) time: about 35 minutes

Calories **76**
Protein **2g.**
Cholesterol **0mg.**
Total fat **5g.**
Saturated fat **1g.**
Sodium **93mg.**

2 zucchini (about 1¼ lb.), ends trimmed
1 large ripe tomato, peeled
2 tbsp. virgin olive oil
¼ tsp. salt
freshly ground black pepper
6 shallots, thinly sliced
2 tbsp. chopped Italian parsley or cilantro
1 tbsp. fresh lemon juice

Put the peeled tomato stem end down on a cutting board. With a small, sharp knife, cut wide strips of flesh from the tomato, discarding the seeds and core. Slice the flesh into ¼-inch-wide strips and set them aside.

Slice the zucchini into 2-inch rounds. Cut each round into six wedges.

Heat the oil in a large, heavy-bottomed skillet over medium-high heat. When the oil is hot, add the zucchini. Cook, stirring frequently, for five minutes. Sprinkle the zucchini with the salt and pepper; add the shallots and cook for another three minutes, stirring often. Add the tomato strips, the parsley or cilantro, and the lemon juice. Cook for four minutes more to blend the flavors, and serve immediately.

Baked Zucchini with Cilantro Pesto

Serves 6
Working time: about 15 minutes
Total time: about 40 minutes

Calories **66**
Protein **3g.**
Cholesterol **3mg.**
Total fat **4g.**
Saturated fat **1g.**
Sodium **157mg.**

6 small zucchini (about 1½ lb.)
½ cup chopped cilantro
½ cup chopped parsley
1 tbsp. pine nuts
1 garlic clove
¼ tsp. salt
freshly ground black pepper
1 tbsp. virgin olive oil
¼ cup freshly grated Parmesan cheese

Preheat the oven to 325° F.

To make the pesto, combine the cilantro, parsley, pine nuts, garlic, salt and pepper in a food processor or blender. Purée until smooth — about three minutes. Add the oil and blend for one minute. Add the Parmesan and blend two minutes more.

Trim the zucchini and cut them in half lengthwise. Spread the pesto on the exposed flesh of one half of each zucchini, and cover with the other half. Wrap the zucchini individually in aluminum foil. Bake them until just tender — 20 to 25 minutes.

Breaded Zucchini Slices with Cheese

Serves 12 as an hors d'oeuvre
Working time: about 30 minutes
Total time: about 40 minutes

Calories **44**
Protein **3g.**
Cholesterol **5mg.**
Total fat **3g.**
Saturated fat **0g.**
Sodium **80mg.**

1 lb. zucchini (3 or 4, depending on size), cut on the diagonal into ¼-inch slices
freshly ground black pepper
½ cup freshly grated Romano cheese
½ cup fresh bread crumbs
1 tbsp. chopped fresh oregano, or 1 tsp. dried oregano
3 egg whites, beaten until frothy
2 tbsp. safflower oil

Preheat the oven to 325° F. Grind pepper liberally over the zucchini slices. In a shallow bowl, combine the cheese, the bread crumbs and the oregano. Dip half of the zucchini slices into the beaten egg whites, then coat them evenly with the cheese-crumb mixture and set them aside.

Heat 1 tablespoon of the safflower oil in a large, ovenproof skillet over medium-high heat. Use a pastry brush to distribute the oil evenly over the bottom. Place the breaded slices in the skillet and put the skillet immediately into the oven. After five minutes, carefully turn the slices over and bake them until they are golden brown — five to seven minutes more. Remove the slices to a warmed serving platter and repeat the process with the remaining zucchini and oil. The zucchini should be eaten hot.

Red and Green Pepper Sauté with Zucchini

Serves 6
Working time: about 35 minutes
Total time: about 40 minutes

Calories **38**
Protein **1g.**
Cholesterol **0mg.**
Total fat **2g.**
Saturated fat **0g.**
Sodium **6mg.**

1 green pepper, seeded, deribbed and cut into 1-inch squares
1 red pepper, seeded, deribbed and cut into 1-inch squares
1 onion, coarsely chopped
6 garlic cloves, finely chopped
¼ tsp. crushed fennel seeds
½ lb. zucchini, trimmed and cut into 1-inch cubes

1 tbsp. virgin olive oil
⅛ tsp. saffron threads, soaked in 2 tbsp. water
1 tbsp. anise-flavored liqueur (optional)
¼ cup chopped fresh basil, or ¼ cup chopped parsley plus 1 tsp. dried basil

In a large skillet, bring 1 cup of water to a boil over high heat. Add the onion, garlic and fennel seeds, and cook until the water has almost evaporated and the onions and garlic are soft — about five minutes. Add the peppers, zucchini, oil, saffron, the liqueur if you are using it, and ¼ cup of water; continue to cook, stirring constantly, until all the vegetables are tender — about five minutes more. Stir in the fresh basil or the parsley and dried basil, and serve immediately.

Red and Yellow Peppers with Arugula

ARUGULA, OR ROCKET, GIVES A PUNGENT, MUSTARDY
ACCENT TO THIS DISH.

Serves 4
Working time: about 45 minutes
Total time: about 1 hour and 15 minutes

Calories **65**
Protein **3g.**
Cholesterol **0mg.**
Total fat **4g.**
Saturated fat **1g.**
Sodium **72mg.**

6 red and yellow peppers, broiled and peeled
5 garlic cloves, unpeeled
1 tbsp. virgin olive oil
1 tsp. balsamic vinegar or fresh lemon juice
⅛ tsp. salt
freshly ground black pepper
1 bunch arugula, washed, leaves coarsely shredded (about 2 cups loosely packed)

Preheat the oven to 350° F. Place the garlic cloves on a piece of aluminum foil, and sprinkle them with 1 teaspoon of the oil. Wrap them up in the foil, then bake until a clove can be pierced easily with a skewer — about 20 minutes.

Remove the stems, ribs and seeds from the peppers, working over a bowl to catch the juices. Strain the pepper juices and reserve them. Slice the peppers lengthwise into ½-inch-wide strips.

Squeeze the softened garlic cloves out of their skins, purée them through a small strainer and add to the pepper juices. Stir in the vinegar or lemon juice, salt and pepper. Heat the remaining 2 teaspoons of oil in a large, heavy-bottomed skillet over medium-high heat. Add the arugula and cook until it wilts — about one minute. Add the sliced peppers and stir in the garlic mixture; cook for one or two minutes more to reheat the peppers. Transfer the peppers and arugula to a serving platter. The dish may be eaten hot, cold or at room temperature.

Corn and Red Pepper Pancakes

Serves 8
Working time: about 30 minutes
Total time: about 45 minutes

Calories **111**
Protein **4g.**
Cholesterol **34mg.**
Total fat **5g.**
Saturated fat **1g.**
Sodium **161mg.**

2 cups fresh corn kernels (about 2 large ears), or 2 cups frozen corn kernels, defrosted
1 egg yolk
¼ cup cornmeal
¼ cup flour
1 tsp. fresh thyme, or ¼ tsp. dried thyme leaves
½ tsp. salt
freshly ground black pepper
1 red pepper, seeded, deribbed and finely chopped (about 1 cup)
4 egg whites
8 tsp. virgin olive oil

Chop 1 cup of the corn finely, by hand or in a blender. Place in a large bowl. Add the egg yolk, cornmeal, flour, thyme, salt and pepper to the bowl, and stir well. Add the red pepper and the remaining 1 cup of corn kernels, and mix to incorporate them. Set aside.

In another bowl, beat the egg whites until soft peaks form. Fold half of the egg whites into the corn-and-red-pepper mixture, and blend well. Then carefully fold in the remaining egg whites; the whites should not be completely incorporated.

Heat a large, heavy-bottomed skillet (preferably one with a nonstick surface) over medium heat. Put 2 teaspoons of the oil in the skillet. When the oil is hot, drop tablespoonfuls of the corn-and-red-pepper mixture into the skillet, taking care not to let the edges touch. Cook until the bottom side of each pancake is golden brown — about three minutes. Turn the pancakes carefully and cook them until the other side browns — about three minutes more. Remove the finished pancakes from the skillet and keep them warm. Repeat the process, using 2 teaspoons of the oil each time, until all of the batter is gone. Serve immediately.

EDITOR'S NOTE: *If you are using frozen corn, whisk 1 teaspoon of sugar into the egg yolk.*

Grilled Vegetables with Herb Marinade

Serves 12
Working (and total) time: about 45 minutes

Calories **88**
Protein **3g.**
Cholesterol **0mg.**
Total fat **5g.**
Saturated fat **1g.**
Sodium **52mg.**

6 medium zucchini
3 medium onions
12 large mushroom caps
4 red sweet peppers
6 ripe plum tomatoes or small tomatoes, halved
3 limes, each cut into 8 wedges

Herb marinade

¼ cup virgin olive oil
1 tbsp. fresh rosemary, or 1 tsp. dried rosemary
1 tsp. fresh thyme, or ½ tsp. dried thyme leaves
¼ tsp. crushed hot red pepper
¼ tsp. salt

About 30 minutes before you plan to cook the vegetables, prepare the coals for grilling.

To make the herb marinade, put the oil, rosemary, thyme, hot red pepper and salt in a small saucepan. Warm the mixture over medium heat until it begins to

bubble gently, then cook it for four minutes more. Remove the marinade from the heat and let it stand while you prepare the vegetables.

Slice the zucchini in half crosswise with a diagonal cut through the middle. Cut each half into a fan by making lengthwise slices ¼ inch apart, leaving the slices attached at the uncut end.

Cut the onions lengthwise into quarters. Thread the onions onto one or two skewers. Wipe the mushroom caps clean and thread them onto a skewer. Cut the red sweet peppers lengthwise into thirds, then derib and seed them. Thread the peppers onto one or two skewers. Thread the tomato halves onto a skewer.

When the grill is hot, lightly brush all the vegetables with the herb marinade. Cook the vegetables, staggering their cooking times so that all the vegetables will be ready at once. Put the zucchini fans on the grill first — they require about 10 minutes' grilling. After two minutes, add the onions; after another two minutes, add the mushrooms. Add the peppers and tomatoes for the last four minutes' grilling. Baste the vegetables with any remaining marinade as they cook, and turn them as they brown.

Remove the vegetables from their skewers and arrange them on a platter. Serve them hot, accompanied by the lime wedges.

Vegetable Mosaic

Serves 10
Working time: about 45 minutes
Total time: about 2 hours

Calories **122**
Protein **4g.**
Cholesterol **0mg.**
Total fat **6g.**
Saturated fat **1g.**
Sodium **195mg.**

4 large onions (about 1¾ lb.), thinly sliced
2 heads of fennel, green stems removed and feathery green tops reserved, bulbs halved lengthwise and thinly sliced
¾ tsp. salt
freshly ground black pepper
1 tbsp. fresh rosemary, or ¾ tsp. dried rosemary, crumbled
¼ cup cider vinegar
3 zucchini (about 1¼ lb.), cut diagonally into ¼-inch-thick slices
2 garlic cloves, finely chopped
2 tbsp. chopped fresh oregano, or 2 tsp. dried oregano
6 ripe plum tomatoes
2 small eggplants (about 1¼ lb.), halved lengthwise and cut into ½-inch-thick slices
4 tbsp. virgin olive oil

Put the onions and fennel in a large, heavy-bottomed casserole with ¼ teaspoon of the salt, some pepper and half of the rosemary. Pour in the vinegar and ¼ cup of water. Cook the vegetables over medium heat, scraping the bottom of the pan frequently to mix in any caramelized bits, until the vegetables are well browned — 30 to 35 minutes.

While the onions and fennel are cooking, prepare the other vegetables. Preheat the broiler. Toss the zucchini slices in a bowl with the garlic, half of the oregano and ¼ teaspoon of the salt. Cut the tomatoes into slices ¼ inch thick. Put the slices on a plate and sprinkle them with some pepper and the remaining ¼ teaspoon of salt. Put the eggplant slices on a baking sheet and brush them with 1 tablespoon of the oil. Broil them two to three inches from the heat source until they are very brown — about eight minutes. Turn the eggplant slices and brush them with another tablespoon of the oil. Broil the slices on the second side until they are brown — six to seven minutes. Set the oven temperature at 375° F.

Spread the browned onions and fennel in the bottom of a large, shallow baking dish. Arrange the eggplant, zucchini and tomato slices on top of the onions. Drizzle 1 tablespoon of the oil over the vegetables and cover the dish with aluminum foil, shiny side down.

Bake the vegetables for 25 minutes. Remove the foil and drizzle the remaining tablespoon of oil over the top. Continue to bake the vegetables, uncovered, until they are soft — about 20 minutes. Sprinkle the vegetables with the remaining rosemary and oregano, and bake them for 10 minutes more. Garnish the dish with the reserved fennel tops.

Summer Vegetable Stew

Serves 10
Working time: about 40 minutes
Total time: about 1 hour

Calories **115**
Protein **4g.**
Cholesterol **3mg.**
Total fat **6g.**
Saturated fat **1g.**
Sodium **147mg.**

3 tbsp. safflower oil
8 small shallots, peeled
½ lb. mushrooms, wiped clean, left whole if small, halved or quartered if large
1 yellow squash, cut into 1-inch cubes
2 celery stalks, cut into 1-inch-long pieces
1 red pepper, seeded, deribbed and cut into 1-inch-wide strips
1 small eggplant, cut into 1-inch cubes
2 garlic cloves, finely chopped
2 medium tomatoes, peeled, seeded and chopped
½ cup dry vermouth
½ tsp. salt
freshly ground black pepper
1 small boiling potato
1 ear of corn, cut into 1-inch-long pieces
½ lb. baby carrots, peeled
½ lb. green beans, trimmed
1 bay leaf
⅛ tsp. saffron threads, steeped in ¼ cup hot water
2 tbsp. chopped fresh marjoram, or 2 tsp. dried marjoram
½ cup freshly grated Parmesan cheese

Heat 1 tablespoon of the safflower oil in a large, heavy-bottomed skillet or shallow casserole over high heat. Sauté the shallots in the oil until they are lightly colored — about one minute. Then add the mushrooms, squash, celery and red pepper, and sauté them for two minutes, stirring frequently to keep them from burning. Transfer the vegetables to a bowl; set them aside.

Heat the remaining 2 tablespoons of oil in the pan over high heat; add the eggplant and sauté it for two minutes. Stir in the garlic and cook it very briefly — no more than 15 seconds. Return the vegetables in the bowl to the pan and stir in the tomatoes and vermouth. Cook the liquid until it is slightly reduced — about five minutes. Add the salt and pepper.

Meanwhile, peel and grate the potato. Stir it into the vegetables along with the corn, carrots, beans, bay leaf and just enough water to cover the vegetables. Simmer the stew, uncovered, until all the vegetables are tender — 25 to 30 minutes. Stir in the saffron mixture and the marjoram. Just before serving the stew, sprinkle it with the Parmesan cheese.

Mediterranean Vegetable Stew

TO PREPARE BABY ARTICHOKES, SIMPLY REMOVE ANY TOUGH OUTER LEAVES AND TRIM THE TOPS.

Serves 6
Working time: about 35 minutes
Total time: about 2 hours and 45 minutes
(includes cooling)

Calories **45**
Protein **2g.**
Cholesterol **0mg.**
Total fat **3g.**
Saturated fat **1g.**
Sodium **175mg.**

2 large tomatoes, peeled, seeded and chopped
6 baby artichokes (about ¾ lb.), trimmed and halved
2 tbsp. fresh lemon juice
2 cups sliced celery
1 fennel bulb, thinly sliced
3 thin leeks, trimmed and sliced into ½-inch rings
1 bay leaf
12 small onions
1 tbsp. virgin olive oil
10 oz. button mushrooms, wiped, trimmed, and halved
½ tsp. salt
freshly ground black pepper
1 tbsp. chopped fennel leaves

In a large, heavy-bottomed saucepan, heat the tomatoes, artichokes, and lemon juice, stirring frequently, until the mixture comes to a boil. Continue to cook the vegetables over high heat, stirring occasionally, for another 10 minutes.

Add the celery, fennel, leeks, and bay leaf to the tomatoes and artichokes, and simmer uncovered, stirring occasionally, until the vegetables are almost tender—about 20 minutes.

Meanwhile, in a small, heavy-bottomed saucepan over medium-low heat, cook the onions in the oil until they are soft and well browned—about 20 minutes. Shake the saucepan frequently to prevent the onions from sticking to the bottom or burning.

When the vegetables in the large pan are nearly cooked, add the mushrooms and simmer for another 10 minutes. Remove the pan from the heat, and mix in the salt, some pepper, and the onions. Allow the mixture to cool for about two hours.

Remove the bay leaf and discard it. Before serving, transfer the stew to a large serving dish and sprinkle the fennel leaves over the top.

7

High in fiber and nutrients, the offerings of garden and orchard afford the salad maker ample room for delicious innovation.

Salads

Basic Dressings with a New Twist

The low-fat, low-calorie dressings that follow were specially developed for this book. Several recipes call for them specifically, but the dressings can also be refrigerated for later use on salads of your own invention.

The vinaigrette suits fresh mixed greens of delicate flavor. The yogurt and buttermilk dressings marry well with assertive vegetables; they also complement meats, grains and pasta. The mayonnaise makes an ideal partner for root vegetables as well as poultry and seafood.

Any of the four may be further enhanced by the addition of herbs, spices or other seasonings. The figures found alongside each recipe give the nutrient analysis for one tablespoon of dressing.

New Mayonnaise

THIS TOFU-BASED MAYONNAISE CONTAINS JUST HALF THE AMOUNT OF EGG YOLKS AND OIL FOUND IN THE TRADITIONAL VERSION.

Makes 1½ cups

¼ lb. firm tofu, cut into small cubes and soaked in cold water for 10 minutes
½ cup plain low-fat yogurt, drained in a cheesecloth-lined colander for 10 minutes
1 egg yolk
1 tsp. dried mustard
½ cup safflower oil
¼ cup virgin olive oil
2 tbsp. white wine vinegar or cider vinegar
½ tsp. salt
½ tsp. sugar
⅛ tsp. white pepper

Calories **70**
Protein **1g.**
Cholesterol **12mg.**
Total fat **7g.**
Saturated fat **1g.**
Sodium **50mg.**

Remove the tofu from its soaking water and drain it on paper towels. Transfer the tofu to a food processor or a blender. Add the yogurt, egg yolk and mustard, and process the mixture until it is very smooth, scraping down the sides at least once.

With the motor still running, pour in the oils in a thin, steady stream, stopping halfway through the process to scrape the sides with a rubber spatula.

Add the vinegar, salt, sugar and pepper, and process the mayonnaise for 15 seconds more. Transfer the mayonnaise to a bowl and refrigerate it; the mayonnaise will keep for at least 10 days.

Vinaigrette

Makes about ½ cup

1 tsp. Dijon mustard
¼ tsp. salt
freshly ground black pepper
2½ tbsp. red wine vinegar
2½ tbsp. safflower oil
2½ tbsp. virgin olive oil

Calories **75**
Protein **0g.**
Cholesterol **0mg.**
Total fat **8g.**
Saturated fat **1g.**
Sodium **75mg.**

In a small bowl, combine the mustard, the salt, a grinding of pepper and the vinegar. Whisking vigorously, pour in the safflower oil in a thin, steady stream; incorporate the olive oil the same way. Continue whisking until the dressing is well combined. Covered and stored in the refrigerator, the dressing will keep for about a week.

Buttermilk Dressing

Makes about ½ cup

½ cup buttermilk
cayenne pepper
¼ tsp. sugar
1 shallot, finely chopped
¼ cup nonfat dry milk
2 tbsp. fresh lemon juice

Calories **15**
Protein **1g.**
Cholesterol **1mg.**
Total fat **0g.**
Saturated fat **0g.**
Sodium **30mg.**

In a small bowl, combine the buttermilk, a pinch of cayenne pepper, the sugar and the shallot. Whisk in the dry milk a tablespoon at a time, then stir in the lemon juice. To allow the dressing to thicken, cover the bowl and refrigerate it for at least 30 minutes. The dressing will keep for three days.

EDITOR'S NOTE: *The inclusion of nonfat dry milk makes for a thick, creamy dressing.*

Creamy Yogurt Dressing

Makes about ½ cup

2 tbsp. cream sherry
2 garlic cloves, finely chopped
1½ tsp. Dijon mustard
½ cup plain low-fat yogurt
1 tbsp. sour cream
⅛ tsp. white pepper

Calories **20**
Protein **1g.**
Cholesterol **2mg.**
Total fat **1g.**
Saturated fat **0g.**
Sodium **25mg.**

Put the sherry and garlic into a small saucepan. Bring the mixture to a simmer over medium heat and cook it until nearly all the liquid has evaporated — about three minutes. Transfer the mixture to a bowl. Stir in the mustard, then the yogurt, sour cream and pepper. Cover the bowl and store the dressing in the refrigerator; it will keep for two to three days.

Leaves of Boston Lettuce in a Garlicky Vinaigrette

Serves 6 as a first course or side dish
Working time: about 10 minutes
Total time: about 25 minutes

Calories **110**
Protein **3g.**
Cholesterol **0mg.**
Total fat **5g.**
Saturated fat **1g.**
Sodium **150mg.**

1 whole garlic bulb, the cloves separated and peeled
1 tbsp. balsamic vinegar, or 1 tbsp. red wine vinegar mixed with ¼ tsp. honey
1 tbsp. virgin olive oil
1 tbsp. safflower oil
⅛ tsp. salt
freshly ground black pepper
2 heads of Boston lettuce, or 4 heads of Bibb lettuce, washed and dried
12 thin French-bread slices, toasted

Put the garlic cloves into a small saucepan and pour in enough water to cover them. Bring the liquid to a boil, then reduce the heat, and simmer the garlic until it is quite tender — about 15 minutes. Increase the heat and boil the liquid until only about 2 tablespoons remain — two to three minutes.

Pour the contents of the saucepan into a sieve set over a small bowl. With a wooden spoon, mash the garlic through the sieve into the bowl. Whisk the vinegar into the garlic mixture, then incorporate the olive oil, safflower oil, salt and some pepper.

Toss the lettuce leaves with the dressing; garnish the salad with the toast and serve at once.

Potato Salad with Roasted Red Pepper Sauce

Serves 8 as a side dish
Working (and total) time: about 40 minutes

Calories **110**
Protein **2g.**
Cholesterol **0mg.**
Total fat **4g.**
Saturated fat **0g.**
Sodium **70mg.**

1½ lb. round red potatoes or other boiling potatoes, scrubbed
2 sweet red peppers
2 garlic cloves, peeled and crushed
1 tsp. chopped fresh rosemary, or ½ tsp. dried rosemary, crumbled
¼ tsp. salt
cayenne pepper
2 tbsp. red wine vinegar
2 tbsp. virgin olive oil
6 oz. arugula, washed and dried, or 2 bunches watercress, stemmed, washed and dried

Put the potatoes into a large saucepan and cover them with cold water. Bring the water to a boil and cook the potatoes until they are tender when pierced with the tip of a sharp knife — about 25 minutes. Drain the potatoes and set them aside to cool.

While the potatoes are boiling, roast the peppers about 2 inches below a preheated broiler, turning them often, until they are blistered on all sides. Put the peppers into a bowl and cover the bowl with plastic wrap; the trapped steam will loosen their skins. Peel the peppers, then seed and derib them. Put the peppers into a food processor or a blender along with the garlic, rosemary, salt and a pinch of cayenne pepper. Purée the mixture to obtain a smooth sauce. With the motor still running, pour in the vinegar, then the oil; continue blending the sauce until it is well combined.

Cut the potatoes in half and then into wedges. Arrange the wedges on a bed of arugula leaves or watercress. Pour some of the sauce over the potatoes and serve the rest alongside.

Endive Salad with Orange and Rosemary

Serves 6 as a first course or side dish
Working (and total) time: about 25 minutes

Calories **70**
Protein **2g.**
Cholesterol **0mg.**
Total fat **4g.**
Saturated fat **1g.**
Sodium **105mg.**

1 garlic clove, cut in half
1 head of curly endive (chicory), washed and dried
3 small heads of Belgian endive, washed, dried and sliced crosswise into ½-inch-wide strips
1 navel orange
1 small red onion, thinly sliced
1 tbsp. chopped fresh rosemary, or 1 tsp. dried rosemary, crumbled
⅛ tsp. salt
2 tbsp. sherry vinegar or red wine vinegar
1 tbsp. grainy mustard
1½ tbsp. virgin olive oil

Rub the inside of a salad bowl with the cut surfaces of the garlic clove. Put all the endive leaves in the bowl.

Working over a bowl to catch the juice, cut away the peel, white pith and outer membrane from the flesh of the orange. To separate the segments from the membranes, slice down to the core with a sharp knife on either side of each segment and set the segments aside. Cut each segment in thirds and add them to the bowl along with the onion and rosemary.

In a small bowl, whisk together the salt, reserved orange juice, vinegar and mustard. Whisking constantly, pour in the oil in a thin, steady stream to create an emulsified dressing. Pour the dressing over the contents of the salad bowl; toss the salad thoroughly and serve it at once.

Belgian Endive and Watercress Salad

Serves 6 as a first course or side dish
Working (and total) time: about 30 minutes

Calories **70**
Protein **2g.**
Cholesterol **0mg.**
Total fat **5g.**
Saturated fat **1g.**
Sodium **140mg.**

2 heads of Belgian endive
1 bunch of watercress, stemmed, washed and dried
12 mushrooms, stems trimmed, caps wiped clean and thinly sliced
18 cherry tomatoes, halved
Dill-mustard vinaigrette
1 tbsp. herb-flavored mustard or Dijon mustard
1½ tbsp. fresh lemon juice
3 scallions, trimmed, the green parts reserved for another use, the white parts finely chopped
2 tbsp. finely cut fresh dill, or 1½ tbsp. dried dill
¼ tsp. salt
freshly ground black pepper
1 tbsp. safflower oil
1 tbsp. virgin olive oil

To make the vinaigrette, combine the mustard, lemon juice, scallions, dill, salt and some pepper in a small bowl. Whisking vigorously, pour in the safflower oil in a thin, steady stream; incorporate the olive oil the same way. Set the vinaigrette aside.

Separate the endive leaves from their cores. Arrange the endive leaves, watercress, mushrooms and tomatoes on individual plates. Spoon the vinaigrette over the salads and serve them immediately.

Red, White and Green Salad

Serves 6 as a first course or side dish
Working time: about 20 minutes
Total time: about 1 hour

Calories **60**
Protein **2g.**
Cholesterol **0mg.**
Total fat **4g.**
Saturated fat **0g.**
Sodium **75mg.**

1 beet (about ½ lb.), rinsed
3 tbsp. raspberry vinegar or red wine vinegar
2 tsp. Dijon mustard
2 tsp. grainy mustard
¼ tsp. honey
freshly ground black pepper
1 ½ tbsp. virgin olive oil

1 head of radicchio, halved, cored, washed, dried and cut into chiffonade
1 large head of Belgian endive, cored, cut in half crosswise, the halves julienned
¼ lb. mâche (corn salad or lamb's lettuce), washed and dried, or 1 small head of Boston or Bibb lettuce, washed, dried and torn into pieces

Put the beet into a saucepan, pour in enough water to cover the beet, and bring the water to a boil. Cook the beet until it is tender — about 30 minutes. Drain the beet and let it cool before peeling and finely dicing it.

Put the diced beet in a small bowl, and toss it with 1 tablespoon of the vinegar.

To make the dressing, combine the mustards, the honey, the remaining 2 tablespoons of vinegar and a liberal grinding of pepper in a bowl. Whisk in the oil.

In another bowl, toss the radicchio and endive with two thirds of the dressing. Separately toss the mâche or lettuce with the remaining dressing.

To assemble the salad, mound the radicchio-endive mixture in the center of a platter and surround it with the mâche or lettuce. Scatter the diced beet on top.

Cutting Chiffonade

1 *ROLLING THE LEAVES. Pluck the leaves from a head of spinach, lettuce or cabbage (here, radicchio). Gently wash and dry the leaves. Stack three to four leaves and roll them into a bundle.*

2 *CUTTING THE ROLL. Holding the bundle with your fingers curled under for safety, square the end by cutting off the rounded tips of the leaves. Slice across the roll at approximately ⅛-inch intervals to produce the thin strips called chiffonade.*

Spinach and Sesame Salad

Serves 6 as a side dish
Working (and total) time: about 30 minutes

Calories **60**
Protein **4g.**
Cholesterol **0mg.**
Total fat **5g.**
Saturated fat **0g.**
Sodium **255mg.**

½ cup unsalted chicken stock
1 tbsp. hulled sesame seeds
1 tbsp. tahini (sesame paste)
1 tsp. dark sesame oil
1 ½ tbsp. low-sodium soy sauce
1 tbsp. fresh lemon juice
1 tsp. finely chopped fresh ginger
1 lb. spinach, washed, stemmed and dried
¼ lb. mushrooms, wiped clean and thinly sliced (about 1 cup)
1 large ripe tomato, sliced into thin wedges
⅛ tsp. salt
freshly ground black pepper

Boil the stock in a small saucepan until only 2 tablespoons remain — about seven minutes.

While the stock is reducing, toast the sesame seeds in a small, heavy-bottomed skillet over medium-low heat until they are golden — about three minutes. Set the skillet aside.

To prepare the dressing, mix the tahini and sesame oil in a small bowl. Whisk in the reduced stock, the soy sauce, lemon juice and ginger.

Put the spinach and mushrooms into a large bowl. Sprinkle the tomato wedges with the salt and pepper and add them to the bowl. Pour the dressing over the vegetables, grind in some more pepper, and toss well. Scatter the sesame seeds over the salad and serve.

Escarole Chiffonade with Mild and Hot Peppers

Serves 6 as a side dish
Working time: about 20 minutes
Total time: about 45 minutes

Calories **55**
Protein **2g.**
Cholesterol **0mg.**
Total fat **4g.**
Saturated fat **1g.**
Sodium **125mg.**

½ cup unsalted veal or chicken stock
2 ancho peppers, seeded, one coarsely chopped, the other very thinly sliced
1 dried hot red pepper, seeded and crushed
1 shallot, coarsely chopped
1 ½ tbsp. red wine vinegar
¾ tsp. sugar
¼ tsp. salt
freshly ground black pepper
1 ½ tbsp. virgin olive oil
1 tbsp. fresh lime juice
1 large head of escarole (about 1 ½ lb.), trimmed, cut in half through the core, washed and dried

In a small skillet, combine the stock, ancho peppers, hot red pepper, shallot, vinegar, sugar, salt and some pepper. Bring the mixture to a simmer and cook it over low heat, stirring frequently, until only about 3 tablespoons of liquid remain — seven to 10 minutes.

Transfer the contents of the skillet to a blender. Add the oil and lime juice and purée the mixture to obtain a smooth dressing. Transfer the dressing to a large bowl; immediately add the sliced ancho pepper. Refrigerate the dressing until it is cool — about 15 minutes.

Lay an escarole half on a work surface cut side down and slice it into chiffonade. Repeat the process with the other half. Toss the chiffonade with the dressing and serve the salad at once.

Gingery Cauliflower Salad

Serves 4 as a first course or side dish
Working time: about 20 minutes
Total time: about 45 minutes

Calories **60**
Protein **1g.**
Cholesterol **0mg.**
Total fat **4g.**
Saturated fat **0g.**
Sodium **150mg.**

1 head of cauliflower, trimmed and cut into florets
one 1-inch piece of fresh ginger, peeled and julienned
1 carrot, julienned
2 tbsp. white vinegar
½ tsp. sugar
¼ tsp. salt
⅛ tsp. cayenne pepper
1 tbsp. safflower oil
¼ tsp. dark sesame oil
1 scallion, trimmed, the green part julienned and soaked in ice water, the white part sliced diagonally into thin ovals

Mound the cauliflower florets on a heatproof plate to resemble a whole head of cauliflower. Scatter the ginger and carrot julienne over the cauliflower.

Combine the vinegar, sugar, salt and cayenne pepper in a small bowl. Whisk in the safflower oil and pour the dressing over the cauliflower.

Pour enough water into a large pot to fill it about 1 inch deep. Stand two or three small heatproof bowls in the water and set the plate with the cauliflower on top of the bowls. Cover the pot, bring the water to a boil and steam the cauliflower until it can be easily pierced with a knife — 15 to 20 minutes.

Remove the lid and let the steam dissipate. Lift the plate out of the pot and let the cauliflower stand until it cools to room temperature. Drizzle the sesame oil over the cauliflower and scatter the green and white scallion parts on top. Serve the salad at room temperature or chilled.

Tomato Fans with Basil, Ham and Provolone

Serves 4 as a first course or side dish
Working time: about 20 minutes
Total time: about 35 minutes

Calories **105**
Protein **5g.**
Cholesterol **11mg.**
Total fat **7g.**
Saturated fat **2g.**
Sodium **280mg.**

2 large, ripe tomatoes, cored
¼ tsp. sugar
⅛ tsp. salt
freshly ground black pepper
2 tbsp. sherry vinegar or red wine vinegar
1 shallot, finely chopped
1 tbsp. virgin olive oil
2 garlic cloves, crushed
1½ oz. thinly sliced prosciutto, julienned
2 thin slices provolone cheese (about 1 oz.), julienned
2 tbsp. thinly sliced fresh basil leaves
1 small head of Boston lettuce or 1 head of Bibb lettuce (about ¼ lb.), washed and dried

Halve the tomatoes from top to bottom, then, with the cut side down, thinly slice each half, and set it aside intact. Transfer the sliced halves to a plate. Gently fan out each half. Sprinkle the tomatoes with the sugar, salt and a generous grinding of pepper, then drizzle 1 tablespoon of the vinegar over them. Refrigerate the tomatoes for about 10 minutes.

Meanwhile, prepare the dressing. Put the shallot and the remaining 1 tablespoon of vinegar into a bowl. Whisk in the oil. Add the garlic, ham, cheese, basil and some more pepper, and stir the mixture to combine it; set it aside.

Arrange the lettuce on a serving platter and place the tomato fans on the leaves. Remove the garlic cloves from the dressing and spoon ¼ of it on each tomato fan. Serve the salad immediately.

Baby Leeks in Caper-Cream Vinaigrette

Serves 6 as a first course
Working time: about 20 minutes
Total time: about 45 minutes

Calories **190**
Protein **2g.**
Cholesterol **3mg.**
Total fat **4g.**
Saturated fat **1g.**
Sodium **200mg.**

12 baby leeks (about 1½ lb.), trimmed, green tops cut to within 2 inches of the white part
2 tsp. fresh thyme, or ½ tsp. dried thyme leaves
2 shallots, finely chopped
¼ tsp. salt
freshly ground black pepper
1 tbsp. fresh lemon juice
1 tbsp. red wine vinegar
1 tsp. capers, rinsed and chopped
1 tbsp. virgin olive oil
2 tbsp. light table cream
2 tbsp. chopped sweet red pepper
1 garlic clove, very finely chopped

Wash each leek to remove the grit: Without splitting the leek or detaching any leaves, gently pry apart the leaves and run cold water between them to force out the dirt. Shake the excess water from the leaves and repeat the washing process. Arrange the leeks in a skillet large enough to hold them in a single layer. Pour in just enough water to cover the leeks; add the thyme, half of the shallots, ⅛ teaspoon of the salt and a lavish grinding of pepper. Poach the leeks over medium-low heat for 10 minutes. Gently turn the leeks over, and continue poaching them until they are tender — about 10 minutes more. Transfer the leeks to a plate lined with a double thickness of paper towels. Refrigerate the leeks until they are cool — at least 20 minutes.

About 10 minutes before the leeks are sufficiently chilled, combine the remaining shallots in a small bowl with the lemon juice, vinegar, capers, the remaining ⅛ teaspoon of salt and some more pepper. Let the vinaigrette stand for five minutes, then whisk in the oil, cream, red pepper and garlic.

Transfer the cooled leeks to a serving dish. Pour the vinaigrette over the leeks and serve them at once.

Braised Endive and Red Pepper Salad

Serves 6 as a side dish
Working time: about 30 minutes
Total time: about 2 hours (includes chilling)

Calories **38**
Protein **1g.**
Cholesterol **0mg.**
Total fat **2g.**
Saturated fat **0g.**
Sodium **108mg.**

2 sweet red peppers	
1 tbsp. olive oil, preferably virgin	
4 heads of Belgian endive (about 1 lb.), trimmed and cut into 1-inch pieces	
1 tbsp. fresh thyme, or 1 tsp. dried thyme leaves	
1 tbsp. fresh lemon juice	
¼ tsp. salt	
3 scallions, trimmed and cut into 1-inch pieces	
freshly ground black pepper	
2 tbsp. sherry vinegar, or 1½ tbsp. red wine vinegar	

To prepare the peppers, place them about 2 inches below a preheated broiler. Broil the peppers, turning them as their sides become scorched, until their skin has blistered all over. Transfer the peppers to a bowl and cover it with plastic wrap, or put them in a paper bag and fold it shut; the trapped steam will make the peppers limp and loosen their skins — about 15 minutes. With a paring knife, peel off the peppers' skins in sections, peeling from top to bottom. Remove the stems, ribs and seeds from the peppers, working over a bowl to catch the juices. Strain the pepper juices into another bowl and set it aside. Slice the peppers lengthwise into ½-inch-wide, 2-inch-long strips and add them to the juices.

Heat the oil in a large, heavy-bottomed skillet over medium heat. Add the endive and the thyme and cook the mixture, stirring constantly, until the endive begins to wilt — about five minutes. Stir in the lemon juice, salt, scallions and some pepper, then cook the mixture for three minutes more, stirring frequently. Add the peppers with their juices and the vinegar; continue cooking for two minutes. Scrape the contents of the skillet into a bowl, then refrigerate the salad until it is cool — about one hour and 30 minutes. The salad may be served chilled or at room temperature.

EDITOR'S NOTE: *This dish can be made a day in advance and refrigerated until serving time.*

Sweet Potato Salad with Curried Yogurt Dressing

Serves 6 as a side dish
Working time: about 30 minutes
Total time: about 2 hours (includes chilling)

Calories **120**
Protein **3g.**
Cholesterol **2mg.**
Total fat **1g.**
Saturated fat **0g.**
Sodium **60mg.**

1 lb. sweet potatoes (yams)
4 celery stalks, thinly sliced
3 scallions, trimmed and thinly sliced
½ cup yogurt dressing mixed with 1 ½ tsp. curry powder
1 tbsp. each finely cut fresh chives and chopped fresh parsley, or 2 tbsp. chopped fresh parsley

Put the sweet potatoes in a deep saucepan and pour in enough water to cover them. Bring the water to a boil and cook the sweet potatoes over medium heat until they are tender — 25 to 30 minutes. Drain the sweet potatoes; when they are cool enough to handle, peel them and cut them into small dice. Put the sweet potatoes in a bowl with the celery and scallions.

Add the dressing to the vegetables and mix gently. Chill the salad for at least one hour. Just before serving, sprinkle the fresh herbs over the top.

EDITOR'S NOTE: *This salad makes a delicious accompaniment to grilled chicken or pork.*

Summer Vegetables in Tomato Aspic

Serves 16 as a side dish
Working time: about 30 minutes
Total time: about 4 hours and 30 minutes
(includes chilling)

Calories **50**
Protein **3g.**
Cholesterol **0mg.**
Total fat **1g.**
Saturated fat **0g.**
Sodium **50mg.**

1½ cups fresh corn kernels (cut from 2 small ears), or 1½ cups frozen corn kernels, defrosted
28 oz. canned unsalted tomatoes, puréed in a food processor or blender
1 hydroponic cucumber, seeded and chopped, or 2 regular cucumbers, peeled, seeded and chopped
½ sweet red pepper, seeded, deribbed and chopped
½ green pepper, seeded, deribbed and chopped
1 small onion, finely chopped
1 tbsp. red wine vinegar
1 tbsp. virgin olive oil
6 drops hot red-pepper sauce

¼ tsp. celery seeds
¼ tsp. salt
freshly ground black pepper
2 tbsp. powdered unflavored gelatin
1½ cups cold unsalted chicken or vegetable stock
1 head of Boston lettuce, or 2 heads of Bibb lettuce, washed and dried

If you are using fresh corn, pour enough water into a saucepan to fill it about 1 inch deep. Set a vegetable steamer in the pan and bring the water to a boil. Put the fresh corn into the steamer; frozen corn does not require steaming. Tightly cover the pan and steam the corn for three minutes.

In a large bowl, combine the puréed tomatoes, the cucumber, red and green pepper, onion, corn, vinegar,

oil, red-pepper sauce, celery seeds, salt and some pepper. Set the bowl aside.

Stir the gelatin into ½ cup of the stock and set the mixture aside for a minute or two. Bring the remaining cup of stock to a boil, then remove it from the heat; add the gelatin-stock mixture and stir until the gelatin is dissolved.

Add the gelatin and stock to the vegetables and stir well to distribute the gelatin evenly. Pour the mixture into an 8-cup mold and chill it until it is firm — at least four hours.

Shortly before serving the salad, run the tip of a knife around the inside of the mold to loosen the sides. Briefly dip the bottom of the mold in hot water. Invert a plate on top of the mold, then turn both over together; if necessary, rap the bottom of the mold to free the salad. Lift away the mold and garnish the salad with the lettuce. Serve the salad immediately.

Broccoli Salad with Oven-Roasted Mushrooms

Serves 8 as a first course or side dish
Working (and total) time: about 1 hour and 15 minutes

Calories **105**
Protein **6g.**
Cholesterol **0mg.**
Total fat **4g.**
Saturated fat **0g.**
Sodium **150mg.**

2 lb. mushrooms, wiped clean, the stems trimmed
4 large shallots, thinly sliced lengthwise
⅓ cup fresh lemon juice
2½ tbsp. fresh thyme, or 2 tsp. dried thyme leaves
¼ tsp. salt
freshly ground black pepper
1 tbsp. safflower oil
2½ lb. broccoli, stemmed and cut into florets
1 head of red- or green-leaf lettuce, washed and dried
Mustard dressing
2 tbsp. grainy mustard
3 tbsp. balsamic vinegar, or 2½ tbsp. red wine vinegar mixed with 1 tsp. honey
1 tbsp. chopped fresh parsley
2 tsp. chopped fresh oregano, or ½ tsp. dried oregano
freshly ground black pepper
1 tbsp. safflower oil

Preheat the oven to 450° F. Put the mushrooms in a large baking dish. Add the shallots, lemon juice, thyme, salt, some pepper and the tablespoon of oil; toss the mixture to coat the mushrooms. Spread the mushrooms in a single layer, then roast them until they are tender and most of the liquid has evaporated — 20 to 25 minutes. Remove the mushrooms from the oven and keep the dish warm.

While the mushrooms are cooking, make the dressing. Combine the mustard, vinegar, parsley, oregano and some pepper in a small bowl. Whisking vigorously, pour in the tablespoon of oil in a thin, steady stream. Continue whisking until the dressing is well combined; set the dressing aside.

Pour enough water into a saucepan to fill it about 1 inch deep. Set a vegetable steamer in the pan and bring the water to a boil. Put the broccoli florets into the steamer, cover the pan, and steam the broccoli until it is tender but still crisp — about four minutes. Add the broccoli to the dish with the mushrooms. Pour the dressing over the vegetables and toss the salad well. Arrange the salad on a bed of the lettuce leaves; it may be served warm or chilled.

Pasta, Corn, and Leek Salad

Serves 6 as a side dish
Working time: about 20 minutes
Total time: about 30 minutes

Calories **260**
Protein **10g.**
Cholesterol **0mg.**
Total fat **4g.**
Saturated fat **1g.**
Sodium **110mg.**

3 oz. pasta spirals
4 ears of corn, husked, or 1 lb. frozen corn kernels
2 cups white parts of leek, cut into thin rounds
2 large tomatoes, cut into thin wedges
2 black olives, pitted and diced
Mustard-basil dressing
1 tbsp. fresh lemon juice
1 tsp. Dijon mustard
⅓ cup low-fat yogurt
¼ tsp. salt
freshly ground black pepper
¼ cup chopped fresh basil

Cook the pasta spirals in 1 quart of boiling water with 1 teaspoon of salt. Start testing the pasta after six minutes, and continue cooking it until it is al dente. Refresh the pasta under cold running water and drain it thoroughly.

If you are using fresh corn, cook it in a saucepan of boiling water for 6 to 10 minutes, until it is just tender. Refresh the ears under cold running water and drain them well. Using a sharp knife, cut off the corn kernels. If you are using frozen corn, blanch it in boiling water and drain it thoroughly.

Parboil the leeks until they are just tender but still have bite—one to two minutes. Refresh them under cold running water and drain them well.

For the dressing, blend the lemon juice and mustard into the yogurt, then stir in the salt, some pepper, and the basil. Transfer the pasta, corn, and leeks to a lidded, nonreactive container, pour on the dressing, and toss the salad gently to combine the ingredients. Cover the salad and chill it until it is needed.

Put the container of dressed salad into a cooler. Pack the tomato wedges and olive dice in separate small containers, and put these in the cooler too. To serve, arrange the tomato wedges around the edge of a serving bowl, pile the salad in the center, and sprinkle the olive dice over the top.

Artichoke and Asparagus Salad

Serves 8 as a side dish
Working time: about 45 minutes
Total time: about 1 hour

Calories **55**
Protein **3g.**
Cholesterol **trace**
Total fat **3g.**
Saturated fat **1g.**
Sodium **105mg.**

1 lemon, cut in half
4 artichokes
1 lb. thin asparagus, trimmed
1 head red-leaf lettuce, leaves separated, washed, and dried, and torn into large pieces
4 heads Bibb lettuce, cut into 1-by-½-inch chunks, washed and dried

Orange-hazelnut vinaigrette

2 tbsp. fresh orange juice
1½ tbsp. hazelnut oil
1 tsp. grainy mustard
½ orange, grated zest only
½ tsp. salt
freshly ground black pepper

Fill a large, nonreactive pan with water. Squeeze the juice from one lemon half into the pan, then add the lemon half itself.

Remove two or three outer layers of leaves from one of the artichokes to expose the tender, yellow-green inner leaves. Using a stainless-steel knife, slice through the artichoke about 1½ inches above the rounded base and discard the top. Cut off the stem flush with the rounded end of the artichoke, and rub the base with the cut surface of the second lemon half. Pare off the dark green bases of the leaves, then trim away the light green parts from the upper half of the artichoke, moistening the cut surfaces with the lemon half as you work. With a teaspoon, scrape out and discard the hairy choke from the center of the vegetable. Drop the artichoke heart that remains into the pan of acidulated water to preserve its color. Prepare the remaining artichokes in the same way.

Bring the pan of artichoke hearts to a boil, and simmer them until they can be pierced easily with the tip of a sharp knife—10 to 12 minutes. Refresh the artichoke hearts under cold running water, then cut each one into 16 pieces.

While the artichokes are cooking, cook the asparagus in a large, shallow pan of boiling water to cover until it is tender—one to two minutes. Refresh the asparagus under cold running water and drain it thoroughly. Cut the spears diagonally into 1-inch pieces, keeping the tips intact.

Put the red-leaf and Bibb lettuce, the artichoke hearts, and the asparagus into a lidded container, and chill them in the refrigerator until they are needed. Put all the ingredients for the vinaigrette into a screw-top jar, and shake them together well. Store the jar of vinaigrette in the refrigerator.

Pack the container of salad and the jar of vinaigrette inside a cooler. At the picnic site, transfer the salad to a bowl. Pour on the dressing and toss the salad gently just before serving.

Salad of Red Leaves, Beans, and Roots

Serves 12 as a side dish
Working time: about 40 minutes
Total time: about 3 hours

Calories **100**
Protein **4g.**
Cholesterol **5mg.**
Total fat **6g.**
Saturated fat **2g.**
Sodium **75mg.**

6 oz. dried red kidney beans (about ¾ cup), picked over
½ lb. red cabbage, finely shredded
1 small red onion, quartered and finely sliced
2 medium beets, peeled and grated
1 head radicchio, leaves washed and dried
1 oz. Stilton cheese, crumbled
1 tsp. poppy seeds
Walnut vinaigrette
1 tsp. grainy mustard
⅛ tsp. hot red-pepper sauce
⅛ tsp. salt
freshly ground black pepper
2 tbsp. red wine vinegar
¼ cup walnut oil

Rinse the kidney beans under cold running water, then put them into a large saucepan with enough cold water to cover them by about 3 inches. Discard any beans that float to the surface. Cover the saucepan, leaving the lid ajar, and slowly bring the liquid to a boil.

Lower the heat and simmer the beans until they are tender—about one hour. Check the water level from time to time and add more hot water if necessary. Drain and rinse the beans when they are cooked. Dry them thoroughly.

Put the shredded red cabbage into a large bowl with the kidney beans, onion, and beets. Mix these ingredients together well. Next, make the dressing. In a small, nonreactive bowl, whisk together the mustard, hot red-pepper sauce, salt, pepper, vinegar, and walnut oil. Pour the dressing over the salad and toss it well. Transfer the salad to a covered, nonreactive container, and chill it until you are ready to leave for the picnic. Place the radicchio leaves in a plastic bag, and the Stilton in a small, sealed container, and chill these too. Fold the poppy seeds in a sheet of paper towel.

At the picnic, line a large salad bowl with the radicchio leaves. Pile the salad in the center, and sprinkle the Stilton and poppy seeds over the top.

EDITOR'S NOTE: *This salad may also be made with canned red kidney beans; rinse the beans thoroughly before use.*

Green and White Rice Salad

Serves 12 as a side dish
Working time: about 25 minutes
Total time: about 45 minutes

Calories **105**
Protein **2g.**
Cholesterol **0mg.**
Total fat **5g.**
Saturated fat **1g.**
Sodium **123mg.**

2 cups unsalted vegetable stock
¾ cup long-grain rice
14 oz. fresh peas, shelled (about 2½ cups), or ¼ lb. frozen peas, thawed
½ cucumber, cut into ¼-inch dice
1 small zucchini, trimmed and julienned
6 scallions, trimmed and thinly sliced diagonally
1 tbsp. finely cut chives
3 tbsp. chopped fresh parsley
1 large head Bibb lettuce, leaves washed and dried
Tarragon vinaigrette
½ tsp. Dijon mustard
⅛ tsp. salt
freshly ground black pepper
2 tbsp. tarragon vinegar
¼ cup walnut or virgin olive oil

Bring the stock to a boil in a small saucepan and add the rice. Lower the heat to a simmer and cook the rice, covered, until it is just tender and all the stock has been absorbed—15 to 20 minutes. Set the rice aside to cool.

Blanch the fresh peas in boiling water for about 30 seconds; if you are using frozen peas, add them to boiling water and just bring the water back to a boil. Drain the peas, refresh them under cold running water, and drain them again.

Transfer the cooled rice to a large bowl, add the peas, cucumber, and zucchini, and mix the ingredients together well. Stir in the scallions, chives, and parsley.

To make the dressing, whisk the mustard, salt, pepper, vinegar, and oil together in a small, nonreactive bowl. Pour the dressing over the salad, and toss it thoroughly. Place the dressed salad in a covered, nonreactive container to take to the picnic, and chill it until you are ready to leave. Place the lettuce leaves in a plastic bag and chill them too.

At the picnic, line a large serving bowl with the lettuce leaves and pile the salad in the center.

Millet Tabbouleh

TABBOULEH, A MIDDLE EASTERN SALAD, IS TRADITIONALLY
MADE WITH BULGUR. HERE MILLET PROVIDES A NEW TOUCH.

Serves 6 as a side dish
Working time: about 15 minutes
Total time: about 1 hour (includes chilling)

Calories **160**
Protein **4g.**
Cholesterol **0mg.**
Total fat **4g.**
Saturated fat **0g.**
Sodium **80mg.**

1 cup millet
⅛ tsp. salt
freshly ground black pepper
⅓ cup raisins
3 cups loosely packed stemmed parsley sprigs
1 shallot, finely chopped
2 tbsp. finely chopped cilantro
2 tbsp. fresh lemon juice
2 tsp. honey
2 tsp. Dijon mustard
1 tbsp. safflower oil
1 head of Boston lettuce, or 2 heads of Bibb lettuce, washed and dried

Pour 2 cups of water into a saucepan and bring it to a
simmer over medium heat. Stir in the millet, salt and a
generous grinding of pepper. Cover the pan and cook
the millet until the water level drops just below the
surface of the millet — 10 to 15 minutes. Stir in the
raisins and reduce the heat to low; continue cooking
the millet, covered, until all the water has been absorbed — about seven minutes more.

Transfer the contents of the pan to a large bowl.
Immediately stir in the parsley sprigs; the hot millet will
cook them slightly. Loosely cover the bowl with plastic
wrap and allow the millet to cool.

Meanwhile, combine the shallot, cilantro, lemon
juice, honey and mustard in a small bowl. Whisk in
the oil. When the millet has cooled to room temperature, pour the dressing over it and toss the salad well.
Serve chilled with the lettuce.

Polenta Salad with Ham

Serves 6 as a first course or side dish
Working time: about 40 minutes
Total time: about 50 minutes

Calories **140**
Protein **4g.**
Cholesterol **5mg.**
Total fat **4g.**
Saturated fat **1g.**
Sodium **220mg.**

¼ tsp. salt
1 tsp. dried oregano, or 1 tbsp. chopped fresh oregano
1 cup stone-ground cornmeal
1 tbsp. virgin olive oil
3 scallions, trimmed and sliced, the white parts kept separate from the green
2 ripe tomatoes (about 1 lb.), peeled, seeded and chopped
¼ cup red wine vinegar
freshly ground black pepper
1 slice of ham (about 2 oz.), diced

Bring 2¼ cups of water to a boil in a large saucepan
with ⅛ teaspoon of the salt and half of the oregano.

Sprinkle in the cornmeal, stirring continuously with a
wooden spoon. Reduce the heat to medium and cook
the polenta, stirring constantly, until all the liquid has
been absorbed and the polenta is quite stiff — 10 to 15
minutes. Spoon the polenta onto a large, lightly oiled
plate and spread it out to a uniform thickness of about
½ inch. Refrigerate the polenta uncovered while you
prepare the dressing. Preheat the oven to 350° F.

Heat the oil in a heavy-bottomed skillet over medium heat. Add the white scallion parts and the remaining oregano, and cook them for one minute. Stir in the
tomatoes, vinegar, the remaining ⅛ teaspoon of salt
and some pepper. Cook the mixture, stirring occasionally, for 15 minutes. Transfer the contents of the pan to
a blender or food processor, and purée the mixture
until a smooth dressing results. Pour the dressing into a
large bowl and chill it while you finish the salad.

Cut the polenta into strips about ½ inch wide and
1½ inches long. Transfer the strips to a lightly oiled
baking sheet and bake them for 10 minutes to dry
them out, turning them occasionally with a metal spatula. Immediately transfer the strips to the bowl with
the dressing. Add the green scallion parts, the ham and
a generous grinding of pepper. Toss the salad well and
serve it without delay.

Brown Rice and Mango Salad

Serves 8 as a side dish
Working time: about 20 minutes
Total time: about 1 hour and 30 minutes

Calories **140**
Protein **2g.**
Cholesterol **0mg.**
Total fat **4g.**
Saturated fat **0g.**
Sodium **70mg.**

1 cup brown rice
¼ cup red wine vinegar
¼ tsp. salt
2 tbsp. safflower oil
1 cubanelle or other mild green pepper, seeded and diced
1 small shallot, finely chopped
⅛ tsp. ground cardamom
mace
cayenne pepper
1 ripe mango, peeled and diced

Bring 6 cups of water to a boil in a large saucepan. Stir in the rice, reduce the heat and simmer the rice, uncovered, until it is tender — about 35 minutes. Drain the rice and put it in a serving bowl. Stir in the vinegar and salt, and allow the mixture to cool to room temperature — about 30 minutes.

When the rice is cool, stir in the oil, pepper, shallot, cardamom and a pinch each of mace and cayenne pepper. Add the mango pieces and stir them in gently so that they retain their shape. Cover the salad; to allow the flavors to meld, let the salad stand, unrefrigerated, for about 30 minutes before serving it.

Kasha with Wild Mushrooms and Peas

Serves 6 as a side dish
Working (and total) time: about 45 minutes

Calories **110**
Protein **4g.**
Cholesterol **0mg.**
Total fat **3g.**
Saturated fat **0g.**
Sodium **90mg.**

¼ oz. dried wild mushrooms
1½ lb. fresh green peas, shelled, or 1½ cups frozen peas, defrosted
1 cup kasha (cracked buckwheat groats)
½ lb. fresh mushrooms, wiped clean, stems trimmed
¼ cup fresh lemon juice
1 tbsp. balsamic vinegar, or ¾ tbsp. red wine vinegar mixed with ¼ tsp. honey
1 small shallot, finely chopped
¼ tsp. salt
freshly ground black pepper
1 tbsp. safflower oil

Soak the dried mushrooms in 1 cup of very hot water for 20 minutes, then drain them, reserving their soaking liquid. Chop the mushrooms and set them aside.

If you are using fresh peas, boil them until they are tender — five to seven minutes. (Frozen peas do not require boiling.) Drain the peas and set them aside.

While the mushrooms are soaking, add the kasha to 2 cups of boiling water and cook it, stirring frequently, until it is tender — about five minutes. Drain the kasha, rinse it well, and drain it again. Transfer the kasha to a large bowl.

Slice the fresh mushrooms and put them into a small bowl with the lemon juice; the juice will prevent them from discoloring. Toss the mushrooms well and set the bowl aside.

To prepare the dressing, strain the reserved soaking liquid through a cheesecloth-lined sieve into a small saucepan. Cook the liquid over medium-high heat until only about 2 tablespoons remain — approximately five minutes. Pour the liquid into a small bowl; add the lemon juice from the bowl containing the fresh mushrooms, then add the vinegar, shallot, salt and some pepper. Stir the ingredients together. Whisking vigorously, pour in the oil in a thin, steady stream. Continue whisking until the dressing is well combined. Set the dressing aside.

Add to the kasha the peas, the dried and fresh mushrooms, and the dressing. Combine the ingredients well and serve the salad at once.

Julienned Carrots, Snow Peas and Endive

Serves 6 as a first course or side dish
Working (and total) time: about 20 minutes

Calories **60**
Protein **2g.**
Cholesterol **0mg.**
Total fat **4g.**
Saturated fat **0g.**
Sodium **70mg.**

1 tbsp. very finely chopped shallot
1 garlic clove, lightly crushed
1 tbsp. herbed vinegar or white wine vinegar
1½ tbsp. almond oil or walnut oil
⅛ tsp. salt
freshly ground black pepper
¾ cup julienned carrot
1 cup julienned snow peas
2 heads of Belgian endive (about ½ lb.), cored and julienned

In a large bowl, combine the shallot, garlic and vinegar. Whisk in the oil and season the dressing with the salt and some pepper. Set the dressing aside while you prepare the vegetables.

Add the carrot julienne to 1 quart of boiling water and cook it for one minute. Add the snow peas and cook the vegetables for only 15 seconds longer. Briefly refresh the vegetables under cold running water, then drain them well. Remove the garlic from the dressing and discard it. Add the cooked vegetables and the Belgian endive to the dressing. Toss the salad well and serve it immediately.

Six-Treasure Asian Medley

Serves 10 as a side dish
Working (and total) time: about 40 minutes

Calories **70**
Protein **2g.**
Cholesterol **0mg.**
Total fat **4g.**
Saturated fat **0g.**
Sodium **220mg.**

¾ lb. carrots
¼ lb. snow peas, strings removed
2 small cucumbers, preferably unwaxed
¼ cup sliced water chestnuts
½ lb. Nappa cabbage, sliced crosswise into ½-inch-thick strips
1 sweet red pepper, seeded, deribbed and julienned
Ginger-sesame dressing
1 tsp. Sichuan peppercorns
1 tsp. dry mustard
2 tsp. sugar
3 tbsp. rice vinegar
3 tbsp. low-sodium soy sauce
2 tsp. dark sesame oil
2 tbsp. safflower oil
1 tbsp. finely chopped fresh ginger
3 garlic cloves, finely chopped

With a small paring knife or a channel knife, cut a shallow groove running the length of each carrot. Repeat the cut on the opposite side of each carrot, then slice the carrots diagonally into ovals about ⅛ inch thick. Put the pieces in a saucepan and pour in enough cold water to cover them by about 2 inches. Bring the water to a boil. Reduce the heat and simmer the carrots until they are barely tender — about two minutes. Drain the carrots and transfer them to a large bowl.

Cut a V-shaped notch in each end of each snow pea. Blanch the snow peas in boiling water for 30 seconds. Refresh the snow peas under cold running water, drain them well, and add them to the bowl with the carrots.

Peel the cucumbers, leaving four narrow strips of skin attached to each one. If you are using waxed cucumbers, peel them completely. Halve the cucumbers lengthwise; scoop out the seeds with a melon baller or a teaspoon. Cut the cucumber halves into ⅛-inch-thick slices. Add the cucumber slices, water chestnuts, cabbage and red pepper to the bowl containing the carrots and snow peas.

To prepare the dressing, put the Sichuan peppercorns into a small skillet and set it over medium-high heat. Cook the peppercorns until you see the first wisps of smoke. Transfer the peppercorns to a mortar or a small bowl and crush them with a pestle or the heel of a heavy knife. Whisk together the mustard, sugar, vinegar, soy sauce, sesame oil, safflower oil, peppercorns, ginger and garlic. Toss the vegetables with the dressing and serve at once.

Bulgur Salad with Raisins and Zucchini

Serves 12 as a side dish
Working time: about 20 minutes
Total time: about 1 hour and 30 minutes
(includes soaking and chilling)

Calories **125**
Protein **4g.**
Cholesterol **0mg.**
Total fat **1g.**
Saturated fat **0g.**
Sodium **5mg.**

2 cups bulgur
2 zucchini, each cut crosswise into ¼-inch slices, each slice cut into eight wedges
5 scallions, trimmed and sliced
½ cup red wine vinegar
1 yellow pepper, seeded, deribbed and cut into ½-inch squares
¼ cup raisins
⅛ tsp. cayenne pepper
⅛ tsp. ground cardamom
⅛ tsp. ground coriander
ground cloves
ground ginger
ground mace

Put the bulgur into a heatproof bowl and pour 3 cups of boiling water over it. Cover the bowl and set it aside for 30 minutes.

At the end of the soaking period, mix in the zucchini, scallions, vinegar, yellow pepper, raisins, cayenne pepper, cardamom, coriander, and a pinch each of cloves, ginger and mace. Let the salad stand for at least 30 minutes before serving it either chilled or at room temperature.

Chick-Pea Purée on Romaine Lettuce Leaves

Serves 8 as a first course or side dish
Working time: about 45 minutes
Total time: about 3 hours (includes soaking)

Calories **70**
Protein **5g.**
Cholesterol **2mg.**
Total fat **3g.**
Saturated fat **0g.**
Sodium **60mg.**

1 cup dried chick-peas, picked over
1 garlic clove, quartered
¼ cup celery leaves
¼ cup freshly grated Parmesan cheese
2 tbsp. pine nuts
¼ cup fresh lemon juice
⅛ tsp. white pepper
2 heads of romaine lettuce, washed and dried
1 small ripe tomato, chopped
2 tbsp. chopped red onion
2 tbsp. chopped green pepper (optional)

Rinse the chick-peas under cold running water, then transfer them to a large pot and pour in enough water to cover them by about 2 inches. Discard any chick-peas that float to the surface. Cover the pot, leaving the lid ajar, and bring the liquid to a boil; cook the peas for two minutes. Turn off the heat, cover the pot, and soak the peas for at least an hour. (Alternatively, soak the peas overnight in cold water.)

At the end of the soaking period, drain the chick-peas and return them to the pot with 3 cups of water. Bring the liquid to a strong simmer, then reduce the heat to medium low, and cook the peas, covered, until they are quite tender — about one hour and 15 minutes. (If the peas appear to be drying out at any point, pour in more water, a cup at a time.)

Drain the chick-peas, catching their cooking liquid in a bowl. Set the bowl aside. Press the chick-peas through a sieve, then put them in a blender or food processor with the garlic, celery leaves, Parmesan cheese, pine nuts, 3 tablespoons of the lemon juice and the white pepper. With the motor running, pour in 1 cup of the reserved cooking liquid in a slow, thin stream — a smooth paste should result. If need be, incorporate as much as ½ cup of additional cooking liquid. (Unsalted chicken stock or water may be used to augment the cooking liquid.)

Remove the outer lettuce leaves and reserve them for another use. Spread about 1 tablespoon of the chick-pea purée over the stem end of each inner leaf. Mound the remaining purée in the middle of a serving plate and arrange the leaves around it. Chill the salad for at least 20 minutes. Just before serving, garnish the salad with the tomato, the onion and the green pepper if you are using it; drizzle the remaining tablespoon of lemon juice over the top of the purée.

Black Bean, Rice and Pepper Salad

Serves 4 as a main course
Working time: about 20 minutes
Total time: about 4 hours (includes soaking and chilling)

Calories **635**
Protein **21g.**
Cholesterol **2mg.**
Total fat **10g.**
Saturated fat **1g.**
Sodium **385mg.**

1 cup black beans, picked over
1 small onion, coarsely chopped
1 garlic clove
2 tsp. fresh thyme, or ½ tsp. dried thyme leaves
1 bay leaf
½ tsp. salt
4 cups unsalted chicken stock
2 cups rice
2 shallots, finely chopped
1 sweet red pepper, seeded, deribbed and sliced into short, thin strips
1 green pepper, seeded, deribbed and sliced into short, thin strips
1 jalapeño pepper, seeded and finely chopped
3 scallions, trimmed and thinly sliced
2 tbsp. chopped cilantro or parsley
Chili dressing
1 tsp. Dijon mustard
1 tbsp. sherry vinegar or white wine vinegar
1 tbsp. unsalted chicken stock
2 tbsp. virgin olive oil
½ tsp. chili powder
4 drops hot red-pepper sauce
1 garlic clove, finely chopped
freshly ground black pepper

Rinse the beans under cold running water, then put them into a large, heavy-bottomed pot, and pour in enough cold water to cover them by about 3 inches.

Discard any beans that float to the surface. Cover the pot, leaving the lid ajar, and slowly bring the water to a boil. Cook the beans for two minutes. Then turn off the heat, cover the pot, and soak the beans for at least an hour. (Alternatively, soak the beans overnight in cold water.)

Add the onion, garlic, thyme and bay leaf to the beans; bring the beans to a simmer over medium-low heat and tightly cover the pot. Cook the beans, occasionally skimming foam from the surface of the liquid, until they are soft — about one hour. Stir in the salt and continue cooking the beans until they are quite tender — 30 minutes to one hour more. If the beans appear to be drying out at any point, pour in more water.

Transfer the cooked beans to a colander. Remove the garlic clove and bay leaf, then rinse the beans, and drain them well.

Bring the stock to a boil in a small saucepan. Add the rice and shallots, and lower the heat to maintain a simmer. Cook the rice, covered, until it is tender and the liquid is absorbed — about 20 minutes.

While the rice is cooking, prepare the dressing. Combine the mustard, vinegar and the tablespoon of stock in a small bowl. Whisk in the oil, then the chili powder, red-pepper sauce, garlic and some pepper.

Transfer the hot rice to a large bowl. Add the peppers, scallions and beans. Pour the dressing over the salad, toss well, and chill the salad for at least one hour. Sprinkle the salad with the cilantro or parsley just before serving.

Red Lentils with White Rice and Pearl Onions

Serves 6 as a side dish
Working time: about 15 minutes
Total time: about 30 minutes

Calories **200**
Protein **8g.**
Cholesterol **0mg.**
Total fat **3g.**
Saturated fat **0g.**
Sodium **20mg.**

1 cup red lentils, picked over
½ cup rice
2 tbsp. sugar
4 tbsp. raspberry vinegar
6 tbsp. unsalted chicken stock
1½ cups pearl onions, blanched for 2 minutes in boiling water and peeled
1 tsp. Dijon mustard
freshly ground black pepper
1 tbsp. safflower oil

Bring the lentils and 3 cups of water to a boil in a small saucepan over medium-high heat. Reduce the heat and simmer the lentils until they are tender — 15 to 20 minutes. Avoid overcooking or the lentils will lose much of their color. Drain the lentils and put them into a large bowl.

Start cooking the rice while the lentils are simmering. Bring the rice and 1 cup of water to a boil in a small saucepan over medium-high heat. Reduce the heat, cover the saucepan, and simmer the rice until the liquid has been absorbed and the rice is tender — about 20 minutes. Add the rice to the lentils.

While the rice is cooking, sprinkle the sugar into a skillet and set it over medium heat. Cook the sugar until it liquifies and starts to caramelize. Pour in 3 tablespoons of the vinegar and 4 tablespoons of the chicken stock. As the liquid comes to a simmer, stir it to incorporate the caramelized sugar, then add the pearl onions. Cook the onions, stirring from time to time, until they are glazed and nearly all the liquid in the skillet has evaporated. Add the onions to the lentils and rice.

To prepare the dressing, combine the remaining tablespoon of raspberry vinegar and 2 tablespoons of chicken stock, the mustard and some pepper in a small bowl. Whisk in the oil, then pour the vinaigrette over the lentil-and-rice mixture, and toss well. This salad is best served cold.

Eggplant, Cucumber and White Bean Salad

Serves 12 as a side dish
Working time: about 30 minutes
Total time: about 3 hours (includes soaking and chilling)

Calories **120**
Protein **7g.**
Cholesterol **0mg.**
Total fat **1g.**
Saturated fat **0g.**
Sodium **95mg.**

1 lb. navy beans, picked over
¾ lb. eggplant, cut into ½-inch cubes
1 onion, chopped
½ tsp. sugar
¼ cup raspberry vinegar or red wine vinegar
1 tsp. chopped fresh sage, or ¼ tsp. dried sage, crushed
1 garlic clove, finely chopped
½ tsp. salt
freshly ground black pepper
1 hydroponic cucumber, cut into ½-inch cubes, or 2 regular cucumbers, peeled, seeded and cut into ½-inch cubes

Rinse the beans under cold running water, then put them into a large, heavy pot, and pour in enough cold water to cover them by about 3 inches. Discard any beans that float to the surface. Cover the pot, leaving the lid ajar, and slowly bring the liquid to a boil. Boil the beans for two minutes, then turn off the heat, and soak the beans, covered, for at least an hour. (Alternatively, soak the beans overnight in cold water.)

Preheat the oven to 500° F.

If the beans have absorbed all of their soaking liquid, pour in enough water to cover them again by about 3 inches. Bring the liquid to a boil, reduce the heat to maintain a strong simmer, and cook the beans until they are tender — about one hour.

While the beans are cooking, put the eggplant cubes into a lightly oiled baking dish and bake them until they are a golden brown — about 20 minutes. Meanwhile, combine the onion with the sugar and 2 tablespoons of the vinegar; set the mixture aside. When the eggplant cubes are browned, transfer them to a bowl; toss the cubes with the remaining 2 tablespoons of vinegar and set the bowl aside until the beans finish cooking.

Drain the cooked beans and rinse them under cold running water. Combine them with the marinated eggplant and onion. Add the sage, garlic, salt, some pepper and the cucumber, and mix well. Serve the salad at room temperature or chill it for at least 30 minutes before serving.

Red and White Bean Salad

Serves 8 as a first course or side dish
Working time: about 25 minutes
Total time: about 2 hours and 20 minutes
(includes soaking)

Calories **200**
Protein **11g.**
Cholesterol **0mg.**
Total fat **3g.**
Saturated fat **0g.**
Sodium **95mg.**

½ lb. red kidney beans, picked over
½ lb. Great Northern beans, picked over
1 small celeriac
1 small onion, thinly sliced
2 tsp. finely chopped fresh ginger
¼ cup red wine vinegar
¼ tsp. salt
freshly ground black pepper
1 tbsp. chopped cilantro
1 large, ripe tomato, chopped
1½ tbsp. safflower oil

Rinse the kidney beans under cold running water, then put them into a large pot with enough cold water to cover them by about 3 inches. Rinse the Great Northern beans and put them in a separate pot; pour in enough cold water to cover them by about 3 inches. Discard any beans that float to the surface. Cover the pots, leaving the lids ajar, and slowly bring the liquid in each one to a boil. Boil the beans for two minutes, then turn off the heat, and soak the beans, covered, for at least an hour. (Alternatively, soak the beans overnight in cold water.)

If the beans absorb all of their soaking liquid, add enough water to cover them again by 3 inches. Bring the liquid in each pot to a boil, reduce the heat to maintain a strong simmer, and cook the beans until they are just tender — 50 to 60 minutes.

While the beans are cooking, peel the celeriac and cut it into ½-inch cubes. Transfer the cubes to a salad bowl and toss them with the onion, ginger and vinegar. Set the bowl aside at room temperature.

Drain the cooked beans and rinse them under cold running water. Drain the beans again and add them to the bowl along with the salt, some pepper, the cilantro, tomato and oil; mix well, and serve chilled or at room temperature.

Lentil and Mushroom Salad

Serves 6 as a side dish
Working time: about 40 minutes
Total time: about 1 hour and 40 minutes
(includes chilling)

Calories **165**
Protein **8g.**
Cholesterol **0mg.**
Total fat **5g.**
Saturated fat **1g.**
Sodium **165mg.**

¾ cup lentils, picked over
1 small onion, studded with 4 whole cloves
1 bay leaf
2 tsp. fresh thyme, or ½ tsp. dried thyme leaves
3 carrots, thinly sliced
3 celery stalks, sliced
3 scallions, trimmed and thinly sliced
6 oz. mushrooms, wiped clean, trimmed and thinly sliced
2 tbsp. fresh lemon juice
3 or 4 leaves romaine lettuce, cut into chiffonade
2 ripe tomatoes, each cut into 8 wedges
1 tbsp. chopped parsley

Spicy mustard vinaigrette
1 tbsp. Dijon mustard
2 tbsp. fresh lemon juice
2 tsp. hot red-pepper sauce
2 garlic cloves, finely chopped
¼ tsp. salt
freshly ground black pepper
2 tbsp. virgin olive oil

Rinse the lentils and put them into a saucepan with 4 cups of water. Add the onion, bay leaf and thyme, and bring the water to a boil. Reduce the heat to maintain a simmer and cook the lentils until they are tender — about 25 minutes. Drain the lentils, discard the onion and the bay leaf, and transfer the lentils to a large bowl. Add the carrots, celery and scallions, and toss the mixture well.

Put the mushrooms and the lemon juice into a

saucepan; pour in enough water to just cover the mushrooms, and bring the water to a boil. Cover the pan, reduce the heat, and simmer the mushrooms until they are tender — about five minutes. Drain the mushrooms and add them to the bowl containing the other vegetables.

To prepare the vinaigrette, whisk together the mustard, lemon juice, hot red-pepper sauce, garlic, salt, some pepper and the oil. Pour the vinaigrette over the lentil mixture, toss well, and refrigerate it for at least one hour.

To serve the salad, mound the lentil mixture in the center of a serving plate and arrange the lettuce around the lentil salad. Garnish with the tomato wedges and sprinkle the chopped parsley over all.

Curried Black-Eyed Peas

Serves 6 as a side dish
Working time: about 20 minutes
Total time: about 2 hours and 30 minutes
(includes soaking and chilling)

Calories **105**
Protein **5g.**
Cholesterol **0mg.**
Total fat **3g.**
Saturated fat **0g.**
Sodium **100mg.**

1 cup dried black-eyed peas, picked over
¼ tsp. salt
½ cup unsalted chicken stock
2 bunches scallions, trimmed and cut into 1-inch lengths
1½ tbsp. fresh lemon juice
1 tbsp. red wine vinegar or white wine vinegar
½ tbsp. honey
1¼ tsp. curry powder
freshly ground black pepper
1 tbsp. virgin olive oil
½ sweet red pepper, seeded, deribbed and cut into bâtonnets

Rinse the black-eyed peas under cold running water, then put them into a large saucepan, and pour in enough cold water to cover them by about 3 inches. Discard any peas that float to the surface. Bring the water to a boil and cook the peas for two minutes. Turn off the heat, partially cover the pot, and soak the peas for at least an hour. (Alternatively, soak the peas overnight in cold water.)

Bring the peas to a simmer over medium-low heat and tightly cover the pot. Cook the peas, occasionally skimming any foam from the surface of the liquid, until they begin to soften — about 45 minutes. Stir in the salt and continue cooking the peas until they are quite tender — about 15 minutes more. If the peas appear to be drying out at any point, pour in more water.

While the peas are cooking, heat the stock in a large skillet over medium heat. Add the scallions and partially cover the skillet. Cook the scallions, stirring often, until almost all the liquid has evaporated — eight to 10

minutes. Transfer the contents of the skillet to a bowl.

In a smaller bowl, combine the lemon juice, vinegar, honey, curry powder and some pepper. Whisk in the oil and set the dressing aside.

Transfer the cooked peas to a colander; rinse and drain them. Add the peas and the red pepper to the scallions in the bowl. Pour the dressing over all and toss the salad well. Chill the salad for at least 30 minutes before serving.

Lentil Salad
with Sweet Red Peppers

Serves 12 as a side dish
Working time: about 1 hour
Total time: about 3 hours (includes chilling)

Calories **130**
Protein **6g.**
Cholesterol **11mg.**
Total fat **5g.**
Saturated fat **1g.**
Sodium **140mg.**

1½ cups dried lentils, picked over and rinsed	3 tbsp. very finely chopped fresh chervil (optional)
¼ cup finely chopped fresh tarragon, or 2 tbsp. dried tarragon	¾ tsp. salt
¼ cup tarragon vinegar	freshly ground black pepper
3 sweet red peppers	1 hard-boiled egg
¼ cup virgin olive oil	1 cucumber, preferably unwaxed
8 large garlic cloves	2 or 3 small ripe tomatoes, sliced
¾ cup fresh lemon juice	
¼ cup finely sliced chives or scallions	

Put the lentils in a large, heavy-bottomed pot with 3 cups of water. Bring the water to a boil, then reduce the heat to medium and simmer the lentils until they are tender — about 20 minutes.

If you are using dried tarragon, combine it with the vinegar in a small, nonreactive pan set over medium heat. Bring the liquid to a simmer, then remove the pan from the heat and allow the tarragon to steep for at least 10 minutes.

While the lentils are cooking, roast the peppers about 2 inches below a preheated broiler, turning them until they are blistered on all sides. Place the peppers in a bowl and cover it with plastic wrap; the trapped steam will loosen their skins. Peel and seed the peppers, then finely chop them; set the chopped peppers aside.

Drain the lentils and transfer them to a large bowl. Combine the oil and vinegar in a small bowl and pour the liquid over the lentils. Add the chopped peppers and stir the mixture well, then refrigerate it.

Preheat the oven to 500° F. Place the garlic cloves in a small, ovenproof dish and bake them until they are soft — seven to 10 minutes. When the cloves are cool enough to handle, peel them and press them through a sieve set over a bowl. Whisk the lemon juice into the garlic purée, then stir the purée into the lentil-pepper mixture. Add the chives or scallions, the fresh tarragon and chervil if you are using them, the salt and some pepper; stir well to combine all the ingredients. Refrigerate the salad for at least two hours before serving it.

At serving time, peel the egg and separate the yolk from the white. Press the yolk through a sieve set over a small bowl. Sieve the egg white the same way. Mound the salad on a serving plate; sprinkle half of the egg white and then half of the yolk over the top. (Of course, the whole egg may be used, but doing so will raise the cholesterol level above our guidelines for a side dish.) Cutting the length of the cucumber with a vegetable peeler, pare off alternating strips of skin to achieve a striped effect. Thinly slice the cucumber. Garnish the salad with the sliced cucumber and tomatoes.

EDITOR'S NOTE: *The flavor of this salad will be even better a day later. If you prepare the salad in advance, store it in the refrigerator; do not add the garnishes until serving time.*

Chick-Pea Salad with Cucumber and Dill Sauce

Serves 6 as a side dish
Working time: about 25 minutes
Total time: about 2 hours and 30 minutes
(includes soaking)

Calories **80**
Protein **5g.**
Cholesterol **3mg.**
Total fat **2g.**
Saturated fat **1g.**
Sodium **115mg.**

1 cup dried chick-peas, picked over
2 hydroponic cucumbers, or 4 regular cucumbers, peeled
1 large tomato, peeled, seeded and coarsely chopped
¼ cup finely cut fresh dill
½ cup plain low-fat yogurt
2 tbsp. sour cream
¼ tsp. salt
freshly ground black pepper

Rinse the chick-peas under cold running water, then put them in a large, heavy pot and pour in enough cold water to cover them by about 3 inches. Discard any that float to the surface. Cover the pot, leaving the lid ajar, and slowly bring the liquid to a boil over medium-low heat. Boil the chick-peas for two minutes, then turn off the heat and soak them for at least one hour. (Alternatively, soak the peas overnight in cold water.) If they absorb all the liquid, add enough water to cover them again by about 3 inches. Bring the liquid to a boil, reduce the heat to maintain a strong simmer, and cook the peas until they are tender — about one hour. Drain the peas, rinse them under cold running water, and transfer them to a salad bowl.

Cut one half of one of the hydroponic cucumbers or one of the regular cucumbers into thin slices and set the slices aside. Peel the remaining cucumbers and seed them. Finely chop their flesh and place it on a large square of doubled cheesecloth. Gather the ends and twist them to wring out as much moisture as possible from the cucumbers. Discard the juice.

Combine the chopped cucumber, tomato, dill, yogurt, sour cream, salt and some pepper with the chick-peas, and gently toss the mixture. Serve the salad garnished with the reserved cucumber slices.

8 Unpacked on a grassy spot, an unhurried brunch awaits picnickers (recipes, pages 208-210).

Brunches and Picnics

The day before this picnic brunch, bake the orange-walnut coffeecake and the spinach spongecake for the roulade. Prepare the filling, and fill, roll and wrap the roulade. Make the eggplant relish and the peach dessert. Prepare the bean salad to the point of adding the tomatoes. Wrap or tightly cover all the dishes. Make the raspberry tea, and refrigerate everything.

On the next day, slice the roulade, the coffeecake and the tomato garnish for the green-bean salad. Pack the spinach garnish for the roulade, and put the salad, the compote and the relish into pretty containers with lids. Pack a platter for the roulade and a napkin-lined container for the cake. Pour the chilled tea into a thermos and, if you like, take along some ice cubes.

Apple-Mushroom Spinach Roulade

Serves 8
Working time: about 1 hour and 15 minutes
Total time: about 1 hour and 45 minutes

Calories **124**
Protein **7g.**
Cholesterol **73mg.**
Total fat **5g.**
Saturated fat **1g.**
Sodium **269mg.**

¾ lb. spinach, washed and stemmed, or 5 oz. frozen spinach
½ cup cake flour
¼ cup whole-wheat flour
1 tsp. baking powder
½ tsp. ground mace
¼ tsp. salt
freshly ground black pepper
2 egg yolks
4 egg whites
Apple-mushroom filling
1 large onion, finely chopped
2 apples, peeled, cored and chopped
½ lb. mushrooms, wiped clean and thinly sliced
¼ tsp. salt
freshly ground black pepper
½ cup part-skim ricotta cheese

Line a 12-by-16-inch jelly-roll pan with parchment or wax paper. Lightly butter the paper, then dust it with flour; shake off the excess flour. Set the pan aside.

If you are using fresh spinach, reserve 10 of the leaves for garnish; put the remaining leaves into a large, heavy-bottomed skillet and cook them over medium heat, stirring occasionally, just until they wilt — about three minutes. (The water clinging to the leaves provides enough moisture.) Transfer the spinach to a colander and let it cool. If you are using frozen spinach, thaw it but do not cook it.

Squeeze the spinach into a ball to extract as much liquid as possible. Purée the spinach in a food processor or chop it very finely by hand. Set the spinach aside.

Sift together the cake flour, whole-wheat flour, baking powder, mace, salt and pepper into a small bowl. In another bowl, beat the egg yolks with an electric mixer on high until they are thick — about four minutes. Bring ¼ cup of water to a boil in a small saucepan; gradually pour the water into the egg yolks, beating continuously. Beat the yolks on high speed until they are pale and very fluffy; gently stir in the spinach.

Preheat the oven to 350° F. In another bowl, beat the egg whites until they form soft peaks. Fold the flour mixture into the spinach-egg-yolk mixture, and then fold in the egg whites.

Spread the batter out evenly on the prepared pan. Bake the spinach spongecake until it is set but still tender and moist — eight to 10 minutes. Remove the spongecake from the oven and loosen the edges with the tip of a knife. Cover the cake with a damp towel.

While the spongecake is cooling, make the apple-mushroom filling. Cook the onion and the apples, covered, in a large, nonstick skillet over low heat until the apples are very soft — about 20 minutes. Add the mushrooms and continue to cook the mixture, still covered, until the mushrooms have released their juice — about five minutes more. Remove the cover, increase the heat to medium high, and stir in the salt and some pepper. Simmer the mixture until almost all of the liquid has evaporated — about three minutes. The filling should be moist but not wet. Remove the skillet from the heat. With a wooden spoon, push the ricotta through a sieve held over the skillet; stir the mixture thoroughly.

To assemble the roulade, invert the jelly-roll pan so that the towel is on the bottom. Lift away the pan and peel off the paper. Spread the apple-mushroom filling onto the cake, leaving a ½-inch border all around. Starting at a long side, roll the spongecake into a tight cylinder, using the towel to help guide the rolling process. Trim the ends, wrap the roulade tightly in aluminum foil, and refrigerate it. When you are ready to serve the roulade, slice it and arrange it on a platter garnished with the reserved spinach leaves.

Eggplant-and-Pepper Relish

Serves 8
Working (and total) time: about 45 minutes

Calories **17**
Protein **0g.**
Cholesterol **0mg.**
Total fat **1g.**
Saturated fat **0g.**
Sodium **14mg.**

2 sweet red peppers
1 tsp. safflower oil
½ lb. eggplant, cut into 2-inch julienne
1 cup finely chopped celery
¼ tsp. celery seeds
¼ tsp. ground coriander
⅛ tsp. cayenne pepper
2 tbsp. cider vinegar

Roast the peppers under a preheated broiler, turning them with tongs as they blister, until their skins are blackened all over — about 15 minutes. Transfer the peppers to a bowl and cover it with plastic wrap; the trapped steam will loosen the peppers' skins. When the peppers are cool enough to handle, peel, seed and derib them. Cut the peppers into julienne strips and set them aside.

Heat the oil in a large, nonstick skillet over medium-high heat. Add the eggplant and celery, cooking them until they are soft and lightly browned — about five minutes. Take the skillet off the heat and stir in the red pepper julienne, celery seeds, coriander, cayenne pepper and vinegar. Let the relish cool completely and spoon it into a serving dish. Serve the relish at room temperature.

Green Beans with Garlic and Canadian Bacon

Serves 8
Working time: about 30 minutes
Total time: about 45 minutes

Calories **67**
Protein **4g.**
Cholesterol **7mg.**
Total fat **2g.**
Saturated fat **1g.**
Sodium **120mg.**

1 tsp. safflower oil
1½ lb. fresh green beans, trimmed and cut into 1-inch pieces
2 tbsp. finely chopped garlic
1 tbsp. grated lemon zest
1½ cups unsalted chicken stock
2 oz. Canadian bacon or lean ham, finely chopped
freshly ground black pepper
1 large ripe tomato, cored and cut into wedges

Heat the oil in a large, nonstick skillet over medium heat. Add the green beans, garlic and lemon zest, and cook them for one minute. Pour in the chicken stock, bring the liquid to a boil, and cook the mixture, stirring frequently, until most of the stock has evaporated and the beans are tender — about five minutes.

Remove the skillet from the heat and stir in the Canadian bacon or ham and some pepper. Transfer the beans to a serving plate and let them cool. Arrange the tomato wedges around the beans. Serve the dish at room temperature or chilled.

Orange-Walnut Coffeecake

Serves 8
Working time: about 30 minutes
Total time: about 1 hour

Calories **230**
Protein **3g.**
Cholesterol **0mg.**
Total fat **9g.**
Saturated fat **0g.**
Sodium **168mg.**

1 cup fresh orange juice
½ cup dark brown sugar
¼ cup safflower oil
grated zest of 2 oranges
1¼ cups cake flour
1 tsp. baking powder
1 tsp. baking soda
¾ cup rolled oats
1 egg white
Streusel topping
½ tsp. cinnamon
1 tsp. pure vanilla extract
2 tbsp. chopped walnuts
2 tbsp. rolled oats

Preheat the oven to 350° F. Lightly butter a 9-by-4-inch loaf pan.

Combine the orange juice, brown sugar, oil and orange zest in a large saucepan and bring the mixture to a boil, stirring constantly. Remove the pan from the heat and let the syrup cool while you prepare the remaining ingredients.

Combine the streusel ingredients in a small bowl; set the bowl aside. Sift the cake flour, baking powder ▶

and baking soda together into a bowl. Put the rolled oats in a food processor or a blender and process them into a powder — about 30 seconds. Stir the ground oats into the flour mixture.

When the orange-juice syrup is cool, whisk in the egg white. Stir in the flour mixture until the ingredients are just blended; do not overmix. Pour half of the batter into the prepared pan and then sprinkle half of the streusel mixture over the batter. Pour the remaining batter into the pan and sprinkle the remaining streusel over the top.

Bake the coffeecake until a cake tester inserted into the center comes out clean — 25 to 30 minutes. Let the cake cool in the pan for 15 minutes, then turn it out onto a rack to cool completely before slicing it. Serve the cake slices topped with Fresh Peach Compote.

Fresh Peach Compote

Serves 8
Working time: about 20 minutes
Total time: about 1 hour and 20 minutes
(includes chilling)

Calories **64**
Protein **1g.**
Cholesterol **0mg.**
Total fat **0g.**
Saturated fat **0g.**
Sodium **0mg.**

1½ lb. ripe peaches, peeled, pitted and thinly sliced
3 tbsp. sugar
3 tbsp. Cointreau or other orange-flavored liqueur
6 tbsp. fresh orange juice

Combine the sugar, liqueur and orange juice in a small saucepan. Bring the mixture to a boil over medium heat and cook it for one minute. Put the peaches into a bowl, pour in the syrup, and stir well. Refrigerate the compote until it is well chilled — about one hour.

Raspberry Iced Tea

Serves 8
Working time: about 20 minutes
Total time: about 1 hour and 20 minutes
(includes chilling)

Calories **45**
Protein **1g.**
Cholesterol **0mg.**
Total fat **0g.**
Saturated fat **0g**
Sodium **1mg.**

1½ to 2 cups fresh or frozen raspberries
zest and juice of 1 orange
3 tbsp. honey
2 jasmine tea bags, or 1½ tbsp. loose jasmine tea
1 lemon, cut into 8 slices, for garnish

If you are using frozen raspberries, thaw them. Purée the raspberries in a blender or food processor, then use a wooden spoon to rub the purée through a fine sieve set over a bowl.

Put the orange zest, orange juice, honey and 6 cups of water into a saucepan. Bring the liquid to a boil and add the tea. Remove the saucepan from the heat and let the tea steep for three minutes. Strain the tea into the purée, stir the mixture, then chill it.

Serve the drink garnished with the lemon slices.

Raspberry Frappé

Makes 6 servings
Working time: about 20 minutes
Total time: about 1 hour and 45 minutes
(includes chilling)

Calories **132**
Protein **3g.**
Cholesterol **4mg.**
Total fat **1g.**
Saturated fat **1g.**
Sodium **31mg.**

3 cups fresh orange juice
2 tbsp. instant tapioca
2 tbsp. sugar, if you are using fresh raspberries
2 cups fresh or frozen raspberries
1¼ cups low-fat milk

Put the orange juice into a nonreactive saucepan; stir in the tapioca and the sugar, if you are using it, and let the mixture stand for five minutes. Bring the liquid to a boil, stirring constantly. Remove the pan from the heat and let the mixture cool completely.

Add the raspberries and purée the mixture, one half at a time, in a blender or a food processor. Strain each batch through a fine sieve. Cover the purée with plastic wrap and chill it for at least one hour, then whisk in the milk. If you like, serve the frappé in chilled glasses.

Banana-Peach Buttermilk Shake

Makes 2 servings
Working time: about 5 minutes
Total time: about 6 hours (includes freezing)

Calories **152**
Protein **5g.**
Cholesterol **5mg.**
Total fat **2g.**
Saturated fat **1g.**
Sodium **129mg.**

1 large banana, peeled and sliced
1 ripe peach, peeled, halved, pitted and sliced, or 1 cup frozen unsweetened sliced peaches
1 cup buttermilk
¼ cup fresh orange juice
2 strawberries for garnish (optional)

Wrap the banana slices in plastic wrap and freeze them for at least six hours. If you are using fresh peach slices, wrap and freeze them at the same time.

When you are ready to prepare the shakes, put the banana and peach slices, the buttermilk and orange juice into a food processor or a blender; process the mixture until it is smooth — about one minute. Pour the purée into tall glasses. If you like, garnish each glass with a strawberry. Serve the shakes at once.

Mixed Vegetable Eye Opener

Makes 2 servings
Working time: about 20 minutes
Total time: about 1 hour (includes chilling)

Calories **63**
Protein **3g.**
Cholesterol **0mg.**
Total fat **0g.**
Saturated fat **0g.**
Sodium **210mg.**

2 celery stalks, trimmed, leaves reserved
1 cucumber, peeled, seeded and coarsely chopped
1½ tsp. fresh lemon juice
8 drops hot red-pepper sauce
14 oz. canned unsalted whole tomatoes, seeded, with their juice
⅛ tsp. salt
½ tsp. sugar
2 scallions, trimmed, the white parts coarsely chopped, the green parts reserved for another use
½ tsp. ground ginger
¼ tsp. dill seeds (optional)
1 carrot, quartered lengthwise, for garnish

Remove the strings from the celery stalks using a vegetable peeler or a paring knife. Cut the stalks into 1-inch pieces and set them aside.

Place the cucumber, lemon juice and hot red-pepper sauce in a food processor or a blender; process the mixture until it is smooth. Add the celery pieces and purée the mixture. Add the tomatoes and their juice, the salt, sugar, scallions, ginger and ⅛ teaspoon of the dill seeds, if you are including them, and process the mixture, using short bursts, until it is smooth again.

Chill the mixture for at least 40 minutes. Pour the drink into glasses; sprinkle each serving with a few of the remaining dill seeds if you are using them, then float the reserved celery leaves on top. Insert one or two carrot sticks into each drink and serve.

EDITOR'S NOTE: *To frost the glasses, place them in the freezer for 30 minutes before serving the drink.*

Chilled Papaya Shake

Makes 4 servings
Working (and total) time: about 15 minutes

Calories **86**
Protein **3g.**
Cholesterol **2mg.**
Total fat **1g.**
Saturated fat **0g.**
Sodium **67mg.**

1 ripe papaya (about 1 lb.), peeled, seeded and cut into chunks
2 tsp. fresh lemon juice
¼ tsp. ground allspice
¾ cup fresh orange juice
2 tsp. honey
1 cup buttermilk
4 ice cubes
lemon slices for garnish

Put the papaya, lemon juice, ⅛ teaspoon of the allspice, and about half of the orange juice into a blender or a food processor, and purée the mixture. Add the honey, buttermilk, the remaining orange juice and the ice, and blend the mixture until it is smooth — about 30 seconds in the blender or one minute in the processor.

To serve the papaya shake, pour it into glasses and sprinkle the drinks with some of the remaining allspice. Garnish each shake with a slice of lemon.

Hot and Spicy Tomato Juice

Makes 4 servings
Working time: about 10 minutes
Total time: about 20 minutes

Calories **39**
Protein **2g.**
Cholesterol **0mg.**
Total fat **0g.**
Saturated fat **0g.**
Sodium **18mg.**

28 oz. canned unsalted whole tomatoes, puréed in a food processor or a blender and sieved
3 tbsp. fresh lime juice
⅛ tsp. ground cayenne pepper
2 tbsp. chopped fresh mint
4 lime slices, for garnish (optional)

Combine the puréed tomatoes, lime juice, cayenne pepper and mint in a nonreactive saucepan. Heat the mixture over low heat and simmer it for 10 minutes. Garnish each serving with a slice of lime, if you like, and serve the drink hot.

Overnight French Toast

ALLOWING THE SOAKED BREAD SLICES TO REST OVERNIGHT
YIELDS SOFT AND CREAMY CENTERS.

Serves 6
Working time: about 30 minutes
Total time: about 8 hours and 30 minutes
(includes chilling)

Calories **298**
Protein **12g.**
Cholesterol **98mg.**
Total fat **4g.**
Saturated fat **2g.**
Sodium **529mg.**

1 loaf (about 1 lb.) unsliced French or Italian bread, the ends trimmed
2 eggs, plus 2 egg whites
⅓ cup sugar
grated zest of 2 lemons
¼ tsp. salt
2 cups low-fat milk
2 tbsp. light or dark rum, or 1 tsp. pure vanilla extract
freshly grated nutmeg

Cut the bread into 12 slices about ¾ inch thick. In a large, shallow dish, whisk together the eggs, egg whites, sugar, lemon zest and salt, then whisk in the milk and the rum or vanilla.

Dip the bread slices into the egg-and-milk mixture, turning them once or twice until they are thoroughly soaked with the liquid. Transfer the slices to a large plate as you work. Drizzle any liquid remaining in the dish over the slices, then sprinkle some nutmeg over them. Cover the slices with plastic wrap and refrigerate them overnight.

Preheat the oven to 400° F. Heat a large griddle or skillet *(box, opposite)* over medium heat until a few drops of cold water dance when sprinkled on the surface. Put as many prepared bread slices as will fit on the griddle or skillet and cook them until the under-sides are golden—about three minutes. Turn the slices and cook them until the second sides are lightly browned—two to three minutes more. Transfer the slices to a baking sheet. Brown the remaining slices and transfer them to the baking sheet.

Place the baking sheet in the oven and bake the French toast until it is cooked through and has puffed up—about 10 minutes. Serve it hot with blueberry syrup *(page at right)* or another topping of your choice.

Blueberry Syrup

Makes about 3½ cups
Working (and total) time: about 15 minutes

Per 3 tablespoons: Calories **54** Protein **0g.** Cholesterol **0mg.** Total fat **0g.** Saturated fat **0g.** Sodium **1mg.**	*2 cups fresh blueberries, picked over and stemmed, or* *2 cups frozen whole blueberries*
	1 cup sugar
	1 lemon, the zest julienned and the juice reserved
	1 navel orange, the zest julienned and the juice reserved
	1 tbsp. cornstarch, mixed with 1 tbsp. water

Combine 1 cup water, the blueberries, sugar, lemon zest and lemon juice, and orange zest and orange juice in a saucepan; bring the mixture to a boil. Reduce the heat to medium low and simmer the blueberries, stirring, for one minute.

Remove the saucepan from the heat and stir in the cornstarch mixture. Return the pan to the heat and simmer the syrup until it becomes thick and clear — about one minute more.

Oiling Griddles and Skillets

While the higher fat content of traditional recipes allows you to cook on the well-seasoned surface of a griddle or skillet without using additional fat, the low-fat recipes in this book often require a slightly different approach to guard against sticking.

A nonstick griddle or skillet that has been maintained according to the manufacturer's instructions need not be oiled. However, if either is beginning to show signs of wear — particularly scratches — it is a good idea to coat the surface with a film of oil. Pour ¼ teaspoon of safflower oil onto the griddle or into the skillet and rub it all over the bottom with a paper towel. Do not discard the towel; it will have absorbed enough oil to allow you to coat the surface several times as needed during the cooking process.

A well-seasoned, heavy griddle or skillet that does not have a nonstick surface should be treated in the same way, but with 1 teaspoon of oil instead of ¼ teaspoon. In both cases, most of the oil will be retained by the towel and thus have little effect on the final calorie count.

Whole-Wheat Yogurt Waffles with Fruit Salsa

Makes about six 7-inch-round waffles
Working (and total) time: about 30 minutes

Calories **393**
Protein **16g.**
Cholesterol **97mg.**
Total fat **11g.**
Saturated fat **2g.**
Sodium **396mg.**

1 cup unbleached all-purpose flour
1 cup whole-wheat flour
1 cup wheat germ
1 tsp. baking powder
½ tsp. baking soda
½ tsp. salt
2 eggs, separated
2 tbsp. safflower oil
3 tbsp. light or dark brown sugar
1 cup low-fat milk
1 cup plain low-fat yogurt
Fruit salsa
2 cups fresh strawberries, hulled and quartered
1 cup diced ripe papaya (or mango, peach, melon or pineapple)
2 tbsp. honey

To make the fruit salsa, combine the fruit with the honey and let the mixture stand at room temperature for 30 minutes.

Put the two flours, the wheat germ, baking powder, baking soda and salt into a bowl. In another bowl, lightly beat the egg yolks with the oil and brown sugar. Stir in the milk and yogurt. Pour the yogurt mixture into the flour mixture. Stir the ingredients together until they are just blended; do not overmix the batter.

Prepare the waffle iron according to the manufacturer's instructions. Beat the egg whites until they form soft peaks and then fold them into the batter. Ladle enough of the batter onto the preheated surface of the grid to cover it by about two thirds. Close the lid and bake the waffle until steam no longer escapes from the sides of the iron and the waffle is crisp and golden — three to five minutes. Serve the waffle at once, topped with the fruit salsa, and continue making waffles in the same manner until all of the batter is used. Although these waffles are best served immediately, you may transfer them as you make them to an ovenproof plate and keep them in a 200° F. oven until all are ready.

Apple French Toast

Serves 6
Working (and total) time: about 30 minutes

Calories **314**
Protein **10g.**
Cholesterol **94mg.**
Total fat **5g.**
Saturated fat **2g.**
Sodium **454mg.**

1 loaf (about 1 lb.) unsliced day-old dense white bread, the ends trimmed
2 eggs, plus 2 egg whites
2 tbsp. sugar
¼ tsp. salt
1 cup low-fat milk
½ cup apple cider or unsweetened apple juice
1 orange (optional), peeled and thinly sliced, the slices halved

Apple compote

1 apple, preferably Granny Smith, peeled, quartered, cored and chopped
1 cup apple cider or unsweetened apple juice
½ cup fresh orange juice
⅓ cup sugar
2 tbsp. currants
grated zest of 1 orange
¼ tsp. grated nutmeg
pinch of salt
1 tbsp. cornstarch, mixed with 1 tbsp. water

Cut the bread into 12 slices about ½ inch thick; cut each slice into four strips. In a large, shallow dish, whisk together the eggs, egg whites, sugar and salt, then whisk in the milk and the cider or apple juice.

Dip the bread strips into the egg-and-milk mixture, turning them once or twice until they are thoroughly soaked with the liquid. Transfer the strips to a large plate or baking sheet as you work. Drizzle any liquid left in the dish over the strips.

To make the apple compote, combine the chopped apple, the cider or apple juice, orange juice, sugar, currants, orange zest, nutmeg and salt in a saucepan. Bring the liquid to a boil, reduce the heat to medium low, and simmer the compote until the apple is barely tender — about five minutes. Remove the pan from the heat and stir in the cornstarch mixture. Return the pan to the heat and simmer the compote, stirring, until it is thick and clear — about one minute. Transfer the compote to a serving bowl and keep it warm.

Heat a large griddle or skillet *(box, page 217)* over medium heat until a few drops of cold water dance when sprinkled on the surface. Cook the prepared strips of bread until the undersides are golden—about three minutes. Turn the strips over and cook them until the second sides are lightly browned—two to three minutes more. Transfer the French toast strips to a platter and keep them warm while you cook the remaining strips.

Serve the French toast at once, garnished with the orange slices, if you are using them, and accompanied by the apple compote.

Frittata with Mozzarella Cheese

Serves 4 as a main dish
Working (and total) time: about 35 minutes

Calories **170**
Protein **11g.**
Cholesterol **83mg.**
Total fat **11g.**
Saturated fat **4g.**
Sodium **320mg.**

1 egg, plus 2 egg whites
¼ tsp. salt
freshly ground black pepper
¼ cup part-skim ricotta cheese
1½ tbsp. olive oil, preferably virgin
3 oz. mushrooms (about 1 cup), wiped clean and sliced
2 garlic cloves, finely chopped
1½ tsp. fresh thyme, or ½ tsp. dried thyme leaves
3 scallions, trimmed and cut into ½-inch pieces, the white and green parts separated
2 small zucchini (about ½ lb.), cut into bâtons
1 sweet red pepper, seeded, deribbed and sliced into thin strips
1½ tsp. fresh lemon juice
2 tbsp. freshly grated Parmesan cheese
2 oz. part-skim mozzarella, cut into thin strips (about ¼ cup)

In a bowl, whisk together the egg, egg whites, ⅛ teaspoon of the salt, some pepper, the ricotta and ½ tablespoon of the oil and set the mixture aside.

Preheat the broiler. Heat the remaining tablespoon of oil in a large, ovenproof, nonstick skillet over high heat. Add the mushrooms, garlic, thyme, the white parts of the scallion and some pepper. Cook the vegetable mixture until the mushrooms are lightly browned — two to three minutes. Add the zucchini, red pepper, the remaining ⅛ teaspoon of salt and the lemon juice, and cook the mixture, stirring frequently, until the vegetables are tender and all of the liquid has evaporated — about five minutes.

Remove the skillet from the heat and stir the scallion greens and the Parmesan cheese into the vegetable mixture. Press the vegetables into an even layer and pour in the egg mixture. Cook the frittata over medium heat for one minute. Sprinkle the mozzarella evenly over the frittata and place the skillet under the preheated broiler. Broil the frittata until the cheese begins to brown — two to three minutes. Slide the frittata onto a warm serving plate and cut it into quarters. Serve the frittata immediately.

Omelets Stuffed with Seafood and Sprouts

Serves 4
Working (and total) time: about 35 minutes

Calories **158**
Protein **13g.**
Cholesterol **106mg.**
Total fat **8g.**
Saturated fat **1g.**
Sodium **86mg.**

3 tbsp. rice vinegar
3 tsp. sugar
1 tbsp. fresh lemon juice
½ lb. bean sprouts
¼ lb. green beans, trimmed and thinly sliced on the diagonal
1 tbsp. plus 2 tsp. safflower oil
1 tsp. curry powder
freshly ground black pepper
2 oz. cooked baby shrimp (about ⅓ cup), chopped
¼ lb. sole or flounder fillets, cut into strips
2 scallions, thinly sliced
1 egg, plus 3 egg whites

Mix the vinegar, 2 teaspoons of the sugar and the lemon juice in a small bowl and set it aside.

Blanch the bean sprouts and the beans in 1 quart of boiling water for 30 seconds. Drain the vegetables and refresh them under cold running water. Squeeze the vegetables in your hands to extract as much liquid as possible. Set the vegetables aside.

Heat 1 teaspoon of the oil in a large, nonstick skillet over medium-high heat. Add the bean sprouts and beans and cook them, stirring frequently, for two minutes. Add ½ teaspoon of the curry, half of the vinegar mixture and a generous grinding of black pepper. Stir the mixture well and continue cooking it until all of the liquid has evaporated — about two minutes. Transfer the vegetable mixture to a bowl and set it aside.

Return the skillet to the heat and pour in 1 tablespoon of the oil. Add the shrimp, sole or flounder, and scallions and cook the mixture, stirring frequently, for one minute. Add the remaining vinegar mixture, then ▶

stir in the vegetable mixture, and cook them, stirring frequently, until all of the liquid has evaporated — two to four minutes. Set the seafood and vegetables aside.

In a bowl, whisk together the egg, egg whites, the remaining ½ teaspoon of curry, the remaining teaspoon of sugar, the remaining teaspoon of oil and some pepper. With a paper towel, wipe out the nonstick skillet that the seafood and vegetables were cooked in and heat the skillet over medium heat. Pour a scant ¼ cup of the egg mixture into the hot skillet and swirl it around. Cook the omelet for 30 seconds, turn it over, and cook it for 10 seconds more. Transfer the omelet to a warm plate. Repeat the process with the remaining egg mixture to make four thin omelets.

Take one fourth of the filling and spread it over one half of one omelet. Fold the omelet over and repeat the process with the remaining omelets and filling. Serve the filled omelets immediately.

Turkey, Apple and Champagne Sausages

Serves 10 as a main dish
Working (and total) time: about 45 minutes

Calories **109**
Protein **14g.**
Cholesterol **32mg.**
Total fat **2g.**
Saturated fat **1g.**
Sodium **162mg.**

1 red apple, cored and finely chopped
1 onion, finely chopped
1 cup fine dry bread crumbs
½ cup dry Champagne or other sparkling dry white wine
1 lb. turkey breast meat, ground
¼ lb. pork loin, trimmed of fat and ground
½ tsp. salt
freshly ground black pepper

Put the apple and onion into a nonstick skillet over low heat and cook them, covered, until they are soft — about four minutes.

Combine the bread crumbs and the wine in a bowl. Add the turkey, pork, salt, some pepper and the apple-onion mixture, kneading the ingredients with your hands to mix them well. Shape the sausage meat into 20 patties about ½ inch thick.

Heat a large, nonstick skillet over medium heat and put half the patties into it. Cook them until the undersides are brown, then turn the patties over, and brown the other sides — about four minutes in all. Remove the browned patties to a platter and keep them warm while you cook the others. Serve the sausages at once.

Spaghetti Omelet

Serves 8 as a side dish
Working (and total) time: about 1 hour

Calories **121**
Protein **7g.**
Cholesterol **6mg.**
Total fat **3g.**
Saturated fat **1g.**
Sodium **262mg.**

28 oz. canned unsalted whole tomatoes, with their juice
4 oz. spaghetti, spaghettini or linguine
1½ tsp. salt
2 egg whites
½ cup low-fat milk
1 tbsp. chopped fresh parsley
3 tbsp. freshly grated Parmesan cheese
freshly ground black pepper
1 tsp. grated lemon zest
2 tsp. olive oil
½ cup grated part-skim mozzarella cheese

Put the tomatoes and their juice into a heavy-bottomed, nonreactive saucepan. Simmer the mixture, stirring it occasionally to prevent it from sticking, until it thickens — 20 to 30 minutes.

While the tomatoes are cooking, prepare the pasta. Add the pasta to 2 quarts of boiling water with 1 teaspoon of the salt. Start testing the pasta after eight minutes and cook it until it is *al dente*. Drain the cooked pasta, rinse it under cold running water and drain it again, thoroughly.

In a large bowl, beat together the egg whites, milk, parsley, Parmesan, a generous grinding of pepper, the remaining ½ teaspoon of salt and the lemon zest. Toss the pasta with the egg-white mixture.

Heat a 9-inch nonstick skillet over medium-high heat. Add the oil, let it heat for 10 seconds and then swirl the pan to evenly coat the bottom with the oil. Put half of the pasta mixture into the skillet; use a rubber spatula to smooth the mixture into an even layer. Reduce the heat to medium. Sprinkle the mozzarella over the pasta mixture and cover it with the remaining mixture. Let the omelet cook slowly until it is firm and the bottom and sides are browned — about eight minutes.

Slide the omelet onto a plate. Invert the skillet over the plate and turn both over together. Cook the second side until it, too, is browned — approximately eight minutes longer.

While the omelet is cooking, make the tomato sauce: Work the cooked tomatoes through a food mill or a sieve and discard the seeds. Keep the tomato sauce warm.

To serve the omelet, slide it onto a warmed serving platter. Cut the omelet into eight wedges and serve it immediately, passing the tomato sauce separately.

Mushrooms and Asparagus in Phyllo Cases

Serves 6
Working (and total) time: about 1 hour

Calories **105**
Protein **5g.**
Cholesterol **0mg.**
Total fat **4g.**
Saturated fat **1g.**
Sodium **90mg.**

4 tsp. safflower oil
6 sheets phyllo pastry, each about 18 by 12 inches
½ lb. asparagus, trimmed and peeled
4 large scallions, trimmed and sliced
1 garlic clove, crushed
¾ lb. mushrooms, wiped clean and sliced
1 cup skim milk
2 tsp. cornstarch
2 large carrots, julienned, parboiled for 5 minutes, and drained
1 tbsp. chopped fresh tarragon
1 tsp. fresh lemon juice
freshly ground black pepper
fresh tarragon sprigs for garnish (optional)

Preheat the oven to 375° F. Brush the bottoms of six ½-cup ramekins or muffin cups with 2 teaspoons of the safflower oil.

Fold each sheet of phyllo pastry in half lengthwise, then in thirds crosswise, to make six 6-inch squares. Trim the three folded edges of each pile of squares, to yield six stacks of pastry, each containing six squares. Take each stack of squares and rearrange the pieces of pastry so that the corners are offset, to resemble the petals of a flower. Place a stack of squares in each ramekin, pressing them into the contours of the dish. Bake the pastry-lined ramekins in the oven until the cases are evenly browned—15 to 20 minutes. Take care not to let the edges burn.

Meanwhile, make the filling. Steam the asparagus in a steamer basket over a saucepan of gently simmering water until it is tender but still crisp—about four minutes. Cut off and reserve twelve 2-inch-long tips for garnish. Coarsely chop the remaining asparagus.

Heat the remaining 2 teaspoons of oil in a small, heavy-bottomed pan, and add the scallions, garlic, and mushrooms. Cook them over medium heat, stirring frequently, until the mushrooms are soft and begin to exude their juices—about three minutes. Add the milk and bring the mixture to a boil. In a small bowl, blend the cornstarch to a smooth paste with 2 tablespoons of water. Add the cornstarch paste to the sauce and bring it back to a boil to thicken it, stirring constantly. Gently mix in the chopped asparagus, carrots, tarragon, lemon juice, and some freshly ground black pepper. Simmer the sauce for one minute, to heat all the ingredients through.

Carefully remove the phyllo cases from the ramekins and place each one on a warmed serving plate. Spoon the vegetable mixture into and around the cases, and garnish each one with two of the reserved asparagus tips and with a sprig of tarragon, if you are using it.

SUGGESTED ACCOMPANIMENTS: *baked tomatoes; new potatoes.*

Baguette and Brie Bake

Serves 4
Working time: about 10 minutes
Total time: about 40 minutes

Calories **220**	3½ oz. Brie or Camembert cheese, chilled
Protein **14g.**	1 small baguette (about 6 oz.)
Cholesterol **80mg.**	1 egg
Total fat **8g.**	2 egg whites
Saturated fat **1g.**	1 scant cup low-fat milk
Sodium **460mg.**	freshly ground black pepper

Preheat the oven to 350° F. Lightly grease a large, shallow ovenproof dish.

Using a sharp knife, slice the cheese lengthwise into ¼-inch-thick slices, then cut each slice into pieces about 1¼ inches wide, to yield 16 small slices. Cut the baguette into sixteen ½-inch slices, and fit the slices of bread and cheese alternately into the prepared dish. Beat the egg and egg whites in a bowl, add the milk and some black pepper, and carefully pour the mixture over the bread and cheese, ensuring that all the bread is thoroughly soaked.

Bake the assembly in the oven until the surface is golden brown and crisp and the custard is just firm in the center—about 30 minutes. Serve at once.

SUGGESTED ACCOMPANIMENTS: *salad of mixed lettuce leaves; tomato, cucumber, and onion salad.*

Irish Soda Biscuits with Currants and Caraway Seeds

Makes 24 biscuits
Working time: about 15 minutes
Total time: about 30 minutes

Calories **86**
Protein **2g.**
Cholesterol **13mg.**
Total fat **2g.**
Saturated fat **1g.**
Sodium **118mg.**

2 cups unbleached all-purpose flour
1 cup whole-wheat flour
2 tbsp. sugar
2 tsp. baking powder
1 tsp. baking soda
¼ tsp. salt
2 tbsp. cold unsalted margarine, preferably corn oil
1 tbsp. cold unsalted butter
1 tbsp. caraway seeds
1 egg
1 cup buttermilk
½ cup currants
2 tbsp. low-fat milk

Preheat the oven to 350° F. In a bowl, combine the two flours, the sugar, baking powder, baking soda and salt. Using a pastry blender or two knives, cut in the margarine and butter until the mixture resembles coarse meal. In another bowl, whisk the caraway seeds, egg and buttermilk together. Stir the buttermilk mixture and the currants into the flour mixture. (The dough will become too stiff to stir before all the flour is mixed in.)

Turn the dough out onto a lightly floured surface and knead it gently just until all the flour is incorporated. Roll or pat out the dough so that it is about ¾ inch thick. Cut out rounds with a 2-inch biscuit cutter or the rim of a small glass, and place the biscuits on an ungreased baking sheet. Gather up the scraps of dough, form them into a ball, and repeat the process. Brush the biscuits with the milk and cut a cross on the top of each with the tip of a sharp knife or a pair of scissors. Bake the biscuits until they are golden brown — about 15 minutes. Serve the biscuits while they are hot.

Spicy Corn Sticks

Makes 18 corn sticks
Working time: about 15 minutes
Total time: about 30 minutes

Calories **94**
Protein **3g.**
Cholesterol **16mg.**
Total fat **2g.**
Saturated fat **0g.**
Sodium **85mg.**

1¼ cups unbleached all-purpose flour
1 cup cornmeal
2 tbsp. sugar
¼ tsp. cayenne pepper
1 tbsp. baking powder
1 cup low-fat milk
1 egg
2 tbsp. safflower oil
⅓ cup diced sweet red pepper
⅓ cup diced green pepper
½ cup fresh or frozen corn kernels

Preheat the oven to 450° F. Lightly oil a corn-stick pan and heat it in the oven for 10 minutes.

Put the flour, cornmeal, sugar, cayenne pepper and baking powder into a bowl and mix them together. In another bowl, whisk together the milk, egg and oil. Pour the milk mixture into the dry ingredients and stir them just until they are blended. Stir in the red and green peppers and the corn.

Spoon the batter into the hot corn-stick pan, filling each mold about three-fourths full. Reduce the oven temperature to 400° F. and bake the corn sticks until a wooden pick inserted into the center comes out clean — 10 to 12 minutes. Keep the corn sticks warm while you bake the remaining batter. Five minutes before the last corn sticks are through baking, return the other corn sticks to the oven to reheat them. Serve the corn sticks at once.

EDITOR'S NOTE: *If a corn-stick pan is not available, the batter can be baked in a 10-inch cast-iron skillet instead. Increase the baking time to about 25 minutes; cut the cornbread into wedges to serve.*

Fruit-Filled Gems

GEMS ARE MINIATURE MUFFINS; GEM PANS ARE AVAILABLE AT
GOURMET AND PROFESSIONAL KITCHEN EQUIPMENT STORES.

Makes 24 gems
Working time: about 45 minutes
Total time: about 1 hour and 15 minutes

Per gem:
Calories **83**
Protein **1g.**
Cholesterol **14mg.**
Total fat **3g.**
Saturated fat **1g.**
Sodium **29mg.**

1 tart cooking apple, peeled, cored and coarsely grated
½ cup chopped dried apricots
½ cup apple cider or unsweetened apple juice
grated zest and juice of 1 lemon
¾ cup sugar
1¼ cup unbleached all-purpose flour
¼ tsp. baking powder
2 tbsp. unsalted butter
2 tbsp. unsalted margarine, preferably corn oil
1 egg, beaten
2 tbsp. chopped almonds, toasted

Combine the apple, apricots, cider or apple juice, lemon zest and juice, and ¼ cup of the sugar in a nonreactive saucepan and bring the mixture to a boil. Reduce the heat and simmer the mixture until the fruit is soft and most of the juice has evaporated — about 15 minutes. Set the filling aside and let it cool.

Combine the remaining sugar with the flour and baking powder in a bowl. Cut the butter and marga-rine into the dry ingredients with a pastry blender or two knives until the mixture resembles coarse meal. With your fingertips, work the egg into the dough just until the egg is incorporated and the dough begins to hold together. Shape two thirds of the dough into a log about 1 inch wide, wrap it in plastic wrap and chill it for 15 minutes. Shape the remaining dough into a round about ½ inch thick; wrap and chill it also.

Preheat the oven to 350° F.

Cut the dough log into 24 pieces and flatten each one slightly. Press one of the pieces into one of the cups of a gem pan to line it, molding the dough along the sides to the top of the cup. Use the remaining pieces of dough to make 23 more cups. Be careful not to leave any holes in the pastry or the gems will stick to the pan after they are baked. Spoon the fruit filling into the lined cups and sprinkle some of the almonds into each one of them.

Roll out the remaining dough on a lightly floured surface until it is about ⅛ inch thick and cut 24 rounds the same size as the tops of the gem cups. Cover each fruit gem with a round of pastry, lightly pressing on the edges of the pastry to seal them.

Bake the fruit gems until they are browned — 25 to 30 minutes. Let them cool slightly. To remove the gems, cover the pan with a baking sheet or a wire rack, turn both over together, and lift off the pan. Serve the fruit gems warm or at room temperature.

Ricotta Muffins with Poppy Seeds

Makes 10 muffins
Working time: about 15 minutes
Total time: about 30 minutes

Per muffin:
Calories **212**
Protein **7g.**
Cholesterol **9mg.**
Total fat **7g.**
Saturated fat **2g.**
Sodium **188mg.**

2 cups unbleached all-purpose flour
½ cup sugar
1 tsp. baking soda
¼ tsp. salt
¼ cup poppy seeds
1 cup part-skim ricotta cheese
2 tbsp. safflower oil
grated zest of 1 lemon
1 tbsp. fresh lemon juice
¾ cup low-fat milk
2 egg whites

Preheat the oven to 400° F. Lightly oil a muffin pan.

Sift the flour, sugar, baking soda and salt into a bowl; stir in the poppy seeds. In another bowl, combine the ricotta, oil, lemon zest and lemon juice, and then whisk in the milk. Add the ricotta mixture to the flour mixture and stir them just until they are blended; do not overmix.

Beat the egg whites until they form soft peaks. Stir half of the beaten egg whites into the batter, then fold in the remaining egg whites. Spoon the batter into the prepared muffin pan, filling each cup no more than two-thirds full, and bake the muffins until they are lightly browned — 12 to 14 minutes. Serve the muffins immediately.

Cheese and Bacon Whole-Wheat Bars

Serves 6
Working time: about 30 minutes
Total time: about 1 hour and 30 minutes
(includes cooling)

Calories **315**
Protein **12g.**
Cholesterol **30mg.**
Total fat **10g.**
Saturated fat **6g.**
Sodium **315mg.**

1½ oz. lean bacon, finely chopped
1 cup whole-wheat flour
1¼ cups unbleached all-purpose flour
3 tsp. baking powder
⅛ tsp. salt
3 tbsp. unsalted butter
1½ oz. sharp cheddar cheese, finely grated (about ½ cup)
1 tbsp. finely grated Parmesan cheese
1 tbsp. chopped fresh oregano, or 1 tsp. dried oregano
1 tbsp. fresh lemon juice
⅔ cup skim milk
Salad filling
½ cup plain low-fat yogurt
¼ head crisp lettuce, sliced
¼ cucumber, thinly sliced
6 scallions, sliced

Preheat the oven to 450° F., and grease and flour a baking sheet.

Put the bacon into a heavy-bottomed, nonstick skillet and cook it over medium heat, stirring frequently, until it is lightly browned—two to three minutes.

Transfer the bacon to paper towels to drain and cool.

Put the whole-wheat flour into a mixing bowl and sift in the all-purpose flour, baking powder, and salt. Using your fingertips, rub in the butter until the mixture resembles fine breadcrumbs. Stir in the bacon, the cheddar and Parmesan cheeses, and the oregano. Add the lemon juice to the milk, and using a wooden spoon, gradually mix sufficient liquid into the dry ingredients to make a soft, but not sticky, dough.

Transfer the dough to a floured work surface, and with floured hands, shape it into a rectangle measuring about 10 by 4 inches. Using a metal spatula, lift the dough onto the prepared baking sheet. With a sharp knife, mark the top of the dough rectangle crosswise into six bars, cutting down about ¼ inch into the dough. Bake the dough until it is well risen, firm to the touch, and a light golden brown—about 20 minutes. Allow the bread to cool on a wire rack.

Cut the bread into the six marked bars and split each one in half. Fill the bars with the yogurt and the lettuce, cucumber, and scallion slices. Wrap the filled bars individually in foil or plastic wrap, and pack them in a covered container. Put the container into a cooler to take to the picnic site.

EDITOR'S NOTE: *The baked bread may be frozen, unfilled, for up to two months. Cover the bread tightly in plastic wrap and foil before putting it into the freezer. Thaw it at room temperature for two hours.*

Turkey and Ham Rolls

Makes 8 filled rolls
Working time: about 45 minutes
Total time: about 2 hours and 15 minutes
(includes rising and cooling)

Per filled roll:
Calories **250**
Protein **19g.**
Cholesterol **30mg.**
Total fat **4g.**
Saturated fat **1g.**
Sodium **370mg.**

1 tsp. virgin olive oil
1 onion, chopped
¾ lb. lean boneless turkey, coarsely chopped
⅓ cup dry white wine
6 oz. celeriac, peeled and coarsely grated
6 oz. lean cooked ham, trimmed of fat and cut into ¼-inch dice
1 tbsp. chopped fresh thyme, or 1 tsp. dried thyme leaves
3 tbsp. chopped fresh parsley
2 tbsp. grated horseradish
freshly ground black pepper
Sesame rolls
3 cups unbleached all-purpose flour
½ tsp. sugar
½ tsp. salt
1½ tsp. fast-rising dry yeast
½ cup skim milk
1 egg white
skim milk for glazing
4 tsp. sesame seeds

First make the dough for the rolls. In a large bowl, mix together the flour, sugar, salt, and yeast. Heat the milk in a saucepan until it is hot to the touch—about 110° F.—then pour it into the dry ingredients together with the egg white. Stir to create a soft dough, adding a little warm water if the mixture is too dry. Turn the dough onto a floured surface, and with well-floured hands, knead it gently until it is smooth—about 10 minutes. Place the dough in a clean bowl, cover it with plastic wrap, and let it rise in a warm place until it has doubled in size—about 30 minutes.

Meanwhile, prepare the turkey and ham filling. Heat the oil in a heavy-bottomed saucepan, add the onion, and cook it over medium heat until it is soft—about three minutes. Add the turkey and cook it, stirring continuously, for about five minutes, or until it is cooked through. Blend the turkey and onion mixture with the wine in a food processor until it is finely chopped but not puréed. Transfer the mixture to a bowl and beat in the celeriac, ham, thyme, parsley, horseradish, and some black pepper. Let the mixture cool completely.

Lightly grease a large baking sheet. On a floured work surface, punch down the risen dough to its original size and divide it into eight equal pieces. Roll out one piece into a round about 6 inches in diameter. Brush the edges of the round with water and spoon one-eighth of the turkey filling into the center. Bring the edges of the dough up over the filling and pleat and press them together neatly to seal the filling inside the roll. Place the filled roll, seam side down, on the baking sheet. Use the remaining dough and filling to make another seven rolls and place them on the baking sheet, leaving a ¼-inch gap between the rolls. Cover the filled rolls with lightly greased plastic wrap and let them rise for 20 minutes. Meanwhile, preheat the oven to 400° F.

Glaze the tops of the rolls lightly with skim milk and sprinkle them with the sesame seeds. Bake the rolls until they turn a deep golden color—about 20 minutes. Cool them on a wire rack.

Take the rolls to the picnic site wrapped in foil inside a covered container. Carry the container in a cooler.

SUGGESTED ACCOMPANIMENT: *a salad of shredded cabbage and flat-leaf parsley, dressed with sour cream.*

The salsa verde and the tomato salads for this brunch can be prepared a day ahead. If you like, the meat can be sliced and the marinade prepared . Freeze the mixture for the lime drink. Refrigerate everything else.

On the day of the brunch, get the pork into its marinade. Make the strawberry-and-grapefruit salad and chill it. Shred the lettuce for the tomato salads, then unmold them onto the lettuce. Transfer the pink lime freeze to the refrigerator to soften for about 45 minutes before processing it. About half an hour before serving time, make the griddlecakes. Keep the griddlecakes warm while you grill the pork.

Cornmeal Griddlecakes

Makes twelve 4-inch cakes
Working (and total) time: about 30 minutes

Calories **111**
Protein **4g.**
Cholesterol **47mg.**
Total fat **2g.**
Saturated fat **1g.**
Sodium **113mg.**

1 cup cornmeal
1 tsp. sugar
¼ tsp. salt
½ cup low-fat milk
1 egg, lightly beaten

Combine the cornmeal, sugar and salt in a bowl. Pour in 1 cup of boiling water all at once and stir until the ingredients are well blended. Let the mixture stand for two minutes.

In a small bowl, whisk together the milk and egg. Pour this mixture into the bowl containing the cornmeal mixture and stir the batter until it is smooth.

Heat a large, nonstick griddle or skillet *(box, page 217)* over medium-high heat until a few drops of cold water dance when sprinkled on the surface. Drop the batter, 2 tablespoons at a time, onto the hot surface, then use the back of the spoon to spread the batter into 4-inch rounds. Cook the griddlecakes until the surface of each is covered with bubbles and the underside is browned—about two minutes. Turn the cakes over and cook them until the other sides are browned ▶

Golden cornmeal griddlecakes are served with grilled pork loin and a bowl of zesty salsa verde. Tomato salads on lettuce and a tomato-lime beverage accompany the meal. For dessert, strawberries are paired with grapefruit segments.

— about one minute more.

Transfer the griddlecakes to a serving plate and keep them warm while you cook the remaining batter. Serve the griddlecakes warm.

Marinated Grilled Pork Loin with Orange Sauce

Serves 6
Working time: about 20 minutes
Total time: about one hour and 10 minutes
(includes marinating)

Calories **107**	¼ cup frozen orange-juice concentrate, thawed
Protein **12g.**	¼ cup malt vinegar
Cholesterol **37mg.**	2 garlic cloves, finely chopped
Total fat **4g.**	freshly ground black pepper
Saturated fat **1g.**	14 oz. pork loin, trimmed of fat and cut into
Sodium **30mg.**	18 thin slices

Mix together the orange-juice concentrate, vinegar, garlic and some pepper in a large, shallow dish. Lay the slices of pork in the marinade, turning them over to coat them. Cover the dish and marinate the pork at room temperature for one hour or in the refrigerator for three hours.

If you plan to grill the pork, light the coals about 30 minutes before cooking time; to broil, preheat the broiler for 10 minutes.

Remove the pork from the marinade. Transfer the marinade to a small saucepan and simmer it over medium-low heat until it has thickened slightly — about three minutes. Set the sauce aside.

Grill or broil the pork slices until they are browned and no longer pink inside — about one minute on each side. Arrange the pork slices on a warmed serving platter. Briefly reheat the sauce and pour it over the meat. Serve at once.

Salsa Verde

Makes about 1½ cups
Working time: about 20 minutes
Total time: about 1 hour and 20 minutes
(includes chilling)

Per 4 tablespoons:	½ lb. tomatillos, husked, cored and finely chopped, or
Calories **16**	½ lb. green tomatoes, seeded and finely chopped
Protein **0g.**	1 jalapeño pepper, seeded, deribbed and finely chopped
Cholesterol **0mg.**	3 garlic cloves, finely chopped
Total fat **0g.**	1 small onion, finely chopped
Saturated fat **0g.**	¼ cup fresh lime juice
Sodium **4mg.**	1 tbsp. chopped cilantro

In a small bowl stir together all of the ingredients. Cover the bowl with plastic wrap and refrigerate the salsa verde until it is cold — about one hour. Serve the salsa with the griddlecakes and the grilled pork.

Individual Molded Tomato Salads

Serves 6
Working time: about 1 hour
Total time: about 3 hours (includes chilling)

Calories **44**	14 oz. canned unsalted whole tomatoes, with their juice
Protein **3g.**	1 tbsp. unflavored powdered gelatin
Cholesterol **0mg.**	½ cup fresh or frozen peas
Total fat **0g.**	2 sweet red peppers, seeded, deribbed
Saturated fat **0g.**	and finely chopped
Sodium **111mg.**	3 scallions, trimmed and finely chopped
	½ cucumber, peeled, seeded and finely chopped
	1 celery stalk, trimmed and finely chopped
	2 tbsp. fresh lemon juice
	1 tsp. sugar
	½ tsp. hot red-pepper sauce
	¼ tsp. salt
	2 cups shredded lettuce

Purée the tomatoes and their juice in a blender or food processor. Strain the purée and discard the seeds. Pour 1¼ cups of the purée into a large bowl.

Pour ½ cup of the remaining purée into a small saucepan; reserve any remaining purée for another use. Sprinkle the gelatin over the purée in the saucepan; let the gelatin stand until it is spongy — about five minutes. Place the pan over low heat and bring the purée to a simmer, whisking to dissolve the gelatin. Remove the mixture from the heat and set it aside.

If you are using fresh peas, cook them in boiling water until they are tender — about three minutes; frozen peas need only be thawed. Add the peas, peppers, scallions, cucumber, celery, lemon juice, sugar, hot red-pepper sauce and salt to the purée in the bowl.

Pour the gelatin mixture into the bowl with the vegetables and stir well. Divide the tomato salad among six ¾-cup ramekins. Refrigerate the ramekins until the tomato salad has set — at least two hours.

To serve, line six plates with the lettuce. Dip the bottoms of the ramekins in hot water, then invert the ramekins onto the lettuce and lift them from the salads.

EDITOR'S NOTE: *The salads can be unmolded two hours in advance and kept in the refrigerator, covered with plastic wrap, until serving time. This recipe can also be used to fill a single 4½-cup mold.*

Strawberry and Grapefruit Salad

Serves 6
Working time: about 30 minutes
Total time: about 1 hour and 30 minutes
(includes chilling)

Calories **93**
Protein **1g.**
Cholesterol **0mg.**
Total fat **0g.**
Saturated fat **0g.**
Sodium **1mg.**

4 grapefruits
2 pints strawberries, hulled, halved if large
3 tbsp. Triple Sec or other orange-flavored liqueur
¼ cup sugar
mint sprigs for garnish (optional)

Use a sharp knife to slice off both ends of one of the grapefruits so the flesh just shows through. With the grapefruit standing on a flat end, cut around the flesh, following the contour of the fruit, to remove vertical strips of the peel and pith. Working over a bowl to catch the juice, hold the peeled grapefruit in one hand and carefully slice between the flesh and membrane to free each segment; let the segments fall into the bowl. Remove the pits from the segments and discard them. Squeeze any remaining juice from the membrane into the bowl. Repeat these steps with the remaining grapefruits.

Put the strawberries, liqueur and sugar into the bowl with the grapefruit segments and juice; toss the fruit gently with a wooden spoon. Cover the fruit and chill it thoroughly—at least one hour. Serve the salad in chilled bowls, garnished with mint sprigs if you like.

Pink Lime Freeze

Makes 6 servings
Working time: about 15 minutes
Total time: about 2 hours and 15 minutes
(includes freezing)

Calories **76**
Protein **0g.**
Cholesterol **0mg.**
Total fat **0g.**
Saturated fat **0g.**
Sodium **2mg.**

½ cup sugar
¾ cup fresh lime juice
1 ripe tomato, peeled, seeded and puréed, or
½ cup low-sodium tomato juice
6 thin lime slices for garnish

Pour 1 cup of water into a saucepan and stir in the sugar. Bring the mixture to a boil, reduce the heat, and simmer the sugar syrup for two minutes. Transfer the syrup to a shallow pan and stir in 3 cups of cold water, the lime juice and the tomato purée. Freeze the liquid for at least two hours, stirring it every half hour.

Just before serving, break the frozen mixture into chunks and process them in two batches in a blender until the mixture is smooth but slushy. Pour the drink into six chilled glasses and garnish each one with a slice of lime.

SUMMER BRUNCH
—
Minted Cucumber Sorbet
Summer Salad with Fresh Tuna
Peppered Bread Sticks
Cherry Summer Pudding

Most of the work for this summer brunch can be done ahead of time. The bread sticks can be made up to two weeks in advance and then frozen; alternatively, bake them the day before the brunch and, when they have cooled, store them in a sealed paper bag. Prepare the sorbet and the cherry pudding a day beforehand; freeze the sorbet and chill the pudding. The pepper dressing, artichokes, beans, potatoes, tuna and greens for the tuna salad also can be prepared a day ahead and kept separately, covered, in the refrigerator.

On the day of the brunch, unmold the cherry pudding. Dress the greens for the tuna salad and then arrange all of its prepared components. If the sorbet is frozen solid, put it in the refrigerator to soften for 30 minutes before serving it.

Minted Cucumber Sorbet

THIS PALATE-AWAKENING SORBET GETS
THE BRUNCH UNDER WAY.

Serves 6
Working time: about 30 minutes
Total time: 1 to 3 hours, depending
on freezing method

Calories **75**
Protein **0g.**
Cholesterol **0mg.**
Total fat **0g.**
Saturated fat **0g.**
Sodium **91mg.**

4 large cucumbers
½ cup sugar
¼ tsp. salt
¼ cup cider vinegar
1 tbsp. chopped fresh mint, or 1½ tsp. dried mint
6 mint sprigs for garnish (optional)

Peel, seed and slice two of the cucumbers. Scrub the remaining two cucumbers to rid them of wax and place them in the refrigerator to chill.

In a small saucepan, bring ½ cup of water and the sugar to a boil over medium-high heat and cook the syrup for two minutes. Add the sliced cucumbers, salt and vinegar to the saucepan, reduce the heat to medium and simmer the mixture, stirring frequently, for five minutes. The cucumbers should be translucent. Remove the pan from the heat and stir in the chopped or ▶

Artichoke wedges form a dramatic garnish for a fresh tuna summer salad, served with red-pepper dressing and peppered bread sticks. Frozen cucumber cups filled with cucumber sorbet, a cherry summer pudding and a pitcher of iced tea complete the brunch.

dried mint. Purée the cucumber mixture in a blender or food processor and set it aside to cool.

Freeze the purée in an ice cream freezer according to the manufacturer's instructions. (Alternatively, the sorbet can be still-frozen in a shallow pan covered with plastic wrap. Stir the sorbet with a whisk every 30 minutes to break the large ice crystals.)

While the sorbet is freezing, prepare the cucumber cups. Using a vegetable peeler or a channel knife, peel stripes down the length of the cucumbers. Cut the cucumbers crosswise into thirds, discarding the rounded ends. With a melon baller or a small spoon, scoop out the centers of the cucumber pieces leaving the bottoms intact and a quarter inch of flesh on the sides. Freeze the cups.

Spoon the frozen sorbet into the cucumber cups, mounding it, and return them to the freezer until serving time. If the cups remain in the freezer for more than one hour, allow them to stand at room temperature for about 15 minutes to soften the sorbet slightly. If you wish, garnish each cup with a sprig of mint.

Summer Salad with Fresh Tuna

THIS UPDATE OF THE CLASSIC *SALADE NIÇOISE* REPLACES THE STANDARD OILY VINAIGRETTE WITH A SPRIGHTLY DRESSING BASED ON ROASTED RED PEPPERS.

Serves 6
Working (and total) time: about 2 hours

Calories **251**	2 artichokes
Protein **14g.**	1 lemon, halved
Cholesterol **14mg.**	¼ lb. fresh green beans, trimmed and cut
Total fat **11g.**	into 1½-inch pieces
Saturated fat **2g.**	½ cup fresh or frozen peas
Sodium **270mg.**	6 red potatoes (about 1 lb.), scrubbed
	½ lb. fresh tuna (or swordfish) steak, about ½ inch thick
	½ lb. assorted salad greens (such as romaine, leaf lettuce, spinach, watercress, endive or radicchio), washed, dried and torn into pieces if necessary

12 cherry tomatoes, halved
1 small red onion, thinly sliced
Red-pepper dressing
2 large sweet red peppers
3 tbsp. olive oil, preferably virgin
8 oil-cured black olives, pitted
3 garlic cloves, chopped
6 tbsp. fresh lemon juice
½ cup loosely packed parsley leaves
¼ tsp. salt
freshly ground black pepper

Preheat the broiler. Place the peppers for the dressing about 2 inches below the preheated broiler. Turn them as their sides become slightly scorched. When the peppers are blistered all over, put them into a bowl, cover them with plastic wrap, and set them aside to cool; the trapped steam will loosen the skins.

While the peppers are cooling, trim the artichokes. Cut 1 inch off the tops, snip off the prickly leaf tips with kitchen scissors, then cut off the stems. Rub the cut edges with a lemon half. Pour enough water into a large, nonreactive saucepan to fill it about 1 inch deep; add the lemon halves and stand the artichokes upright in the water. Cover the pan and bring the water to a boil, then reduce the heat to medium low. Steam the artichokes until a knife slides easily into the stem end and a leaf gently tugged pulls free easily— about 30 minutes. Refresh the artichokes under cold running water and set them upside down on paper towels to drain.

Meanwhile, pour enough water into another large saucepan to fill it 1 inch deep. Set a vegetable steamer in the pan, and put the green beans into the steamer along with the fresh peas, if you are using them. Cover the pan and bring the water to a boil over medium-high heat. Steam the vegetables until they are just tender — about four minutes. Lift the steamer from the saucepan but leave the water in the pan to use again.

Refresh the green beans and the fresh peas under cold running water, then put them into a bowl. If you are using frozen peas, add them at this point. Cover the vegetables with plastic wrap and refrigerate them.

Add water to the saucepan, if necessary, to bring the level back to 1 inch. Replace the steamer, add the potatoes, and steam them until they are tender — about 15 minutes.

To make the dressing, use a paring knife to peel the peppers and slice them open. Remove the stems, ribs and seeds, working over a bowl to catch any juices. Put the peppers into a blender or a food processor along with the pepper juices, oil, olives, garlic, lemon juice, parsley, salt and a generous grinding of pepper. Purée the mixture.

Remove the cooked potatoes from the steamer and let them cool slightly. Cut the potatoes into ½-inch cubes, put them into a bowl, and toss them with ⅔ cup of the dressing. Set the bowl aside.

Preheat the broiler again. Rinse the tuna under cold running water and pat it dry with paper towels. Broil the tuna until its flesh is opaque and feels firm to the touch — about three minutes per side. Cut the fish into ½-inch chunks and toss them gently with the dressed potatoes. Cover the bowl with plastic wrap and refrigerate the mixture.

Cut the artichokes in half lengthwise and remove the hairy chokes with a small spoon or paring knife. Cut each half into thirds.

In a large bowl, toss the greens with all but approximately ½ cup of the remaining dressing; line a large chilled serving platter with them. Arrange the potato-tuna salad, artichokes and tomatoes on the greens, then scatter the beans, peas and onion slices over the top. Pass the remaining dressing as a dip for the artichoke leaves.

Peppered Bread Sticks

Makes 12 bread sticks
Working time: about 20 minutes
Total time: about 1 hour

Per bread stick:
Calories **111**
Protein **3g.**
Cholesterol **0mg.**
Total fat **1g.**
Saturated fat **0g.**
Sodium **179mg.**

1 envelope fast-rising yeast (about 1 tbsp.)
½ tsp. salt
1 cup unbleached all-purpose flour
¼ cup bread flour
½ tsp. freshly ground black pepper
1 tsp. olive oil
3 tbsp. cornmeal

Combine the yeast, salt, ¾ cup of the all-purpose flour, the bread flour and the pepper in a large bowl. Heat ½ cup of water and the oil in a saucepan just until they are hot to the touch (130° F.). Stir the hot water and oil into the flour mixture to combine the ingredients thoroughly.

Turn the dough out onto a floured surface and knead in the remaining ¼ cup of all-purpose flour. Continue to knead the dough until it is smooth and elastic — four to five minutes more.

Gather the dough into a ball and place it in a lightly oiled large bowl, turning the ball once to coat it with the oil. Cover the bowl with a damp towel or plastic

wrap and let the dough rise in a warm, draft-free place until it has doubled in bulk — 30 to 40 minutes.

When the dough has risen, punch it down, then transfer it to a floured surface, and knead it for two minutes. Divide the dough into 12 equal pieces. Roll each piece into a 10-inch-long rope.

Preheat the oven to 400° F. Sprinkle a baking sheet with the cornmeal. Lay the dough ropes on the sheet, cover them with the towel or plastic wrap, and let the ropes rise in a warm place for 10 minutes.

Bake the bread sticks until they are dry and lightly browned — 10 to 15 minutes. Transfer them to a rack to cool or serve them at once, piping hot. If you plan to use the bread sticks the following day, store them in an airtight container.

Cherry Summer Pudding

Serves 6
Working time: about 1 hour
Total time: about 9 hours (includes chilling)

Calories **288**
Protein **6g.**
Cholesterol **0mg.**
Total fat **3g.**
Saturated fat **1g.**
Sodium **256mg.**

4 cups pitted fresh or frozen sweet cherries
6 tbsp. honey
2 tbsp. fresh lemon juice
26 very thin slices white bread, crusts removed
1 cup fresh cherries for garnish (optional)

Put the 4 cups of fresh or frozen cherries into a non-reactive saucepan. Add the honey and lemon juice to the saucepan; bring the mixture to a boil. Reduce the heat and simmer the cherries for 10 minutes. Purée the cherries in a blender or a food processor.

Spoon enough of the purée into a 1½-quart mold or bowl to coat the bottom. Cover the purée with a single layer of bread, trimming the slices to allow them to fit snugly. Fill the mold with alternating layers of cherry purée and bread, pouring any remaining purée over the last layer. Cover the mold with plastic wrap and put it into the refrigerator for at least eight hours or overnight.

To serve the pudding: Run a knife around the edge of the mold and set an inverted plate over it. Turn both over together and lift off the mold, gently shaking it until the pudding slides out. Garnish the pudding with the fresh cherries if you are using them.

9 *An antique scoop holds a very modern peach ice cream made with part-skim ricotta cheese (recipe, page 274).*

Desserts

Summer Fruit Salad

Serves 6
Working time: about 25 minutes
Total time: about 1 hour and 25 minutes

Calories **191**
Protein **4g.**
Cholesterol **2mg.**
Total fat **2g.**
Saturated fat **0g.**
Sodium **35mg.**

1 watermelon (about 6 lb.), cut in half crosswise
juice of 1 lime
juice of 1 orange
¼ cup honey
2 cups blueberries, picked over and stemmed
2 kiwi fruits, each peeled and cut into 8 pieces
1 cup plain low-fat yogurt
2 tbsp. Grand Marnier or other orange-flavored liqueur

With a melon baller, scoop the watermelon flesh from the shell. Set the watermelon balls aside. (If you do not have a melon baller, remove the flesh with a curved grapefruit knife and cut it into uniform cubes, discarding the seeds.) Scrape out and discard any remaining flesh. Notch the rim of one watermelon shell half with a decorative zigzag and refrigerate the shell. Discard the other half.

To make the dressing, combine the lime juice, orange juice and 2 tablespoons of the honey in a large bowl. Add to the dressing the watermelon balls, blueberries and kiwis. Toss the fruit well, then refrigerate the salad for one hour.

To prepare the sauce, whisk together the yogurt, the remaining 2 tablespoons of honey and the liqueur. Refrigerate the sauce.

At serving time, set the watermelon shell on a large platter. Toss the salad once more to coat the fruit with the dressing, then spoon the fruit into the watermelon shell. Serve the chilled sauce in a separate bowl.

Strawberry Blossoms with Pears and Red-Wine Sauce

Serves 8
Working (and total) time: about 45 minutes

Calories **224**
Protein **1g.**
Cholesterol **4mg.**
Total fat **3g.**
Saturated fat **1g.**
Sodium **5mg.**

2 ½ cups red wine
⅔ cup sugar
3 lb. firm, ripe pears, peeled, quartered and cored
1 tbsp. unsalted butter
2 tbsp. fresh lemon juice
5 cups hulled strawberries

Combine the wine and ⅓ cup of the sugar in a heavy-bottomed saucepan over medium heat. Cook the wine, stirring occasionally, until it is reduced to about 1 cup — about 30 minutes. Transfer the sauce to a bowl and refrigerate it until it is cool.

While the wine is reducing, cut the pears into thin strips. Melt the butter in a large, heavy-bottomed skillet over medium heat. Add the pears, lemon juice and the remaining ⅓ cup of sugar; cook the mixture, stirring frequently, until almost all the liquid has evaporated — 15 to 20 minutes. Transfer the pear mixture to a plate and refrigerate it until it is cool.

Set eight of the smaller berries aside. Stand the remaining strawberries on a cutting board and cut them into vertical slices about ⅛ inch thick.

Spoon about ¼ cup of the chilled pear mixture into the center of a large dessert plate. Arrange some of the larger strawberry slices in a ring inside the pear mixture, overlapping the slices and propping them at a slight angle to resemble the petals of a flower. Form a smaller ring of strawberry slices inside the first and stand a whole berry in the center. Repeat the process with the remaining pear mixture and strawberries to form eight portions in all.

Just before serving, pour a little of the red-wine sauce around the outside of each blossom, letting a few drops fall onto the petals themselves.

Fresh Fruit in Ginger Syrup

Serves 6
Working time: about 25 minutes
Total time: about 2 hours (includes chilling)

Calories **149**
Protein **1g.**
Cholesterol **0mg.**
Total fat **0g.**
Saturated fat **0g.**
Sodium **3mg.**

1 tart green apple, quartered, cored and cut into ½-inch pieces
2 ripe peaches or nectarines, halved, pitted and cut into ½-inch pieces
1 pear, peeled, cored and cut into ½-inch pieces
1½ cups blueberries, picked over and stemmed
3 tbsp. fresh lemon juice
2 tbsp. julienned orange zest
2-inch length of ginger root, cut into ¼-inch-thick rounds
⅔ cup sugar

Place the cut fruit and the blueberries in a large bowl. Pour the lemon juice over the fruit and toss well, then refrigerate the bowl.

Pour 4 cups of water into a large, heavy-bottomed saucepan over medium-high heat. Add the orange zest, ginger and sugar, and bring the mixture to a boil. Reduce the heat to medium and simmer the liquid until it is reduced to about 2 cups of syrup. Remove the ginger with a slotted spoon and discard it.

Pour the syrup into a large bowl and let it stand at room temperature for 10 minutes. Add the fruit to the syrup and stir gently to coat the fruit. Refrigerate the dessert, covered, until the fruit is thoroughly chilled — about 1 hour and 30 minutes.

Fig Flowers with Cassis Sauce

Serves 6
Working time: about 25 minutes
Total time: about 40 minutes

Calories **156**
Protein **1g.**
Cholesterol **0mg.**
Total fat **0g.**
Saturated fat **0g.**
Sodium **5mg.**

2 cups dry white wine
1 tbsp. sugar
¼ cup crème de cassis
12 fresh figs
fresh mint leaves

Combine the wine and sugar in a saucepan over medium-high heat. Cook the liquid until it is reduced to approximately ¾ cup — about 15 minutes. Pour the reduced wine into a bowl and refrigerate it until it is cool — approximately 20 minutes. Stir the crème de cassis into the cooled liquid, then return the sauce to the refrigerator.

With a small, sharp knife, cut a cross in the top of each fig, slicing no more than halfway through. Carefully cut each quarter halfway down into two or three small wedges, leaving the wedges attached at the bottom; each fig will have eight to 12 wedges in all. With your fingers, press the base of the fig to spread the wedges outward like the petals of a flower in bloom. (More cutting may be needed to separate the wedges.)

Set two fig flowers on each of six chilled dessert plates. Drizzle some of the cassis sauce over the flowers, then garnish each serving with a few mint leaves.

duced by half — about 15 minutes. (There should be about ¼ cup of thick sauce.) Stir in the kirsch and the vanilla, then pour the sauce over the cherries. Broil the cherries for two or three minutes; serve them hot, with a spoonful of sauce dribbled over each portion.

Black Forest Cherries

Serves 4
Working (and total) time: about 30 minutes

Calories **224**	1 lb. sweet cherries
Protein **2g.**	¼ cup sugar
Cholesterol **21mg.**	1 tbsp. unsweetened cocoa powder
Total fat **7g.**	⅛ tsp. salt
Saturated fat **4g.**	¼ cup heavy cream
Sodium **73mg.**	¼ cup kirsch
	½ tsp. pure vanilla extract

Pit the cherries as shown at right.

Combine ¼ cup of water and the sugar in a heavy-bottomed saucepan set over medium-high heat, and bring the mixture to a boil. Add the cherries and stir gently to coat them with the syrup. Cook the cherries for one minute. Using a slotted spoon, transfer the poached cherries to a gratin dish or other heatproof serving dish, and set the dish aside. Remove the syrup from the heat.

Preheat the broiler.

In a bowl, combine the cocoa and salt. Pouring in a steady stream, whisk the cream into the cocoa and salt. Stir the mixture into the syrup in the saucepan. Bring the sauce to a boil, then reduce the heat, and simmer the mixture, stirring occasionally, until it is re-

Pitting a Cherry

1 *INSERTING THE BLADE. Grip a swivel vegetable peeler on either side of the blade, avoiding the cutting edges. Insert the tip into the top of a cherry from which the stem has been removed, and work the peeler's curved tip around the pit.*

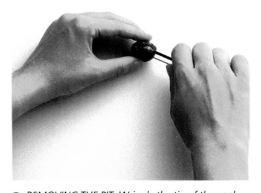

2 *REMOVING THE PIT. Wriggle the tip of the peeler back and forth to loosen the pit from the surrounding flesh. Then pry the pit up through the top of the fruit to dislodge it.*

Poached Peaches with Berry Sauce

Serves 8
Working time: about 30 minutes
Total time: about 2 hours and 30 minutes
(includes chilling)

Calories **122**
Protein **1g.**
Cholesterol **11mg.**
Total fat **3g.**
Saturated fat **2g.**
Sodium **4mg.**

8 firm but ripe freestone peaches
2 cups dry white wine
1 cup sugar
2-inch strip of lemon peel
8 mint sprigs (optional)
Berry sauce
1½ cups fresh or frozen blackberries or raspberries
2 tbsp. sugar
¼ cup heavy cream

Blanch the peaches in boiling water until their skins loosen — 30 seconds to one minute. Remove the peaches and run cold water over them to arrest the cooking. When the peaches are cool enough to handle, peel them and cut them in half lengthwise, discarding the pits.

Put the wine, sugar and lemon peel into a large saucepan. Bring the liquid to a boil, then reduce the heat, and simmer the mixture for five minutes. Add the peach halves to the liquid and poach them until they are just tender — three to five minutes. Using a slotted spoon, transfer the peach halves to a plate. Discard the poaching syrup. Cover the plate and refrigerate it for at least two hours.

To make the berry sauce, purée 1 cup of the berries with the sugar in a food processor or a blender, then strain the purée through a fine sieve into a bowl. Stir the cream into the purée.

To serve, arrange two peach halves on each of eight dessert plates and pour a little of the berry sauce over each portion. Garnish each serving with a few of the remaining berries and, if you like, a sprig of mint.

Mixed Berry Cobbler

Serves 8
Working (and total) time: about 30 minutes

Calories **179**
Protein **2g.**
Cholesterol **11mg.**
Total fat **6g.**
Saturated fat **3g.**
Sodium **5mg.**

2 cups fresh blueberries, picked over and stemmed, or 2 cups frozen blueberries, thawed
2 cups fresh or frozen red raspberries, thawed
2 cups fresh or frozen black raspberries or blackberries, thawed
¼ cup fresh lemon juice
¼ cup sugar
Oatmeal topping
1 cup rolled oats
¼ cup dark brown sugar
3 tbsp. unsalted butter

Preheat the oven to 350° F.

To prepare the topping, combine the oats and brown sugar in a small bowl. Spread the mixture in a baking pan and bake it until it turns light brown — eight to 10 minutes. Cut the butter into small pieces and scatter them in the pan. Return the pan to the oven until the butter has melted — about one minute. Stir the oats to coat them with the butter and bake the mixture for five minutes more. Set the oatmeal topping aside to cool. (The topping may be made ahead and stored, tightly covered, for several days.)

Put 1 cup of each of the berries into a 2-quart bowl and set them aside. Combine the lemon juice with the sugar in a saucepan and bring the mixture to a boil. Add the remaining cup of blueberries to the syrup; reduce the heat to low and cook the fruit for three minutes. Add the remaining cup of red raspberries along with the remaining cup of black raspberries or blackberries. Bring the mixture to a simmer and cook it, stirring constantly, for three minutes. Pour the cooked fruit into a sieve set over the bowl of reserved berries; use the back of a wooden spoon to press the fruit through the sieve. Stir gently to coat the whole berries with the sauce.

To serve, spoon the warm fruit mixture into individual ramekins or small bowls. Sprinkle some of the topping over each portion.

EDITOR'S NOTE: *If you prefer not to add the oatmeal topping, the fruit mixture may be served on its own, or it may be spooned over frozen yogurt.*

Blueberry-Peach Crumble

Serves 8
Working time: about 30 minutes
Total time: about 1 hour and 15 minutes

Calories **202**
Protein **3g.**
Cholesterol **38mg.**
Total fat **3g.**
Saturated fat **1g.**
Sodium **133mg.**

6 ripe peaches
1 tbsp. fresh lemon juice
¼ cup sugar
3 cups fresh blueberries, picked over and stemmed, or 3 cups frozen whole blueberries
Crumble topping
¾ cup whole-wheat flour
1 tsp. baking powder
¼ tsp. salt
1 tbsp. cold unsalted butter
½ cup plus 1 tbsp. sugar
1 egg
½ tsp. ground cinnamon
1 tbsp. wheat germ

Preheat the oven to 375° F.

Blanch the peaches in boiling water until their skins loosen — 30 seconds to one minute. Peel the peaches and halve them lengthwise, discarding the pits. Cut each peach half into five or six slices. In a bowl, gently toss the slices with the lemon juice and the sugar.

To prepare the crumble topping, put the flour, baking powder, salt, butter and ½ cup of the sugar into a food processor; mix the ingredients just long enough to produce a fine-meal texture. Alternatively, put the dry ingredients into a bowl and cut the butter in using a pastry blender or two knives. Add the egg and blend it in — five to 10 seconds. The topping should have the texture of large crumbs.

Arrange the peach slices in an even layer in a large, shallow baking dish. Scatter the blueberries over the peach slices, then sprinkle the topping over the blueberries. Stir together the cinnamon, wheat germ and the remaining tablespoon of sugar, and strew this mixture over the topping. Bake the dish until the topping is brown and the juices bubble up around the edges — 45 to 55 minutes.

EDITOR'S NOTE: *For added fiber, leave the peach skins on.*

Pineapple Gratin

Serves 6
Working time: about 20 minutes
Total time: about 30 minutes

Calories **170**
Protein **2g.**
Cholesterol **0mg.**
Total fat **1g.**
Saturated fat **0g.**
Sodium **22mg.**

1 large ripe pineapple
2 tbsp. dark raisins
2 tbsp. golden raisins
5 tbsp. pure maple syrup
3 tbsp. bourbon or white rum
1 egg yolk
½ tsp. pure vanilla extract
¼ tsp. ground ginger
1 tbsp. cornstarch
2 egg whites, at room temperature
2 tbsp. dark brown sugar

Preheat the oven to 500° F.

Trim and peel the pineapple. Stand the pineapple upright and cut it in half from top to bottom. Remove the core from each half by cutting a shallow V-shaped groove down the center, then cut each half crosswise into nine slices.

Overlap the pineapple slices in a large, shallow baking dish. Scatter the dark raisins and golden raisins over the pineapple slices. Drizzle 2 tablespoons of the maple syrup over the top, then sprinkle the dish with 2 tablespoons of the bourbon or rum. Cover the dish and set it aside at room temperature.

In a small bowl, blend the egg yolk with the vanilla, ginger, cornstarch, the remaining 3 tablespoons of maple syrup and the remaining tablespoon of bourbon or rum. In a separate bowl, beat the two egg whites until they form soft peaks. Stir half of the beaten egg whites into the yolk mixture to lighten it. Gently fold the yolk mixture into the remaining beaten egg whites.

Bake the dish containing the pineapple until the slices are heated through — about three minutes. Remove the dish from the oven and spread the egg mixture evenly over the fruit. Rub the sugar through a sieve over the top of the egg mixture. Return the dish to the oven and bake the pineapple until the sugar melts and the topping browns and puffs up slightly — about five minutes. Serve the gratin immediately.

Fruit-and-Nut-Filled Phyllo Roll

Serves 6
Working time: about 40 minutes
Total time: about 1 hour and 10 minutes

Calories **186**
Protein **4g.**
Cholesterol **8mg.**
Total fat **6g.**
Saturated fat **2g.**
Sodium **2mg.**

1 egg white
¼ cup part-skim ricotta cheese
1 orange
1 tsp. grated lemon zest
¼ tsp. ground cinnamon
⅛ tsp. grated nutmeg
⅛ tsp. ground allspice
⅛ tsp. salt
3 tbsp. coarsely chopped pecans
½ cup raisins
1 tbsp. pure maple syrup
¼ cup sugar
2 slices whole-wheat bread, toasted
2 sheets frozen phyllo dough, thawed
1 tbsp. unsalted butter, melted

To make the filling, first mix together the egg white and the ricotta. With a vegetable peeler or a paring knife, remove the zest from the orange and reserve it. Cut away all the white pith and discard it. Working over a bowl to catch the juice, segment the orange dropping the segments into the bowl. Squeeze the last drops of juice from the pulpy core of membranes into the bowl. Coarsely chop the orange zest and orange segments, and add them to the ricotta mixture along with the juice that has collected in the bowl. Stir in the lemon zest, cinnamon, nutmeg, allspice, salt, pecans, raisins, maple syrup and sugar. Cut the toasted bread slices into cubes and mix them into the filling. Set the filling aside.

Preheat the oven to 350° F.

Lay one of the phyllo sheets on a piece of wax paper that is slightly larger than the phyllo. Lightly brush the phyllo with some of the butter. Set the second sheet of phyllo squarely atop the first.

Spoon the filling down one of the longer sides of the doubled phyllo sheet, leaving about 1½ inches uncovered at both ends of the filling. To avoid tearing the phyllo, lift the edge of the wax paper and roll the phyllo once around the filling. Continue rolling the phyllo and filling away from you to form a compact cylinder. Tuck under the two open ends of the roll and transfer it to a lightly oiled baking sheet. Brush the top of the roll with the remaining butter and bake it until it is golden brown — about 30 minutes. Allow the roll to cool, then slice it into serving rounds.

Raspberries and Figs Brûlées

Serves 4
Working (and total) time: about 10 minutes

Calories **116**
Protein **1g.**
Cholesterol **5mg.**
Total fat **3g.**
Saturated fat **2g.**
Sodium **11mg.**

1 cup of fresh or frozen whole raspberries, thawed

2 ripe figs, quartered and thinly sliced lengthwise

¼ cup sour cream

¼ cup light brown sugar

Preheat the broiler. Divide the raspberries evenly among four 4-ounce ramekins. Arrange one quarter of the fig slices in each ramekin, overlapping the slices as necessary to fit them in. Spread 1 tablespoon of the sour cream over the fig slices in each ramekin, then top each layer of sour cream with 1 tablespoon of the brown sugar rubbed through a sieve. Set the ramekins on a baking sheet and broil them until the brown sugar melts and the sour cream bubbles — one to two minutes. Serve immediately.

Chocolate Chiffon Cake with Raspberry Filling

Serves 12
Working time: about 40 minutes
Total time: about 2 hours

Calories **207**
Protein **3g.**
Cholesterol **46mg.**
Total fat **6g.**
Saturated fat **1g.**
Sodium **112mg.**

¼ cup unsweetened cocoa powder
¾ cup cake flour
¾ cup sugar
1 tsp. baking soda
⅛ tsp. salt
¼ cup safflower oil
2 eggs, separated, plus 2 egg whites, the whites at room temperature
1 tsp. pure vanilla extract
¼ tsp. cream of tartar
Raspberry filling
2 cups fresh or frozen whole raspberries
½ cup sugar
Raspberry-Champagne sauce
2 cups fresh or frozen whole raspberries, thawed
½ tsp. fresh lemon juice
¾ cup chilled dry Champagne
2 tbsp. sugar (if you are using fresh raspberries)

Spoon the unsweetened cocoa powder into a small heatproof bowl and stir ½ cup of boiling water into it. Set the bowl aside.

Preheat the oven to 350° F.

Sift the flour, 6 tablespoons of the sugar, the baking soda and salt into a large bowl. Stir in the oil, egg yolks, the cocoa mixture and the vanilla; mix to blend the ingredients.

Pour the egg whites into a bowl and beat them until they are frothy. Add the cream of tartar, then continue beating the whites until soft peaks form. Gradually adding the remaining 6 tablespoons of sugar, beat the whites until they form stiff peaks.

Mix one third of the beaten whites into the flour mixture to lighten it; gently fold in the remaining whites. Pour the mixture into a 9-by-5-by-3-inch loaf pan. Bake the cake until a wooden pick inserted in the center comes out clean — about 55 minutes. Invert the pan on a cake rack and let the cake cool completely.

While the cake is cooling, make the raspberry filling. Combine the 2 cups of raspberries, ½ cup of sugar and ▶

2 tablespoons of water in a heavy saucepan over medium heat; cook the mixture, stirring constantly, until it has the consistency of fruit preserves — about 25 minutes. Refrigerate the filling.

For the sauce, purée the 2 cups of raspberries with the lemon juice in a food processor or a blender. (If you are using fresh raspberries, include the 2 tablespoons of sugar in the purée.) Strain the purée into a bowl; discard the solids. Refrigerate the purée.

Run a knife blade around the sides of the loaf pan, then invert the pan again and rap it sharply against the work surface to unmold the cake. Cut the cake into two horizontal layers. Spread the chilled raspberry filling over the bottom layer, then set the top layer back in place. Just before serving, stir the Champagne into the chilled raspberry purée. Cut the cake into serving slices, and surround each one with a little raspberry-Champagne sauce.

EDITOR'S NOTE: *If you are using Dutch-process cocoa powder, which is more alkaline than domestic brands, substitute 1½ teaspoons of baking powder for the teaspoon of baking soda. A split of Champagne will yield ¾ cup.*

Papaya Porcupines with Coconut Quills

Makes about 20 porcupines
Working time: about 30 minutes
Total time: about 45 minutes

Per porcupine:
Calories **49**
Protein **1g.**
Cholesterol **0mg.**
Total fat **1g.**
Saturated fat **1g.**
Sodium **14mg.**

2 egg whites
2 tbsp. fresh lemon juice
½ cup unbleached all-purpose flour
6 tbsp. sugar
⅔ cup sweetened dried coconut
1 papaya (about 1 lb.), peeled and cut into about 20 chunks

Preheat the oven to 400° F.

Prepare the coating for the papaya: In a small bowl, thoroughly whisk the egg whites, lemon juice, flour and 2 tablespoons of the sugar. Set the coating aside.

Spread out the coconut on a sheet of wax paper.

Toss the papaya pieces with the remaining ¼ cup of sugar. Dip a piece of papaya into the coating, then hold the piece over the bowl to allow the excess coating to drip off. Roll the papaya piece in the coconut, then transfer it to a baking sheet. Repeat the process to coat the remaining pieces.

Bake the papaya porcupines until the coating has set and is lightly browned — about 15 minutes. Serve the papaya porcupines warm.

Rhubarb Tartlets
Topped with Meringue

Serves 4
Working (and total) time: about 1 hour and 30 minutes

Calories **202**
Protein **3g.**
Cholesterol **7mg.**
Total fat **5g.**
Saturated fat **2g.**
Sodium **180mg.**

1 tart green apple, peeled, cored and cut into ½-inch cubes
2 tbsp. dry white wine
1 lb. fresh rhubarb, trimmed and cut into ½-inch pieces, or 1 lb. frozen rhubarb, thawed
¼ cup light brown sugar
¼ tsp. pure vanilla extract
½ tbsp. fresh lemon juice
¼ tsp. ground cinnamon
grated nutmeg
⅛ tsp. salt
4 frozen phyllo-dough sheets in a stack, thawed
1 tbsp. unsalted butter, melted
1 egg white
1½ tbsp. sugar

Put the apple cubes and wine into a saucepan and simmer them, covered, for five minutes. Add the rhubarb, reduce the heat to low, and cook the mixture, uncovered, for five minutes more. Stir in the brown sugar, vanilla, lemon juice, cinnamon, a pinch of nutmeg and the salt. Continue cooking the mixture, stirring occasionally, until most of the liquid has evaporated — five to 10 minutes. Set the mixture aside.

Preheat the oven to 350° F.

To prepare the pastry, fold the stack of phyllo sheets in half, then fold it in half again and trim off the edges to produce a stack of sixteen 5-inch squares. Lay one of the phyllo squares on a work surface; using a pastry brush, lightly dab the square with a little of the melted butter. Set a second square atop the first and brush it with butter. Set a third square on top of the second at a 45-degree angle, forming an eight-pointed star. Dab the top of the third square with butter and cover it with a fourth square.

Lightly oil four cups of a muffin tin. Transfer the stacked phyllo to one of the cups and gently press it in place, taking care that the edges of the phyllo come as far as possible up the sides of the cup. Prepare the remaining phyllo squares in the same manner, making four tartlets in all.

Bake the tartlets until they are light brown and crisp — about eight minutes. Remove the muffin tin from the oven and unmold the tartlets, then set them aside. Let the tartlets cool to room temperature.

Increase the oven temperature to 500° F.

To make the meringue, whip the egg white in a small bowl until the white forms soft peaks. Continue beating, gradually adding the sugar, until stiff peaks form when the beater is lifted from the bowl.

Set the tartlets on a cookie sheet and divide the rhubarb mixture among them. Using a pastry bag or a spoon, top each with some of the meringue; bake the tartlets until the meringue browns — about three minutes. Serve the tartlets within two hours.

Cherry Cheese Tartlets

Makes 12 tartlets
Working time: about 45 minutes
Total time: about 1 hour and 10 minutes

Per tartlet:
Calories **100**
Protein **5g.**
Cholesterol **20mg.**
Total fat **3g.**
Saturated fat **1g.**
Sodium **110mg.**

3 sheets phyllo pastry, each about 18 by 12 inches
1 tbsp. unsalted butter, melted
Spicy cheese filling
8 oz. low-fat cream cheese, softened
½ cup plain low-fat yogurt
1 egg
1 tbsp. honey
1 tsp. pure vanilla extract
½ tsp. ground cinnamon
Glossy cherry topping
1 tbsp. cherry jam
½ tsp. cornstarch
12 oz. sweet cherries, pitted and halved

Preheat the oven to 375° F.

Trim 2 inches off one of the short edges of each sheet of phyllo, then cut each sheet into twelve 4-inch squares. Keep the squares covered with a damp cloth to prevent them from drying out, removing them as needed. Brush twelve 3-inch round tart pans with a little of the melted butter. Stack three squares of phyllo pastry in each pan, fold the edges over to neaten them, then brush the tops lightly with melted butter. Bake the cases in the oven until they are crisp and lightly browned—about three minutes. Allow the cases to cool in the pans.

In the meantime, prepare the cheese filling. Put the cheese, yogurt, egg, honey, vanilla extract, and cinnamon into a mixing bowl. Beat the ingredients together with a wooden spoon until smooth, or blend the mixture in a food processor. Divide the filling equally among the pastry cases, spreading it evenly with the back of a teaspoon. Return the tartlets to the oven and cook them until the filling has set—8 to 10 minutes. Remove the tartlets from the oven and cool them in the pans.

While the tartlets are cooling, prepare the cherry topping. First, make a glaze by stirring the cherry jam with 3 tablespoons of water in a small saucepan set over low heat. Blend the cornstarch to a smooth paste with 1 tablespoon of water. Add the cornstarch paste to the jam solution, bring the mixture to a boil, and cook, stirring, until it thickens and becomes translucent—about two minutes. Arrange the cherry halves on top of the cheese mixture, and brush them with the cherry glaze.

Allow the glaze to set for a few minutes before unmolding and serving the tartlets.

Cherry Triangles

Makes 12 triangles
Working time: about 40 minutes
Total time: about 1 hour and 20 minutes

Per triangle:	
Calories **90**	6 tbsp. plain low-fat yogurt
Protein **2g.**	1 tbsp. sugar
Cholesterol **0mg.**	1 tbsp. kirsch
Total fat **6g.**	1 lb. sweet cherries, pitted
Saturated fat **trace**	8 sheets phyllo pastry, each about 18 by 12 inches
Sodium **25mg.**	3 tsp. safflower oil
	confectioners' sugar to decorate

First, make the filling. Place the yogurt, sugar, and kirsch in a mixing bowl. Reserve 12 cherries for decoration. Quarter the remainder and gently fold them into the yogurt mixture.

Preheat the oven to 400° F. Keep the sheets of phyllo covered with a damp cloth to prevent them from drying out, removing them as needed.

Lay one sheet of phyllo on a work surface. Brush it lightly with oil and cover it with a second sheet. Cut this double sheet of phyllo lengthwise into three strips, each 4 inches wide. Place one tablespoon of filling at one end of a strip, then fold a corner of the phyllo over the filling to form a neat triangle. Continue folding the filled triangle until you reach the end of the strip, keeping the shape as you work. Tuck in the loose end of the phyllo and transfer the triangular parcel—seam side down—to a lightly oiled baking sheet. Make up the two remaining strips in the same way, then repeat the process with the rest of the phyllo and filling to make nine more triangles.

Brush the phyllo triangles with the remaining oil, and bake them until they are crisp and golden—9 to 10 minutes. Transfer them to a wire rack to cool.

Before serving, halve the reserved cherries. Sift a little confectioners' sugar over the top of each triangle and serve with the cherries.

Rice and Apricot Ring

Serves 8
Working time: about 1 hour and 10 minutes
Total time: about 3 hours and 30 minutes
(includes chilling)

Calories **125**
Protein **6g.**
Cholesterol **trace**
Total fat **1g.**
Saturated fat **trace**
Sodium **60mg.**

2½ cups skim milk
⅓ cup short-grain rice, washed
½ tsp. pure almond extract
5 large ripe apricots, peeled, halved, and pitted, or 14 oz. canned apricot halves in their own juice, drained
¼ cup plain low-fat yogurt
1 tbsp. powdered gelatin
2 egg whites
⅓ cup sugar
6 oz. fresh raspberries (about ¾ cup)

Bring the milk to a boil in a heavy-bottomed saucepan. Reduce the heat to low, and add the rice and the almond extract. Simmer the mixture uncovered, stirring from time to time, until the rice has absorbed all of the milk—about 50 minutes.

If you are using fresh apricots, place them cut sides down in a nonreactive saucepan and pour in ¾ cup of boiling water. Simmer the fruit gently until it is just tender—two to three minutes—then drain it.

Arrange eight apricot halves in the bottom of an 8-inch ring mold. Reserve the remaining apricot halves.

When the rice has absorbed the milk, remove it from the heat and allow it to cool slightly, then stir in the yogurt. Dissolve the gelatin in 2 tablespoons of cold water and stir it into the rice mixture. Beat the egg whites until they stand in soft peaks. Beat in all but 1 tablespoon of the sugar in three batches, ensuring that the mixture is stiff and glossy each time before adding more sugar.

Stir a spoonful of the egg whites into the rice to lighten the mixture, then fold in the remainder of the egg whites. Spoon the mixture into the prepared ring mold, being careful not to disturb the apricot halves. Level the surface of the mixture and refrigerate the ring until it is set—at least two hours.

Meanwhile, put the raspberries in a nonreactive saucepan and add the remaining sugar. Heat the berries and sugar gently until the juice runs, then simmer the berries until they fall apart—two to three minutes. Allow them to cool.

Purée the cooked raspberries with the reserved apricot halves in a food processor or blender. Press the purée through a fine sieve to remove the seeds.

To unmold the dessert, dip the bottom of the ring mold in hot water for two to three seconds, then turn the contents out onto a flat serving plate. Serve the dessert cut into slices and garnished with the raspberry-apricot purée.

SUGGESTED ACCOMPANIMENT: *fresh raspberries, placed in the center of the ring.*

EDITOR'S NOTE: *The ring may be stored in the refrigerator for up to four days, but it should not be frozen.*

Molded Chocolate Mousse with Orange-Caramel Sauce

Serves 8
Working time: about 25 minutes
Total time: about 3 hours and 25 minutes

Calories **210**
Protein **5g.**
Cholesterol **5mg.**
Total fat **7g.**
Saturated fat **4g.**
Sodium **50mg.**

1 tbsp. powdered gelatin
5 oz. semisweet chocolate
1 tbsp. dark rum (optional)
½ cup sour cream
1 cup plain low-fat yogurt
1 orange, grated zest only
2 egg whites
1 tbsp. sugar
2 tangerines, peeled and segmented, all pith removed

Orange-caramel sauce

1 cup fresh orange juice
½ cup sugar
1 tsp. ground cinnamon

Line a 2-cup decorative mold with plastic wrap, pulling the wrap as tight as possible and pressing it into the contours of the mold.

Dissolve the gelatin in 2 tablespoons of water. Melt the chocolate, with the rum if you are using it, in a flameproof bowl set over a pan of simmering water; stir the chocolate until it is smooth. In a mixing bowl, whisk together the sour cream and yogurt, then whisk in the melted chocolate, the orange zest, and finally the dissolved gelatin.

In a separate bowl, beat the egg whites until they form soft peaks. Add the sugar, and beat again until the whites are stiff and glossy.

Gently fold the beaten egg whites into the chocolate mixture, then turn the mixture into the prepared mold. Level the surface of the mousse and put it in the refrigerator to set—three to four hours.

To make the sauce, put 3 tablespoons of the orange juice in a heavy-bottomed pan with the sugar. Heat these ingredients gently until the sugar has dissolved, then increase the heat and bring the liquid to a boil. Add the remaining orange juice to the pan (cover your hand with a towel when doing this, in case the mixture splatters), and stir in the cinnamon. Boil the sauce for five minutes, to reduce it a little. Strain the sauce into a bowl through a paper coffee filter or a layer of cheesecloth, to remove the sediment. Allow the sauce to cool thoroughly.

To serve the mousse, invert the mold onto a flat serving dish and carefully peel off the plastic wrap. Pour the sauce around the mousse, and arrange the tangerine segments decoratively along the top of the mousse and in the sauce.

the meringues stand at room temperature until they cool — they will become quite crisp.

Purée the ricotta with the yogurt in a food processor or a blender. Divide the cheese mixture among the meringue baskets, and top each with some of the strawberries and blueberries.

Berry-Filled Meringue Baskets

Serves 8
Working time: about 50 minutes
Total time: about 5 hours (includes drying)

Calories **150**
Protein **4g.**
Cholesterol **5mg.**
Total fat **2g.**
Saturated fat **1g.**
Sodium **45mg.**

3 egg whites
1 cup sugar
½ cup part-skim ricotta cheese
¼ cup plain low-fat yogurt
2 cups hulled, sliced strawberries
1 cup blueberries, stemmed, picked over and rinsed

Line a baking sheet with parchment paper or with a paper bag that has been cut open and flattened. Preheat the oven to 160° F. If your oven does not have a setting this low, set it just below 200° F. Keep the oven door propped open with a ball of crumpled foil.

To prepare the meringue, put the egg whites and sugar into a large, heatproof bowl. Set the bowl over a pan of simmering water, and stir the mixture with a whisk until the sugar has dissolved and the egg whites are hot — about six minutes. Remove the bowl from the heat. Using an electric mixer, beat the egg whites on medium-high speed until they form stiff peaks and have cooled to room temperature.

Transfer the meringue to a pastry bag fitted with a ½-inch star tip. Holding the tip about ½ inch above the surface of the baking sheet, pipe out the meringue in a tightly coiled spiral until you have formed a flat disk about 3½ inches across. Pipe a single ring of meringue on top of the edge of the disk, forming a low wall that will hold in the filling. Form seven more meringue baskets the same way.

Put the baking sheet into the oven and let the meringues bake for at least four hours. The meringues should remain white and be thoroughly dried out. Let

Rolled Cherry-Walnut Cake

Serves 8
Working time: about 1 hour
Total time: about 1 hour and 30 minutes

Calories **142**
Protein **5g.**
Cholesterol **70mg.**
Total fat **4g.**
Saturated fat **1g.**
Sodium **72mg.**

¼ cup walnuts, finely chopped
1½ tbsp. unbleached all-purpose flour
½ tsp. baking powder
2 eggs, separated, plus 1 egg white, the whites at room temperature
2 tbsp. dark brown sugar
½ tsp. pure vanilla extract
¼ cup sugar
2 tsp. confectioners' sugar
Cherry filling
½ tsp. pure vanilla extract
1 cup plain low-fat yogurt
2 tbsp. sugar
½ lb. fresh cherries, pitted and quartered

Dot the corners and center of a baking sheet with butter. Line the sheet with parchment paper or wax paper — the butter will hold the paper in place. Lightly butter the top of the paper, then dust it with flour and set the pan aside. Heat the oven to 350° F.

Mix together the walnuts, flour and baking powder in a small bowl; set the mixture aside.

Beat the two egg yolks with the brown sugar and 1½ tablespoons of very hot water until the mixture is thick enough to fall in a ribbon when the beater is lifted from the bowl — about four minutes. Stir in the vanilla and set the bowl aside.

Beat the three egg whites on medium speed in a bowl until they form soft peaks. Increase the speed to medium high and continue beating, gradually adding the ¼ cup of sugar, until stiff peaks form.

Stir about one fourth of the egg whites into the yolk mixture to lighten it. Gently fold one third of the remaining egg whites into the yolk mixture, then fold in half of the nut-and-flour mixture, followed by half of the remaining egg whites. Finally, fold in the remaining nut-and-flour mixture and the last of the egg whites.

Transfer the batter to the baking sheet and spread it

out, forming a rectangle about 11 by 7 inches. Bake the cake until it is lightly browned and springy to the touch — about 20 minutes. Let the cake cool completely — at least 30 minutes.

Sprinkle a sheet of parchment paper or wax paper with confectioners' sugar and invert the cake onto the paper. Gently remove the paper on which the cake baked from the bottom of the cake. Trim the edges of the cake with a serrated knife or scissors. Stir the vanilla into the yogurt, then spread this mixture onto the cake, leaving a ½-inch border uncovered all around. Sprinkle the sugar over the yogurt mixture, then scatter the cherries evenly on top. Starting at a long side, roll the cake into a cylinder. Set the cake on a platter; sprinkle the confectioners' sugar over the top just before serving.

Freezing Sorbets, Sherbets and Ice Creams

Frozen desserts count among everyone's favorites. Three different methods for preparing them are examined below. For efficiency, make sure that the dessert mixture is well chilled before you freeze it.

Hand-whisking method

This basic procedure involves placing the dessert mixture in a freezer, then whisking it from time to time as it firms up to break the ice crystals and aerate the mixture. Before starting, turn your freezer to its coldest setting. Use as large a nonreactive metal bowl as will fit into the freezer, or resort to metal ice-cube trays. (Vessels made of glass, a poor conductor of heat, will retard the freezing process.) Place the bowl containing the dessert in the freezer. When a ring of crystals about half an inch wide has formed around the outside edge of the mixture, usually after an hour or two, whisk the mixture. Return the bowl to the freezer and allow another ring of crystals to form before whisking the mixture again. Repeat the whisking a few more times until the dessert is frozen through. After the final whisking, allow the dessert to freeze an additional 15 minutes, then serve it.

Food-processor method

This fast and easy method utilizes a food processor once the dessert mixture has set. Freeze the mixture in a nonreactive metal bowl; when the dessert has solidified — the center may still be soft — break it into chunks and place them in a food processor. (Return the empty bowl to the freezer; you will need it later.) Process the frozen chunks until the dessert has a smooth consistency; be careful not to overprocess it or it will melt. Return the dessert to the chilled bowl and let it sit in the freezer — a process that cooks call "ripening" — for another 15 minutes until it firms up.

Frozen desserts consisting only of fruit juice and a moderate amount of sugar or those containing alcohol will melt faster than those made with fruit purée, a high amount of sugar, egg white, milk or yogurt. They should be broken into chunks, then processed quickly to break down the crystals without melting. Sorbets and sherbets prepared according to the food-processor method will keep, covered, for several days in the freezer; to restore their consistency, however, they will likely need reprocessing followed by 15 minutes in the freezer.

Churning method

The old-fashioned ice-cream maker that demanded half an hour or more of laborious hand-cranking is quickly being replaced by electric and other convenience models, some containing coolants. In using them, be sure to follow the manufacturer's instructions carefully.

Blueberry Sorbet

Serves 6
Working time: about 10 minutes
Total time: 1 to 3 hours, depending on freezing method

Calories **223**
Protein **1g.**
Cholesterol **0mg.**
Total fat **0g.**
Saturated fat **0g.**
Sodium **7mg.**

4½ cups fresh blueberries, picked over and rinsed, or 4 cups frozen unsweetened blueberries
1¼ cups sugar
1 tbsp. fresh lemon juice

Purée all but ½ cup of the blueberries in a food processor or a blender. If you are using frozen blueberries, purée them all; they do not make a suitable garnish. Strain the purée through a fine sieve into a bowl. Discard any solids remaining in the sieve. Add the sugar and lemon juice to the purée, then stir the mixture until the sugar has dissolved.

Freeze the sorbet, using one of the methods described at left *(box)*. Blueberry sorbet is best when served within 24 hours. Just before serving, garnish the sorbet with the reserved fresh blueberries.

Apple Sorbet with Candied Almonds

Serves 8
Working time: about 50 minutes
Total time: 1 to 3 hours, depending on freezing method

Calories **249**
Protein **1g.**
Cholesterol **0mg.**
Total fat **2g.**
Saturated fat **0g.**
Sodium **2mg.**

10 tart green apples
juice of 5 lemons
1⅔ cups sugar
¼ cup slivered almonds
1 tbsp. brown sugar

Cut off and discard the top quarter of one of the apples. Using a melon baller or a spoon, scoop the flesh, core and seeds from the apple, leaving a ¼-inch-thick wall. Reserve the flesh; discard the core and seeds. Sprinkle the inside of the apple and the reserved flesh with some of the lemon juice. Repeat the process with all but two of the remaining apples, then freeze the hollowed apples. Peel, seed and chop the two remaining apples, and add them to the reserved flesh.

Put 2 cups of water, 1 cup of the sugar and about half of the remaining lemon juice in a saucepan. Bring the liquid to a boil, then reduce the heat to medium, and simmer the mixture for three minutes. Add the reserved apple flesh and simmer it until it is tender — three to four minutes. With a slotted spoon, transfer the cooked apple flesh to a food processor or a blender. Discard the poaching liquid. Purée the apple; put 2 cups of the purée into a bowl and allow it to cool. If any purée is left over, reserve it for another use.

Stir the remaining lemon juice and the remaining ⅔ cup of sugar into the apple purée. Freeze the mixture, using one of the methods opposite *(box)*.

While the sorbet is freezing, put the slivered almonds in a small, heavy-bottomed skillet over medium heat. Toast the almonds, stirring constantly, until they turn golden brown — about five minutes. Stir in the brown sugar, increase the heat to high, and cook the almonds until they are coated with melted sugar — about one minute more. Set the almonds aside.

When the sorbet is firm, scoop or spoon it into the prepared apple cups, then sprinkle some of the candied almonds over each apple. Keep the apples in the freezer until they are served.

EDITOR'S NOTE: *These sorbets are best when consumed within 24 hours of their preparation.*

Lemon Cups

Serves 8
Working time: about 30 minutes
Total time: 1 to 3 hours, depending on freezing method

Calories **52**
Protein **0g.**
Cholesterol **0mg.**
Total fat **0g.**
Saturated fat **0g.**
Sodium **0mg.**

4 lemons, plus ½ tsp. grated lemon zest
½ cup sugar
16 citrus leaves or fresh mint leaves (optional)

Halve the lemons lengthwise, cutting the rind in a zigzag pattern. Remove the pulp and seeds from the halves with a melon baller or a small, sturdy spoon. Transfer the pulp to a sieve set over a bowl, and press down on it with the bottom of a ladle or the back of a wooden spoon to extract all the juice. Discard the pulp and seeds and reserve the juice. With a sharp knife, lightly pare the bottom of each lemon shell to stabilize it. Freeze the lemon halves.

Strain ½ cup of the lemon juice into a bowl. (Any excess juice may be reserved for another use.) Whisk 1½ cups of water, the grated zest and the sugar into the strained lemon juice, stirring until the sugar has dissolved. Freeze the sorbet, using one of the methods described on page 262.

When the sorbet is firm, spoon or pipe it into the lemon halves and return them to the freezer. If you like, garnish each lemon cup with two of the citrus or mint leaves before serving.

Lime Cups

Serves 8
Working time: about 30 minutes
Total time: 1 to 3 hours, depending on freezing method

Calories **52**
Protein **0g.**
Cholesterol **0mg.**
Total fat **0g.**
Saturated fat **0g.**
Sodium **0mg.**

8 limes, plus 1 tsp. grated lime zest
2 tbsp. fresh lemon juice
½ cup sugar
1 egg white (optional)
8 citrus leaves or fresh mint leaves (optional)

Cut each lime in half lengthwise. Remove the pulp from the shells with a melon baller or a small spoon. Transfer the pulp to a sieve set over a bowl, and press down on the pulp with the bottom of a ladle or the back of a wooden spoon to extract all the juice. Discard the pulp and seeds, and reserve the juice. Lightly pare the bottom of the shells to stabilize them. Freeze the lime shells.

Strain 6 tablespoons of the lime juice into a bowl. (Any extra juice may be reserved for another use.) Whisk in the lemon juice, 1½ cups of water, the lime ▶

zest, sugar and egg white, and stir until the sugar has dissolved. Freeze the sorbet, using one of the methods described on page 262.

When the sorbet is firm, pipe or spoon it into the lime shells and return them to the freezer. If you like, garnish each lime shell with a citrus or mint leaf.

EDITOR'S NOTE: *The egg white called for here keeps the sorbet from freezing too hard, making it easier to pipe. An egg white may likewise be added to any citrus sorbet in this section.*

Kiwi Sorbet

Serves 4
Working time: about 15 minutes
Total time: 1 to 3 hours, depending on freezing method

Calories **190**
Protein **2g.**
Cholesterol **0mg.**
Total fat **1g.**
Saturated fat **0g.**
Sodium **8mg.**

8 kiwi fruits
2 tbsp. fresh lemon juice
½ cup sugar

Cut a thin slice from both ends of a kiwi fruit. Stand the fruit on a cutting board. Remove the rest of the skin by slicing vertical strips from the sides of the fruit, taking care not to cut off too much of the flesh. Peel the remaining kiwis the same way.

Quarter each kiwi fruit and put the pieces into a food processor or a blender. Process the kiwis just long enough to purée them without cracking their seeds. Add the lemon juice and sugar, and blend them in.

Freeze the mixture, using one of the methods on page 262. Serve the kiwi sorbet in scoops.

Plum and Red Wine Sorbet with Raisin Sauce

Serves 10
Working time: about 25 minutes
Total time: about 1 day

Calories **181**
Protein **1g.**
Cholesterol **0mg.**
Total fat **0g.**
Saturated fat **0g.**
Sodium **3mg.**

2½ cups red wine
1¼ cups sugar
1 lb. ripe red plums, quartered and pitted, two of the quarters sliced for garnish
2 tbsp. fresh lemon juice
¼ cup dark raisins
¼ cup golden raisins

Combine 2 cups of the wine with the sugar in a heavy-bottomed saucepan over medium heat. Bring the mixture to a boil, stirring to dissolve the sugar. When the liquid reaches a boil, reduce the heat, cover the pan, and simmer the syrup for two minutes. Stir in the plum quarters; as soon as the syrup returns to a simmer, cover the pan again and cook the plums for four minutes more. Strain ½ cup of the syrup into a small bowl and set it aside for the sauce.

To prepare the sorbet, first purée the plum-wine mixture in a blender or food processor. Blend in the remaining ½ cup of wine and the lemon juice. Let the mixture cool to room temperature, then chill it.

Using one of the methods described on page 262, freeze the sorbet mixture until it is firm but not hard. Transfer the frozen sorbet to a metal mold or bowl. Rap the bottom of the mold or bowl on the counter once or twice to collapse any large air bubbles. Cover the container tightly with plastic wrap and freeze the sorbet overnight.

To prepare the sauce, combine the reserved ½ cup of syrup with the dark and golden raisins in a small, heavy-bottomed saucepan. Quickly bring the mixture to a boil, then immediately remove the pan from the heat. Let the sauce cool to room temperature before refrigerating it; the raisins will plump up.

Shortly before serving time, unmold the sorbet. Dip the bottom of the mold into hot water for 15 seconds; invert a chilled platter on top and turn both over together. If the dessert does not unmold, wrap it in a towel that has been soaked in hot water. After 15 seconds, remove the towel and lift the mold away. Garnish the sorbet with the plum slices, then cut the sorbet into wedges with a cake knife that has been dipped into hot water. Serve some of the raisin sauce with each portion.

Frozen Peach Yogurt

Serves 6
Working time: about 15 minutes
Total time: 1 to 3 hours, depending on freezing method

Calories **147**
Protein **5g.**
Cholesterol **3mg.**
Total fat **1g.**
Saturated fat **1g.**
Sodium **58mg.**

1½ lb. ripe peaches
2 tbsp. fresh lemon juice, plus 1 tsp. grated lemon zest
1 tbsp. grated orange zest
1½ cups plain low-fat yogurt
2 egg whites
⅓ cup honey
3 tbsp. cognac or brandy (optional)

Leaving the peaches unpeeled, halve and pit them. Set one of the peach halves aside. Put the remaining peach halves into a food processor or a blender, along with the lemon juice, lemon zest and orange zest; purée the mixture. Add the yogurt, the egg whites, the honey, and the cognac if you are using it, and blend the mixture for five seconds.

Freeze the mixture, following one of the techniques described on page 262.

Before serving, thinly slice the reserved peach half and use the slices to garnish the frozen yogurt.

Frozen Vanilla Yogurt

Serves 4
Working time: about 10 minutes
Total time: 1 to 3 hours, depending on freezing method

Calories **164**
Protein **9g.**
Cholesterol **9mg.**
Total fat **2g.**
Saturated fat **2g.**
Sodium **123mg.**

½ cup low-fat milk
one 2-inch length of vanilla bean, or 1 tsp. pure vanilla extract
2 cups plain low-fat yogurt
2 egg whites
⅓ cup sugar

If you are using the vanilla bean, warm the milk in a saucepan over low heat. Split the vanilla bean lengthwise and add it to the milk. Remove the pan from the heat and let the vanilla bean steep until the milk has cooled to room temperature — about 15 minutes.

Remove the bean from the milk and scrape the seeds inside it into the milk. If you are using vanilla extract, simply combine the unheated milk with the vanilla.

Whisk the yogurt, egg whites and sugar into the milk. Freeze the mixture using one of the methods described on page 262.

Frozen Raspberry Yogurt

Serves 6
Working time: about 15 minutes
Total time: 1 to 3 hours, depending on freezing method

Calories **138**
Protein **5g.**
Cholesterol **5mg.**
Total fat **1g.**
Saturated fat **1g.**
Sodium **70mg.**

2½ cups fresh or whole frozen raspberries, thawed
2 cups plain low-fat yogurt
½ cup sugar
2 egg whites
¼ cup cassis (optional)

Purée the raspberries in a food processor or a blender. Then, to remove the raspberry seeds, pass the purée through a fine sieve into a bowl; use a spatula to force the purée through the wire mesh. Combine the purée with the yogurt and sugar, whisk in the egg whites, then freeze the mixture using one of the methods described on page 262.

Pass the cassis separately so that each diner can pour a little over the yogurt.

EDITOR'S NOTE: *If desired, two yogurts can be swirled together. Make vanilla frozen yogurt (recipe above). Spoon the frozen raspberry yogurt inside a pastry bag, keeping it to one side; spoon the frozen vanilla yogurt on top of the raspberry yogurt, filling the other side of the bag. Pipe out the two yogurts together in a mounting spiral.*

Two-Melon Ice with Poppy Seeds and Port Sauce

Calories **183**
Protein **2g.**
Cholesterol **0mg.**
Total fat **1g.**
Saturated fat **0g.**
Sodium **22mg.**

Port sauce:
Calories **64**
Protein **0g.**
Cholesterol **0mg.**
Total fat **0g.**
Saturated fat **0g.**
Sodium **2mg.**

Serves 8
Working time: about 15 minutes
Total time: 1 to 3 hours, depending on freezing method

1 ripe honeydew melon (about 5 lb.)
1 ripe cantaloupe (about 3 lb.)
1 tsp. poppy seeds
⅛ tsp. ground mace
¼ cup fresh lemon juice
1 to 1⅓ cups sugar, depending on the sweetness of the melon
Port sauce (optional)
1½ cups ruby port
2 tsp. cornstarch

With a narrow-bladed knife, halve the honeydew melon crosswise, using a zigzag cut to produce a sawtooth pattern in the rind. Remove and discard the seeds. Select the most attractive half of the melon for serving; with a melon baller, scoop from it 1 to 1½ cups of melon balls. Refrigerate the melon balls in a large bowl. Cut enough 1-inch chunks from the flesh of the other melon half to measure 2¾ cups. Purée the chunks in a food processor or a blender — there should be about 2 cups of purée. If the purée measures less than 2 cups, process more melon chunks; if it measures more than 2 cups, reserve the excess for another use. Refrigerate the purée.

Slice the cantaloupe in half with a simple crosswise cut. Scoop out 1 cup of cantaloupe balls and refrigerate them with the honeydew balls until serving time. Cut the remaining cantaloupe into chunks and purée the chunks to produce 2 cups of purée. Stir the cantaloupe and honeydew purées together and chill them.

Discard all the melon shells except the honeydew half you selected for serving. Scrape the inside of the shell clean. Pare a thin slice from the bottom so that the melon will stand upright, then freeze the shell.

Combine the chilled melon purée with the poppy seeds, mace, lemon juice and sugar. Freeze the mixture, using one of the methods described on page 262.

To make the sauce, bring 1¼ cups of the port to a boil in a saucepan. Combine the remaining port with the cornstarch and stir the mixture into the boiling port. Cook the sauce, stirring constantly, until it thickens — about one minute. Allow the sauce to cool to room temperature, then chill it.

Use an ice-cream scoop to fill the frozen honeydew shell with balls of the melon ice. Scatter the chilled melon balls over the top and pass the sauce separately.

Cappuccino Parfaits

Serves 8
Working time: about 35 minutes
Total time: 1 to 3 hours, depending on freezing method

Calories **130**
Protein **1g.**
Cholesterol **11mg.**
Total fat **3g.**
Saturated fat **2g.**
Sodium **16mg.**

zest of 1 orange
2 tbsp. instant espresso coffee
1 cup sugar
¼ cup heavy cream
½ tsp. ground cinnamon
2 egg whites
powdered cocoa

In a heatproof bowl, combine the orange zest, espresso, ¾ cup of the sugar and 2 cups of boiling water. Stir to dissolve the sugar, then let the orange zest steep for 10 minutes. Remove the zest and discard it. Using one of the techniques described on page 262, freeze the espresso mixture.

When the mixture is frozen, divide it among eight glass coffee cups or glasses; freeze the containers.

In a small bowl, whip together the cream and cinnamon until soft peaks form; set the mixture aside. In another bowl, whip the egg whites until they can hold soft peaks when the beater is lifted from the bowl. Continue whipping, gradually adding the remaining ¼ cup of sugar, until the whites are glossy and form stiff peaks. Fold the whipped cream into the egg whites. Fill each of the cups or glasses with some of the egg white-cream mixture. Freeze the parfaits until they are firm — about 30 minutes.

Just before serving the parfaits, dust each one with some of the cocoa.

The five ice-cream recipes that follow contain no heavy cream, yet each is a delightfully smooth dessert.

Spiced Coffee Ice Cream

Serves 8
Working time: about 15 minutes
Total time: 1 to 3 hours, depending on freezing method

Calories **158**
Protein **6g.**
Cholesterol **15mg.**
Total fat **5g.**
Saturated fat **3g.**
Sodium **68mg.**

1 ½ cups part-skim ricotta cheese
½ cup plain low-fat yogurt
⅔ cup sugar
1 cup freshly brewed triple-strength coffee, chilled
½ tsp. ground cinnamon
½ tsp. ground cardamom, or ¼ tsp. grated nutmeg
½ tsp. pure vanilla extract
1 oz. semisweet chocolate, grated

Purée the ricotta, yogurt and sugar in a food processor or a blender, stopping at least once to scrape down the sides; the goal is a very smooth purée.

Whisk the coffee, cinnamon, cardamom or nutmeg, vanilla and chocolate into the purée. Freeze the mixture, using one of the techniques described on page 262. If you are using the food-processor method, add the chocolate after you have processed the mixture.

Strawberry Ice Cream

Serves 8
Working time: about 30 minutes
Total time: 1 to 3 hours, depending on freezing method

Calories **157**
Protein **7g.**
Cholesterol **15mg.**
Total fat **4g.**
Saturated fat **2g.**
Sodium **81mg.**

4 cups hulled ripe strawberries
½ cup sugar
1 ½ tbsp. fresh lemon juice
2 tbsp. Grand Marnier, or 1 tbsp. grated orange zest
1 ½ cups part-skim ricotta cheese
½ cup plain low-fat yogurt
2 egg whites

In a food processor or a blender, purée the strawberries with the sugar, lemon juice and the Grand Marnier or orange zest. Transfer the purée to a large bowl and set it aside.

Rinse out the food processor or blender. Add the ricotta cheese and the yogurt and purée them, stopping at least once to scrape down the sides; the goal is a very smooth purée. Whisk the ricotta-yogurt purée and the egg whites into the strawberry purée, then freeze the mixture, using one of the methods described on page 262.

Peach Ice Cream

Serves 8
Working time: about 30 minutes
Total time: about 1 to 3 hours, depending
on freezing method

Calories **193**
Protein **8g.**
Cholesterol **18mg.**
Total fat **5g.**
Saturated fat **3g.**
Sodium **95mg.**

2 lb. ripe peaches
1½ tbsp. fresh lemon juice
1½ cups part-skim ricotta cheese
½ cup plain low-fat yogurt
2 tbsp. sour cream
½ cup low-fat milk
½ cup light brown sugar
2 egg whites
½ tsp. pure vanilla extract
¼ tsp. almond extract

Bring 2 quarts of water to a boil in a large pot. Add the peaches and blanch them until their skins loosen — 30 seconds to one minute. Remove the peaches with a slotted spoon and set them aside; when they are cool enough to handle, peel them, cut them in half and remove their pits.

Cut enough of the peaches into ½-inch dice to measure 2 cups. Purée the remaining peaches with the lemon juice in a food processor or a blender. Transfer the purée to a large bowl and set it aside.

Put the ricotta, yogurt and sour cream in the food processor or blender; purée the mixture until it has a creamy consistency, stopping at least once to scrape down the sides. Blend in the milk, brown sugar, egg whites, and the vanilla and almond extracts, then whisk the mixture into the peach purée.

Stir the reserved peach dice into the purée and freeze it, using one of the methods described on page 262. If you use the food-processor method of freezing, do not add the peach dice until after you have processed the ice cream.

Ginger-Date Ice Cream

THE CREAMY TEXTURE OF THIS LOW-FAT ICE CREAM
COMES FROM THE PAIRING OF RICOTTA CHEESE AND YOGURT.

Serves 8
Working time: about 25 minutes
Total time: 1 to 3 hours, depending on freezing method

Calories **122**
Protein **6g.**
Cholesterol **12mg.**
Total fat **3g.**
Saturated fat **2g.**
Sodium **77mg.**

1 cup low-fat milk
¼ lb. dried dates, cut into small pieces (about 1 cup)
⅓ cup plain low-fat yogurt
1 cup part-skim ricotta cheese
2 tbsp. sugar
2 egg whites
1 tbsp. finely chopped candied ginger
½ tbsp. fresh lemon juice

Warm the milk in a saucepan over very low heat. Remove the pan from the heat and add all but 2 tablespoons of the dates; steep the dates for 10 minutes.

Purée the date-milk mixture in a food processor or a blender, then transfer the purée to a large bowl.

Purée the yogurt, ricotta cheese and sugar in the food processor or blender, stopping at least once to scrape down the sides; the goal is a very smooth purée. Add the yogurt-ricotta purée to the date-milk purée in the bowl, and whisk the two together. Refrigerate the bowl for 15 minutes.

Blend the egg whites into the refrigerated purée, then freeze the mixture using one of the techniques described on page 262. If you plan to use an ice-cream maker, stir the candied ginger and reserved dates into the mixture before freezing it. If you are using the hand-whisking method, stir in the lemon juice, ginger and reserved dates when the mixture is almost solid. For the food processor method, add the lemon juice during the processing, then blend in the ginger and reserved dates.

Cherry Ice Cream

Serves 8
Working time: about 30 minutes
Total time: 1 to 3 hours, depending on freezing method

Calories **178**
Protein **8g.**
Cholesterol **16mg.**
Total fat **6g.**
Saturated fat **3g.**
Sodium **90mg.**

¾ lb. sweet cherries
½ cup sugar
1½ cups part-skim ricotta cheese
½ cup plain low-fat yogurt
½ tsp. almond extract
½ tsp. pure vanilla extract
½ cup low-fat milk
2 tbsp. toasted almonds, crushed
2 egg whites

Pit and quarter the cherries, working over a large bowl to catch any juice. Put the pitted cherries, the sugar and ½ cup of water in a heavy saucepan. Bring the liquid to a boil over medium-high heat, then reduce the heat and simmer the cherries for 10 minutes.

Remove the cherries from the syrup with a slotted spoon and continue cooking the syrup until it is reduced by one half — about five minutes. Refrigerate the cherries and half of the syrup.

Put the ricotta, yogurt, almond extract and vanilla into a food processor or a blender. Purée the mixture, stopping at least once to scrape down the sides; the goal is a very smooth purée. Stir the cherries and the syrup into the ricotta mixture, then add the milk, almonds and egg whites, and mix well. Freeze the mixture, using one of the techniques described on page 262. If you are using the food processor method, do not add the cherries and almonds until after you have processed the mixture.

Avocado and Grapefruit Bombe with Candied Zest

THIS ELEGANT PRESENTATION OF GRAPEFRUIT SORBET AND AVOCADO ICE MILK MAKES AN ELABORATE BUT PERFECT ENDING TO A SPECIAL MEAL.

Serves 12
Working time: about 1 hour
Total time: 2 to 4 hours, depending on freezing method

Calories **263**
Protein **3g.**
Cholesterol **4mg.**
Total fat **9g.**
Saturated fat **2g.**
Sodium **29mg.**

Grapefruit sorbet
4 large grapefruits
1½ cups sugar
Avocado ice milk
2 large ripe avocados
1 cup whole milk
1 cup low-fat milk
½ cup sugar
2 tbsp. finely chopped crystallized ginger

Put a 6-cup round mold into the freezer. Using a vegetable peeler or a paring knife, remove the zest from two of the grapefruits. Cook the zest in a saucepan of boiling water for 10 minutes, then drain it. Julienne half of the zest and candy it *(box, right)*. Set the candied zest aside. Put the uncandied zest into a food processor or a blender.

Pare the pith from the two zested grapefruits and discard it. Cut away all of the peel from the remaining two grapefruits and discard it, too. Working over a bowl to catch the juice, cut between the membranes of the grapefruits to free the segments. Discard the seeds. Transfer the juice and the segments to the food processor or blender, and purée them with the uncandied zest. Add the sugar and process until it is dissolved. Freeze the grapefruit sorbet, using one of the methods described on page 262.

Remove the mold from the freezer and line it evenly with the sorbet, leaving a large hollow at the center for the avocado mixture. Return the mold to the freezer.

Peel and seed the avocados, and purée their flesh. Blend in the whole milk, low-fat milk and sugar. Freeze the mixture, using one of the methods on page 262. Add the ginger halfway through the freezing process.

When the ice milk is frozen, spoon it into the hollow in the grapefruit sorbet. Then freeze the mold for one and a half hours. Before serving, dip the bottom of the mold in hot water, then invert a chilled platter over the top and turn the two over together. Lift the mold away. Garnish the bombe with the candied grapefruit zest, and serve immediately.

Candied Citrus Zest

Makes about ¾ cup
Working time: about 20 minutes
Total time: about 35 minutes

½ cup julienned citrus zest
(orange, grapefruit, lemon or lime)

¼ cup sugar

Per tablespoon:
Calories **16**
Protein **0g.**
Cholesterol **0mg.**
Total fat **0g.**
Saturated fat **0g.**
Sodium **0mg.**

Put the citrus zest into a saucepan with 1 cup of water and bring the water to a boil. Cook the zest for 15 minutes, then remove it with a slotted spoon, and spread it on paper towels to drain. Pour the water out of the saucepan. Add the sugar, 2 tablespoons of cold water and the drained zest to the pan. Cook the mixture over high heat, stirring constantly, until the zest is coated with white, crystallized sugar — about 3 minutes. Remove the candied zest from the pan and set it on wax paper to dry.

EDITOR'S NOTE: *Candied zest may be stored in an airtight container at room temperature for up to a week.*

Frozen Lemon-Meringue Torte

Serves 8
Working time: about 1 hour and 15 minutes
Total time: 1½ to 4 hours, depending on freezing method

Calories **242**
Protein **4g.**
Cholesterol **0mg.**
Total fat **5g.**
Saturated fat **0g.**
Sodium **28mg.**

| 8 lemons |
| 1¼ cups sugar |
| 2 egg whites |
| 2 tbsp. unsweetened cocoa powder |
| **Almond meringues** |
| 2 egg whites |
| ⅓ cup sugar |
| ½ cup blanched almonds, ground |
| 2 tbsp. confectioners' sugar |

Grate the zest from three of the lemons and put it into a blender or a food processor. Working over a bowl to catch the juice, peel and segment one of the lemons. Squeeze the pulpy core of membranes over the bowl to extract every bit of juice. Repeat the process with the remaining lemons. To remove the seeds, strain the lemon juice into the blender or food processor. Add the lemon segments, the 1¼ cups of sugar, the two egg whites and 2¼ cups of water to the zest and juice, and purée the mixture.

Freeze the lemon mixture using one of the methods described on page 262. While the mixture is freezing, make the almond meringues.

Preheat the oven to 200° F. Line a cookie sheet with parchment paper, or butter the sheet lightly and then dust it with flour.

Whip the two egg whites until they form soft peaks. Beat in the ⅓ cup of sugar a tablespoon at a time; when all the sugar has been incorporated, continue beating the whites until they are glossy and hold stiff peaks. Sprinkle the ground almonds over the whites and fold them in.

Fit a pastry bag with a ½-inch plain tip and spoon the meringue into the bag. Pipe the meringue onto the prepared cookie sheet in strips nearly the length of the sheet; the strips should be about 1 inch wide and 1 inch apart. (If you have no pastry bag, shape the strips with a spoon.) Sprinkle the strips evenly with the confectioners' sugar, then bake them for one hour.

Turn off the oven and let the strips dry, with the oven door ajar, for another hour; if necessary, use a wooden spoon to prop the oven door open. Remove the cookie sheet from the oven and gently loosen the meringues. Break the meringues into bars about 3 inches long; when they have cooled, store them in an airtight container until you are ready to decorate the torte.

When the lemon sorbet is frozen, transfer it to an 8- or 9-inch springform pan. Use a rubber spatula to distribute the sorbet evenly in the pan. Rap the bottom of the pan on the work surface to collapse any large air bubbles, then smooth the top of the sorbet with the spatula. Freeze the torte until it is firm — about one hour.

Remove the sides of the springform pan. Slide a knife or a long metal spatula between the torte and the base of the pan, and transfer the torte to a serving platter. Smooth the sides of the torte with a knife dipped in hot water. Press the meringue bars in place in a random pattern over the top and on the sides of the torte. (The torte can be kept in the freezer with the meringue bars attached.)

Just before serving, dust the torte with the cocoa powder: Put the cocoa into a sieve, then tap the sieve gently as you move it over the torte.

Frozen Nectarine and Plum Terrine

Serves 10
Working time: about 45 minutes
Total time: about 1 day (includes freezing)

Calories **192**
Protein **1g.**
Cholesterol **0mg.**
Total fat **1g.**
Saturated fat **0g.**
Sodium **1mg.**

Nectarine sorbet
1 lb. nectarines, halved and pitted
½ cup fresh orange juice
¼ cup fresh lemon juice
¾ cup sugar
Plum sorbet
1 lb. plums, halved and pitted
¾ cup fresh orange juice
¾ cup sugar
Garnish
1 nectarine, halved, pitted and sliced into thin wedges
2 plums, halved, pitted and sliced into thin wedges

To prepare the nectarine sorbet, purée the nectarines, orange juice, lemon juice and sugar in a food processor or blender. Transfer the purée to a freezer container and freeze it, using one of the methods described on page 262. Prepare the plum sorbet the same way and freeze it as well.

When both sorbets are firm but not hard, line a 6-cup loaf pan with plastic wrap.

Put half of the nectarine sorbet into the lined pan, smoothing it out with a rubber spatula. Top the nectarine sorbet with half of the plum sorbet; smooth its top the same way. Repeat the layering process with the remaining sorbet to make four layers in all. To collapse any air bubbles, tap the bottom of the loaf pan on the work surface. Cover the top of the sorbet with plastic wrap and freeze the terrine overnight.

Remove the plastic wrap from the top. Invert the terrine onto a chilled platter. Unwrap the terrine and cut it into ½-inch-thick slices, dipping the knife into hot water and wiping it off between slices. Garnish the slices with the wedges of nectarine and plum.

Brandy Snaps

Makes 12 cookies
Working time: about 10 minutes
Total time: about 20 minutes

Per cookie:
Calories **54**
Protein **0g.**
Cholesterol **5mg.**
Total fat **2g.**
Saturated fat **1g.**
Sodium **3mg.**

2 tbsp. unsalted butter
2 tbsp. sugar
2 tbsp. light corn syrup
1 tsp. molasses
1 tsp. ground ginger
½ tsp. grated lemon zest
2 tbsp. brandy
⅓ cup unbleached all-purpose flour

Preheat the oven to 400° F.

Put all the ingredients but the flour into a small saucepan and bring the mixture to a boil. Cook the mixture for one minute, then remove it from the heat and let it cool for one minute. Add the flour and whisk the batter until it is smooth.

Lightly oil a heavy baking sheet. Drop the cookie batter onto the sheet in heaping teaspoonfuls at least 3 inches apart. (It may be necessary to bake the cookies in two batches; if you are using two baking sheets, stagger the cooking to allow enough time to shape the cookies after they are baked.) Bake the cookies until they turn slightly darker — three to four minutes.

Remove the baking sheet from the oven and let it sit for one minute while the cookies firm up a little. With a metal spatula, remove some of the still-soft cookies and drape them over a clean rolling pin to cool. Remove the curved cookies from the rolling pin as soon as they harden — about 30 seconds. Immediately repeat the procedure to fashion the remaining cookies. If any of the cookies become hard while they are still on the baking sheet, return them to the oven for a few seconds to soften them.

Iced Apple Mousse Cake with Brandy Snaps

Serves 12
Working time: about 1 hour
Total time: 2½ to 4 hours, depending
on freezing method

Calories **174**
Protein **2g.**
Cholesterol **10mg.**
Total fat **4g.**
Saturated fat **2g.**
Sodium **29mg.**

2 lb. Golden Delicious apples (about 4 apples)
¼ cup fresh lemon juice
½ tsp. ground cloves
½ tsp. ground cinnamon
2 tbsp. unsalted butter
½ cup sugar
6 egg whites
12 brandy snaps
Apple fans
2 Golden Delicious apples
2 tsp. honey

To make the apple mousse, peel and core the 2 pounds of apples, then cut them into ½-inch chunks. Toss the apples with the lemon juice, cloves and cinnamon.

Melt the butter in a large, heavy-bottomed skillet over medium heat. Add the apple mixture and cook it, stirring frequently, for 10 minutes. Sprinkle in the sugar and continue to cook the mixture, stirring often, for five minutes more.

Put the apple mixture into a food processor or a blender and process it until it is very smooth, stopping at least once to scrape down the sides. Transfer the mixture to a shallow bowl and whisk in the egg whites. Freeze the mixture, using one of the methods described on page 262.

Preheat the oven to 350° F.

To prepare the apple fans, peel the remaining two apples and cut them in half lengthwise. Remove the cores, then slice the apple halves thinly, keeping the slices together. Fan out each sliced apple half on a baking sheet. Drizzle the honey over the apple fans and bake them until they are tender — about 15 minutes. Allow the fans to cool to room temperature, then refrigerate them.

Transfer the apple mixture to a 9-inch springform pan and freeze it until it is solid — about one hour.

To unmold the cake, run a knife around the inside of the pan, then place a hot, damp towel on the bottom for about 10 seconds. Invert a plate on the cake; turn both cake and plate over together. Remove the sides of the pan, and smooth the surface of the cake with a long knife or spatula.

Arrange the chilled apple fans atop the cake; decorate the sides of the cake with brandy snaps.

Homemade Stocks: Foundations of Flavor

The elixir that is stock comes from humble beginnings indeed — inexpensive cuts of meat, fish bones, or chicken wings and backs. Attention to details will reward you with a rich and beautifully limpid stock: Any large fat deposits should be trimmed away beforehand; large bones, if they are to cede the treasured gelatin that gives body to a stock, should be cracked first. During cooking, remove the scum that collects occasionally atop the liquid. Scum consists of protein particles released by meat and bones; these float to the surface, where they gather in a foam. As nutritious as it is, the foam must be removed lest it cloud the stock. Skim off the scum as it forms at the start of cooking; skim thereafter only as the recipe directs. After its initial rapid cooking, a stock must not be allowed to return to a full boil; the turbulence would muddy the liquid. As a final cleansing, the stock should be strained through a fine sieve or a colander lined with cheesecloth.

To prepare stock for storage, divide it among containers surrounded with ice water. Wait until the stock has cooled to cover the vessels; otherwise, it may sour. Refrigerated in covered containers, any of these stocks will keep for up to three days. Because the fat atop the stock will form a temporary seal, helping to keep it fresh, you need not degrease the stock until shortly before you are ready to use it. To prolong the life of a refrigerated stock, first remove and discard the congealed fat, then boil the stock for five minutes; either freeze the stock or boil it again every two or three days. As always, cool it quickly — and uncovered — before storing it once more.

Fish stock and vegetable stock may be frozen for two months; the other three may be frozen for as long as four months. Stock destined for the freezer must first be degreased; frozen fat can turn rancid.

The recipes that follow yield differing amounts of stock. Brown stock and veal stock, for example, are made from large bones, which require more water for cooking. But like any stock, these two freeze well, meaning an abundance is never too much.

Vegetable Stock

Makes about 2 quarts
Working time: about 25 minutes
Total time: about 1 hour and 30 minutes

4 celery stalks with leaves, cut into 1-inch pieces
4 carrots, scrubbed and cut into 1-inch pieces
4 large onions (about 2 lb.), coarsely chopped
3 large broccoli stems (optional), coarsely chopped
1 medium turnip, peeled and cut into ½-inch cubes
6 garlic cloves, crushed
½ cup coarsely chopped parsley leaves and stems
10 black peppercorns
4 fresh thyme sprigs, or 1 tsp. dried thyme leaves
2 bay leaves, crumbled

Put the celery, carrots, onions, broccoli if you are using it, turnip, garlic, parsley and peppercorns into a heavy stockpot. Pour in enough cold water to cover the contents by about 2 inches. Bring the liquid to a boil over medium heat, skimming off any scum that rises to the surface. When the liquid reaches a boil, stir in the thyme and the bay leaves. Reduce the heat and let the stock simmer undisturbed for one hour.

Strain the stock into a large bowl, pressing down lightly on the vegetables to extract all their liquid. Discard the vegetables.

Chicken Stock

Makes about 2 quarts
Working time: about 20 minutes
Total time: about 3 hours

4 to 5 lb. uncooked chicken trimmings and bones (preferably wings, necks and backs), the bones cracked with a heavy knife
2 carrots, cut into ½-inch-thick rounds
2 celery stalks, cut into 1-inch pieces
2 large onions (about 1 lb.), cut in half, one half stuck with 2 cloves
2 fresh thyme sprigs, or ½ tsp. dried thyme leaves
1 or 2 bay leaves
10 to 15 parsley stems
5 black peppercorns

Put the chicken trimmings and bones into a heavy stockpot; pour in enough water to cover them by about 2 inches. Bring the liquid to a boil over medium heat, skimming off the scum that rises to the surface. Reduce the heat and simmer the liquid for 10 minutes, skimming and adding a little cold water to help precipitate the scum.

Add the vegetables, herbs and peppercorns, and submerge them in the liquid. If necessary, pour in enough additional water to cover the contents of the pot. Simmer the stock for two to three hours, skimming as necessary to remove the scum.

Strain the stock, discard the solids, and degrease the stock.

EDITOR'S NOTE: *The chicken gizzard and heart may be added to the stock. Wings and necks — rich in natural gelatin — produce a particularly gelatinous stock, ideal for sauces and jellied dishes.*

Turkey, duck or goose stock may be prepared using the same basic recipe.

Veal Stock

Makes about 3 quarts
Working time: about 30 minutes
Total time: about 4½ hours

3 lb. veal breast or shank meat, cut into 3-inch pieces
3 lb. veal bones (preferably knuckles), cracked
2 onions, quartered

2 celery stalks, sliced
1 carrot, sliced
8 black peppercorns
3 unpeeled garlic cloves (optional), crushed
1 tsp. fresh thyme, or ¼ tsp. dried thyme leaves
1 bay leaf

Fill a large pot halfway with water. Bring the water to a boil, add the veal meat and bones, and blanch them for two minutes to clean them. Drain the meat and bones in a colander, discarding the liquid. Rinse the meat and bones under cold running water and return them to the pot.

Add the onions, celery, carrot, peppercorns, and garlic if you are using it. Pour in enough water to cover the contents of the pot by about 3 inches, and bring the water to a boil over medium heat. Reduce the heat to maintain a simmer, and skim any impurities from the surface. Add the thyme and bay leaf, and simmer the stock very gently for four hours, skimming occasionally.

Strain the stock into a large bowl; allow the solids to drain thoroughly into the bowl before discarding them. Degrease the stock.

EDITOR'S NOTE: *Any combination of veal meat and bones may be used to make this stock; ideally, the meat and bones together should weigh about six pounds. Ask your butcher to crack the bones.*

Brown Stock

Makes about 3 quarts
Working time: about 40 minutes
Total time: about 5½ hours

3 lb. veal breast (or veal-shank or beef-shank meat), cut into 3-inch pieces
3 lb. uncooked veal or beef bones, cracked
2 onions, quartered
2 celery stalks, chopped
2 carrots, sliced
3 unpeeled garlic cloves, crushed
8 black peppercorns
3 cloves
2 tsp. fresh thyme, or ½ tsp. dried thyme leaves
1 bay leaf

Preheat the oven to 425° F. Place the meat, bones, onions, celery and carrots in a large roasting pan and roast them in the oven until they are well browned — about one hour.

Transfer the contents of the roasting pan to a large pot. Pour 2 cups of water into the roasting pan; with a spatula, scrape up the browned bits from the bottom of the pan. Pour the liquid into the pot.

Add the garlic, peppercorns and cloves. Pour in enough water to cover the contents of the pot by about 3 inches. Bring the liquid to a boil, then reduce the heat to maintain a simmer and skim any impurities from the surface. Add the thyme and bay leaf, then simmer the stock very gently for four hours, skimming occasionally during the process.

Strain the stock; allow the solids to drain thoroughly into the stock before discarding them. Degrease the stock.

EDITOR'S NOTE: *Thoroughly browning the meat,*

Quick Stocks from Supplies at Hand

Canned stocks are no substitute for homemade, but they can be used in a pinch. A handful of readily available ingredients will invigorate them. Similar treatment will transform bottled clam juice into a creditable fish stock.

To enliven canned beef stock (called broth or bouillon), combine several tablespoons each of minced onion and carrot and a tablespoon or two of minced celery with 2 cans of stock. Next pour in ½ cup of red or dry white wine and 2½ cups of water, then add two sprigs of parsley, a small bay leaf and a pinch of dried thyme. Simmer the mixture for 20 to 30 minutes, then strain and degrease it.

To add spark to two cans of low-sodium chicken broth, use vegetables and herbs in the same proportion as for beef stock, but do not add water; instead use ¼ cup of white wine. If you wish, toss in a few celery leaves. Simmer the stock for 20 to 30 minutes, then strain it. In the case of beef stock, a good low-sodium stock is unavailable, so reduce or omit the salt in the recipe.

To every 2 cups of clam juice, add 1 cup of water, ½ cup of dry white wine, a sliced onion and four black peppercorns. (Be sure to reduce or omit the salt in the dish.) Simmer the stock for 10 minutes, then strain it.

---

bones and vegetables should produce a stock with a rich mahogany color. If your stock does not seem dark enough, cook 1 tablespoon of tomato paste in a small pan over medium heat, stirring constantly, until it darkens — about three minutes. Add this to the stock about one hour before the end of the cooking time.

Any combination of meat and bones may be used to make the stock; ideally, the meat and bones together should weigh about six pounds. Ask your butcher to crack the bones.

Fish Stock

Makes about 2 quarts
Working time: about 15 minutes
Total time: about 40 minutes

2 lb. lean-fish bones, fins and tails discarded, the bones rinsed thoroughly and cut into large pieces
2 onions, thinly sliced
2 celery stalks, chopped
1 carrot, thinly sliced
2 cups dry white wine
2 tbsp. fresh lemon juice
1 leek (optional), trimmed, split, washed thoroughly to remove all grit, and sliced
3 garlic cloves (optional), crushed
10 parsley stems
4 fresh thyme sprigs, or 1 tsp. dried thyme leaves
1 bay leaf, crumbled
5 black peppercorns

Put the fish bones, onions, celery, carrot, wine, lemon juice, 2 quarts of cold water, and the leek and garlic if you are using them, in a large, nonreactive stockpot. Bring the liquid to a boil over medium heat, then reduce the heat to maintain a strong simmer. Skim off all the scum that rises to the surface.

Add the parsley, thyme, bay leaf and peppercorns, and gently simmer the stock for 20 minutes more.

Strain the stock; allow the solids to drain thoroughly before discarding them. If necessary, degrease the stock.

EDITOR'S NOTE: *Because the bones from oilier fish produce a strong flavor, be sure to use only the bones from lean fish. Sole, flounder, turbot and other flatfish are best. Do not include the fish skin; it could discolor the stock.*

Index

Picture Credits